BODY, MIND, AND SPORT

"Everyone is slowly trying to kill themselves to get better. Dr. Douillard really explains how less can be more."

Scott Molina,
Ironman winner,
world-class triathlete

"Your practical training on Invincible Athletics principles attracted great attention from trainers, coaches, and listeners, and has received an excellent mark from all the participants."

A. Tsarik and Y. Belous,
USSR State Committee for
Physical Culture and Sports

"I've never used anabolic steroids. I know they have a destructive effect on the mind-body connection and give only the illusion of invincibility. Now, with Dr. Douillard's course, you're offered an opportunity to experience true invincibility, the ability not to be destroyed: to be powerful and limitless."

Joanne Arnold Madden,
Ms. Maine 1989, Ms.
Natural New England 1989

"I was suffering injuries due to overtraining. Now, one year after training with Dr. Douillard, I can run 'in the zone' for 17 miles or more at a pace of 6 minutes per mile with a heart rate of 115 beats per minute and a breath rate of 10 breaths per minute."

Warren Wechsler, runner

"After going through the Invincible Athletics program, I do the physical and mental techniques of Ayurveda every day. At the end of the year at the state tournament I was in the 'zone' for the whole singles tournament. I felt like I was in control every match throughout the tournament."

Kyle Cleveland,
1991 Iowa State
High School Singles
Tennis champion

"I have two children under four, and my body has been transformed by only four months of this program. Even when I'm fatigued before exercise, I feel clarified and energized and never tired afterward."

Sheila Ross, homemaker

"What I notice when I follow Dr. Douillard's training is that I perform like you would not believe. I'm totally in a blissful state. I'm just running on air, and that's the way it should be every time."

> Colleen Cannon, 1990
> National Sprint Triathlon
> champion

"Since I met Dr. Douillard and started practicing his techniques, I have found that I can accomplish just as much or more as I used to, but I don't get as tired and I have plenty of energy left when I have to compete."

> Gigi Fernandez, ranked #1
> in Women's Professional
> Tennis Doubles

"After I added just this simple program of Invincible Athletics, my body looks more youthful. My face looks younger."

> Barbara Levinson,
> aerobics instructor

"Dr. Douillard has written a wonderfully clear, entertaining, and useful book for all athletes and exercisers. He logically outlines a method of exercise and diet that is comfortable, health promoting, and doable, and, best of all, leads to personal best performances.

> Julie Anthony, Sports
> psychologist, coach, and
> former touring tennis pro.

"Exercise is safer and much more effective when prescribed according to your body type."

> Willy Draper, ski coach,
> master's racer,
> former U.S. ski team
> member

"I apply John's principles to my personal fitness program every day. It makes exercise easy and enjoyable, and I heartily recommend it."

> Dr. Wayne Dyer, author of
> *Your Erroneous Zones*

"Now, with my performance in the zone each time, I'm hitting shots I always dreamed about but never did."

> Nancy Kalil, ranked #1 in
> U.S. Professional Women's
> Handball

BODY, MIND

A N D

SPORT

THE MIND-BODY GUIDE

TO LIFELONG FITNESS AND

YOUR PERSONAL BEST

JOHN DOUILLARD

FOREWORDS BY BILLIE JEAN KING
AND MARTINA NAVRATILOVA

HARMONY BOOKS • NEW YORK

Published by Harmony Books, a division of
Crown Publishers, Inc., 201 East 50th Street,
New York, New York 10022. Member of the Crown
Publishing Group.

Random House, Inc. New York, Toronto, London, Sydney, Auckland

HARMONY and colophon are trademarks of Crown Publishers, Inc.

Manufactured in U.S.A.

Design by Debbie Glasserman

Library of Congress Cataloging-in-Publication Data

Douillard, John.
Body, mind, and sport : the mind-body guide to lifelong fitness and your personal best/
by John Douillard.—1st ed.
Includes index.
1. Exercise. 2. Physical fitness. 3. Mind and body.
4. Medicine, Ayurvedic. 5. Sports. I. Title.
RA781.D625 1994
613.7′1—dc20
93-26446
CIP

ISBN 0-517-59455-2

10 9 8 7 6 5 4 3 2 1

First Edition

CONTENTS

ACKNOWLEDGMENTS

Thanks to all those whose enjoyment of these principles has kept this project alive.

To my wife, Ginger, and children, Janaki, Devaki, and Austin, for keeping my priorities in perspective. You are my happiness.

To Linda Hensley, whose artistic talent made these concepts easier to understand.

To my agent, Muriel Nellis, and Peter Guzzardi at Harmony Books; to Dr. Karen Blasdell for her selfless enthusiasm and vision; to my assistant David Therault and Robert and Tracy Liptak, who believed in the invincible athlete from the beginning—I thank you all.

To Jack Forem, who made my seven-year search for an editor worth every minute. His brilliance is deeply appreciated.

And most of all, for teaching me how to live in the eye of the hurricane, for the formula of the exercise high and the knowledge of life itself, my deepest thanks and appreciation to Maharishi Mahesh Yogi.

FOREWORD

BILLIE JEAN KING

Dr. John Douillard's teachings can change your life as it has mine and thousands of others of all ages. He makes it very clear we are all athletes.

Adults can start this program immediately, whether they are recreational, highly competitive, or professional athletes. This knowledge and practice can guide and support children to experience exercise at their speed as unique individuals who will prosper, grow, and learn integration of mind and body. Generally, "working" out has usually been a struggle, except during early childhood. Personally I have always had huge swings with my weight of fifty to sixty pounds. What kept me going was my tennis career, my goals, and an insatiable desire to be the best I could be. But the process was difficult and on many occasions very stressful. I was taught that stress-recovery methods were the only way to excel. No pain, no gain, no more! Dr. John Douillard's *Body, Mind, and Sport* information is on the cutting edge. It is based on the principles of Ayurveda, the "Science of Life," which is thousands of years old. By adopting these principles my life is finally on track physically, mentally, emotionally, and spiritually; for our body and mind are one. "Working" out is no longer work but an entire, enjoyable, slow, steady building process of being connected, whole, and playful once again.

As Martina Navratilova's part-time coach (Craig Kardon's her full-time coach), I am pleased to see that she has thoroughly embraced the knowledge of *Body, Mind, and Sport* to enhance her already record-breaking career. We are both enjoying mind-body breathing techniques to maximize our respiratory efficiency, performing mind-body stretching exercises, implementing specific dietary recommendations and daily and seasonal routines all according to the needs of our individual and unique body types. Wherever you are in your journey toward health and fitness, reading *Body, Mind, and Sport* will elevate your quality of life.

Thank you, Dr. John Douillard, for bringing health and fitness back into my life as a fun, safe, exhilarating daily experience. Every day can be a "Zone" experience by learning to listen to yourself, your Body and Mind.

FOREWORD

MARTINA NAVRATILOVA

In all my years of trying to become the best athlete possible I have gone through a lot of different methods of training and different kinds of programs. The one thing those programs had in common is fatigue. None of those methods took into consideration the most important part of the training—the body itself. You just simply go through the process come hell or high water. Whatever you feel like—it doesn't matter—just guts it out and do the sprints, suck it up and run for an hour, suffer through a two-hour bike ride, and by God, you are going to lift those weights! That's where John Douillard is different. You listen to your body—it will tell you exactly what you need to do. I have been on John's program for eight months now and never have I felt better. I still work hard but I let my body dictate the pace. As a result, I feel good, look good, and everything about me is balanced—the emotional, mental, and physical are working in balance.

PREFACE

John Douillard's book *Body, Mind, and Sport* is sensational. This revolutionary book is not only for athletes, it is for you and me. It's a book that guarantees longer life and a greater quality of life for everyone. It's a must read! It should be required reading for every student, coach, athlete, and indeed anybody and everybody who is interested in living longer and living better. Physical education programs and athletic departments that are keen on developing health and fitness should incorporate the tenets of this book into all aspects of the education and training. Parents should own this knowledge so they can ensure the fun, safety, and benefits of exercise for their children. The stress and strain of exercise we all considered a requirement is eloquently diasrmed, leaving us with the permission to enjoy exercise and develop our god-given physical potential without pain. John looks to nature for this formula to enhance both performance and enjoyment. As in nature, less is more, and when this notion is properly implemented, exercise, health, and fitness will become a way of life instead of a chore for all of us. We have all forced fitness either to compete, lose weight, or accomplish a goal. We have been taught to push through exhaustion and stress, leaving many of us either injured, overworked, or all too often sedentary. Exercise is a must for everyone at every level of fitness but in the right amounts. John's book will guide the beginner and the competitive athlete to a more enjoyable and productive result according to their individual requirements determined from a body type analysis.

Personally, using John's program I immediately felt better after my workouts, refreshed instead of exhausted. I have consistently watched my performance steadily increase while enjoying a surprisingly low level of exertion. Instead of rating myself on how much I can do or how fast I can go, I now rate myself on how much I can do with how little effort. It's about using your body more efficiently and rejuvenating it along the way.

In other words you get fit while removing stress rather than incurring it. With these principles in place we will see performance rise to entirely new levels. This revolutionary book will set the pace for all future athletic training and fitness programs to come.

> Bill Simon, former United States Secretary of the Treasury and former President of the United States Olympic Committee

Introduction

We all know we should exercise, but relatively few of us do it. Those who do rarely maintain it as a way of life. Even athletes search for the competitive edge in all the wrong places. Here in America, overweight kids and sedentary adults make up the majority of the population. Why?

It's a little-known fact that 50 percent of American children experience their first major failure in life in the field of sports. Our children are often humiliated at tryouts, by being the last one selected when choosing teams or by not measuring up in outdated fitness testing—so how can we expect they'll be motivated to become fit? By the end of high school, the vast majority of children have left organized sports, and few get enough exercise after they graduate.

This lack of interest in exercise continues into our adult lives. Add to that the stresses of business, relationships, raising a family, and financial burdens, and exercise quickly finds its way to the back of the closet with our workout shoes.

Many of us suddenly look up to find ourselves, in our forties and fifties, overweight and out of shape. We are overcome by a compelling, now-or-never desire to exercise. But now we are not quite as resilient as we were in our early twenties and thirties. So, to play it safe, we join a health club, seeking better health and a higher level of fitness.

We walk into the health club for the first time, only to relive the exercise-related humiliation and frustration we encountered in childhood. The place is filled with buffed, tucked, perfectly sculpted bodies! Their perfection is intimidating, to say the least. Although everyone is very upbeat and cordial, it seems more a place to *be* fit than to *get* fit.

As a result, we retreat to the privacy of our living rooms with the latest home exercise video and workout machine. Soon the video is shelved and the exercise bicycle sits dormant. Again I ask: Why?

The root of the problem, I believe, is that exercise is not fun. It is a *work*out, based on the theory that in order to build up the body, you must first break it down. This concept, although primitive, does get results. But at what cost? It requires that we push our bodies to exhaustion. Exercise, which was so much fun in childhood (outside of school, that is), is now hard work. And it is boring.

We are told by the so-called experts to listen to music or watch TV while we work out, to distract the mind from the body in order to prevent boredom. Unfortunately, when you disconnect your mind from your body, you distract yourself not only from what your body is doing but from how exhausted and miserable you feel!

The key lies in the opposite approach. Increased mind-body integration is the secret ingredient for an enjoyable, safe fitness program that can last for the rest of your life.

Athletes seek the elusive exercise high, the Zone of peak performance where there are no thoughts and the crowd and the contest disappear into a magical moment of perfection, a total harmony of mind and body. As Olympic gold medal decathlete Bruce Jenner described it, "I started to feel there was nothing I couldn't do. I was rising above myself, doing things I had no right to be doing." In 1954, Roger Bannister gave us the formula for the Zone when he broke the 4-minute mile. "I felt no pain," he said. "There was no strain."

This exercise high, in which dynamic physical activity coexists with the inner experience of composure and calm, is not exclusive to athletes; it can be reached by anyone, regardless of his or her level of fitness. The Zone has been heralded throughout the ages as the key to developing not only our physical potential but our full human potential. The formula for reaching the Zone is the same as that required to achieve optimum health and to access the untapped 90 percent of human potential.

In nature, this coexistence of opposites, dynamic activity and silence, is vividly apparent. A striking example is a hurricane, in which the silence of the eye coexists with shattering winds. The earth spins on its axis, yet we feel still and solid. Vast galaxies, teeming with activity, float through the perfect silence of outer space.

Man, as part of nature, can tap this inexhaustible reservoir of power and peace. Preliminary findings among athletes using the techniques described in this book showed exercise to be more fun (as measured by a subjective feeling of less exertion) when compared to conventional exercise methods. Both heart and breath rates were lower along with a more composed nervous system when compared to the usual fight-or-flight exercise stress response. The most remarkable finding was the reproduction of alpha brain waves during exercise, indicating a state of inner calm. The mind is composed, the body is functioning in an efficient, relaxed way—*in the midst of the most dynamic physical activity.* The athlete, like Mother Nature, is doing less and accomplishing more. Our preliminary (Travis, et al., 1993) studies indicate that anyone can experience the Zone or "runner's high" at will. This gives us a new, uniquely challenging fitness goal. We're no longer content to see how much we can do; we want to know how effortlessly we can do it!

As you use the techniques in this book, your performance will soar, while your exertion and your breath and heart rates decrease. You will also learn the history of this unique mind-body experience. The Zone is referred to, in various ways, in the ancient teachings of China's Tao and Japan's Zen, but the oldest references come from India, the land of the Veda, where historians believe the original martial arts were taught. I spent over a year there, studying with some of the foremost experts in Vedic knowledge.

Although this book brings together knowledge from many branches of the Vedic literature, the principles of Ayurveda, the Science of Life, most closely apply, as you will see in part II. My training was in Maharishi Ayur-Ved, a revival and authentication of the principles and techniques according to the original Vedic texts.

In ancient cultures exercise was a piece of a much larger puzzle. The original Kung Fu masters, for example, spent hours not to master the art of breaking bricks but to unleash their full human potential, to achieve what they called *enlightenment*. In this book we will go deeply into the original principles of exercise and see how they can help you to consistently produce an exercise high and carry that experience into your daily life. For most people, exercise is entirely separate from daily life; thus it is hard to find or make time for it. I aim to show you how to use exercise as one of the most powerful and enjoyable means of achieving a healthy, happy, productive way of life.

The first step in this program is to determine your individual nature. Each person has a unique psychophysiological constitution or mind-body type. Your mind-body type will be your natural guide to sports selection, diet, best time of day to exercise, breathing, stretching, and much more. In addition, this book will show you how to adjust every aspect of your daily routine and fitness program to your individual requirements.

The next step in designing your health and fitness program is to choose a level that best suits your needs. To make this book equally useful for both the elite athlete and the person seeking general health and fitness, Level 1 and Level 2 programs have been structured. These programs are offered throughout the book, and from them you can select the sport, breathing technique, workout design, and stretching program most appropriate for you.

Level 1 is for people who are looking for general health and fitness, with little or no concern for performance and competition. Level 2 is for those who are more serious about exercise; this program includes sports and athletic training for both recreational and competitive purposes.

This book is designed to set you on the road to perfect health and fitness. To do it right, to make it fun and safe, and to make it last, it is essential that you learn the following points.

• How to determine your mind-body type and shape your health and fitness program to your requirements
• How to select the most appropriate exercise, sport, and cross-training sport for your body type
• How to guide your children into exercise, and to the sports most suitable for them, providing them with the most enjoyment and the greatest success
• How to listen to the needs of the your body during exercise
• How to decrease heart and breath rates while improving both fitness and performance
• How to perform specific stretching exercises to tone and strengthen the whole body during warm-ups and cool-downs and as a workout by itself
• How to incorporate body-type–specific dietary recommendations and daily and seasonal routines into your life for maximum health and fitness
• How to experience the Zone or exercise high at will

In my seminar, which I call Invincible Athletics, I have taught professional athletes and thousands of other people around the world, including the national team coaches and athletes from the former USSR State Committee for Physical Culture and Sports in Moscow. I've seen this knowledge transform children. I've seen adults begin to enjoy exercise for the first time in their lives. In my life, these principles have transformed my capacity, desire, and love for exercise, and I invite you to experience the same.

PART ONE

1

LIVING IN THE ZONE

Pele, the great soccer player whose spectacular performance almost single-handedly inspired American awareness and appreciation of his sport, wrote of his experience of the Zone in his autobiography, *My Life and Beautiful Game*. "In the middle of a match, I felt a strange calmness I hadn't experienced before. It was a type of euphoria. I felt I could run all day without tiring, that I could dribble through any or all of their team, that I could almost pass through them physically. It was a strange feeling and one that I had not had before. Perhaps it was merely confidence, but I have felt confident many times without that strange feeling of invincibility."

Baseball players are famous for their exotic pregame rituals in hopes of entering the Zone, in hopes of seeing baseballs as big as watermelons floating to the plate. Superstitions such as wearing dirty socks or garter belts for weeks on end are not unusual. Former Boston Red Sox third baseman Wade Boggs was famous for his pregame chicken dinners. Almost all professional athletes, in their own ways, search for the effortless performance of the Zone.

It has been called many things. Researchers speak of it as "peak experience" or the "flow state"; they say it is an "altered state" of human consciousness that cannot be intentionally created. Athletes find it difficult to describe when they return from it, although they may attribute it to supernatural concentration, religious mysticism, Zen, visualization, or biorhythms. More commonly, athletes refer to the Zone as the "exercise high," the "runner's high," the "groove," being "unconscious," or being "locked in."

Byron Scott, of the Los Angeles Lakers, said that when he finds himself in the Zone, "All you can hear is this little voice inside you, telling you 'Shoot' every time you touch the ball, because you know it's going in. Nobody outside can penetrate this world and the person guarding you wishes he wasn't. . . . I could shoot blindfolded from half court over my head and it would go in."

Joseph Campbell, considered the world's foremost authority on mythology, was interviewed for a PBS series shortly before his death in 1987, when he was in his eighties. During the interview, Bill Moyers asked him, "How do you explain what the psychologist Maslow called 'peak experiences'?" After a pause, Campbell replied, "My own peak experiences, the ones I knew were peak experiences after I had them, all came in athletics."

The field of sports psychology, which was developed in part to help athletes reproduce the highly coveted experience of the Zone, has failed in its attempts. Dr. Keith Henschen of the University of Utah, who specializes in the field, recognizes the elusive nature and apparently unreproducible experience of the Zone, but at the same time he believes it can be randomly accessed by anyone. That is, it can come to anyone, but it comes when it comes, not necessarily when you want it to. Perhaps the most certain limiting factor, according to Henschen, is that "the harder you try to get there, the less likely it is that you will."

This generates an interesting paradox. Modern exercise theory revolves around one central pivot, the stress-and-recover cycle, which boils down to this: We must repeatedly push ourselves to our limits and then let the body recover; that is how we become stronger, faster, and so on. The Zone is defined antithetically: The harder you try to reach that state, the less likely it is that you will. Conventional training demands that we put out tremendous effort; the Zone is an experience of absolute effortlessness.

Before 1954, the 4-minute mile was considered beyond human capability. Then Roger Bannister, an English medical student, cracked the barrier, running a mile in 3:59:4. Bannister said, "We seemed to be going so slowly. . . . I was relaxing so much that my mind seemed almost detached from my body. There was no strain. There was no pain. Only a great unity of movement and aim. The world seemed to stand still or even not exist."

Bannister's experience was not "No pain, no gain," but rather, "No strain, no pain = historic world record." Although Bannister told the world his formula for success, during the forty years since his achievement, athletes have continued to train using the stress-and-recover method.

If we want to reproduce the Zone, doesn't it make more sense that we should reproduce its qualities? If the experience is effortless, then we should cultivate effortlessness, rather than push the body to its limits. It seems naïve and foolish to expect the light, comfortable, euphoric feeling of the Zone to come with any regularity after the mind has driven the body into exhaustion.

This is one of the strategies you will learn in this book: capture the ease of the Zone from the first step of each workout, and gracefully build on that experience without dis-integrating the mind from the body.

DO LESS AND ACCOMPLISH MORE

Warren Wechsler had never considered himself an athlete. He had spent most of his adult life developing his mind, while paying little attention to his body. A successful businessman at 33, Warren suddenly found himself with a burning desire to run and set himself the goal of running a marathon by age 40.

He had a long way to go. He was overweight, stressed from his job, and completely out of shape. But he bought a pair of top-quality running shoes and started jogging. Very quickly he realized that he felt happier and healthier than before and that he had a natural talent for the sport.

After four months of pounding the pavement, Warren developed Achilles tendonitis. To alleviate it, he stretched more, went for physical therapy, and took more rest days, but the tightness on long runs persisted. He decided to "run through it"—a common technique among die-hard runners—hoping that the pain would disappear. After four more months Warren's ankle pain worsened. It soon developed into calf pain as well, then worked its way up to the knee. Undaunted, Warren continued his workouts, convinced that "all good things have their price." The aches and pains soon appeared in the other knee. When they reached his back, he was forced to hang up his running shoes.

Three years later, in 1989, Warren attended my Invincible Athletics seminar. He wanted to get back to running, but, afraid of reinjury, he didn't let himself get his hopes up too high. On hearing the principle that "less is more," and that running, if done properly, should remove strain rather than produce it, Warren decided to give it another go. He began exercising again, cautiously this time, following the specific advice for his body type and listening carefully to the needs of his body. (Body types are fully explained in chapter 4.)

Warren was so conditioned to expect strain and pain that he found it strange not to hurt during his workouts. At first he noticed that his heart rate would jump from 75 BPM (beats per minute) to 170 or 180 as soon as he started exercising with even moderate exertion. After three months of reconditioning his body to do less and accomplish more on his exercise bike, he found that he could pedal for over an hour with his heart rate around 120 and his breath rate even and comfortable at around 15 breaths per minute.

In January 1990, Warren felt ready to run and rejoined his health club, which featured an indoor track. At first, finding himself lapped by his old running partners, he had to struggle against his desire to keep up with them. Listening carefully to his body—not to the ambitions of his mind or to his sense of pride—he let them pass him. Gradually he picked up speed. Soon he surpassed his former running partners, only this time he did so without injury or pain.

He called me at my office eighteen months after starting the Invincible Athletics program and gave me this report:

> John, I'm 38 years old. I've never been an athlete in my life. I took your course to give my running one last try. Since then, I've lost 30 pounds and 6 inches of girth without trying or dieting. I don't get sick or anxious anymore, and I've got more vitality than I've ever known.
>
> Yesterday, running on my indoor track, I ran 17 miles. I felt absolutely fantastic the whole way. I felt as good when I stopped as I did when I started. The amazing thing was that I ran a 6-minute-mile pace for the entire 17 miles. It was unbelievable. I was in the Zone, I felt like I was running on air. It was the easiest thing I've ever done.
>
> The most incredible thing was that my heart rate averaged about 120 BPM during the entire run. Sometimes it went even lower, but it never went over 130 BPM while I maintained the 6-minute pace. When I counted my breath rate, it was between 12 and 15 breaths per minute. [The average breath rate at rest is 18 breaths per minute.] At this rate, when I'm 40 I could be running marathons with the best runners in the world, having the runner's high experience the entire time.

For Warren, exercise had become a means of removing stress. The more he ran, the more rejuvenated he felt.

We had been working with many athletes at our health center and finding some dramatic decreases in exertion during high-level exercise using our techniques, but a heart rate of 120 BPM while maintaining a 6-minute-mile pace was hard to believe. I figured that perhaps Warren's monitoring equipment wasn't first-rate and invited him to our health center to verify his findings.

When he came, I put him on the treadmill. It wasn't long before he had the equipment "maxed out" at 10.5 miles per hours (a little better than a 6-minute mile), and, sure enough, his heart rate was stable at about 125 BPM and he was breathing easily at just the rate he had reported. The average runner would have to strain pretty hard to run a 6-minute mile, showing heart rates up to 180 BPM and breath rates up to 40 or 50 breaths per minute.

Warren's success came because he was determined not to incur stress but to let his body gracefully improve from the inside out. He never put pressure on himself to reach any specific time, either to meet an arbitrary deadline or to compete in a given race. He simply wanted to see how fast he could run and with how little effort.

Lowering heart and breath rates while running faster and faster is like driving a big old Cadillac and getting 50 miles per gallon. This possibility provides a new level of motivation: to see not only what one can do, but with how little effort and with how much efficiency it can be done. (I discuss how to do this in chapters 13 and 14, which describe the Three Phase Workout.)

Not long after Warren's visit to me at the health center, he ran his first marathon. He cruised at a comfortable 6½-minute-mile pace the whole way, finishing with ease and comfort at 2 hours 53 minutes. The next day he went out and ran 5 miles. Even more amazing, four days later he did a 10-mile run in a time that was his personal best.

Warren's strategy was to treat every race as a training race. He felt that if he could stay within himself, taking his cues from himself and not from any preconceived or outward standard, he would continue to rejuvenate himself with each run and steadily get better. More important, he would *enjoy* every race.

With this attitude, Warren fell in love with exercise. He was becoming fit, but this time it wasn't a case of his body being whipped into shape by his mind. He was feeling a deep sense of integrity and efficiency, as if he could run all day without strain. As he continued to improve, he would monitor his heart and breath rates and watch them remain low while he effortlessly attained competitive speeds and distances. To his amazement and delight, the harmony of his mind and body was reflected in his increasing ability to be in the Zone.

The principles described in this book are derived from ancient teachings that far predate the sports psychologists' discouraging pronouncements that the Zone is not reproducible. I believe—on the basis of my professional experience—that not only should the runner's high or Zone experience be expected with every workout, but that reaching this experience is the primary *purpose* of exercise. Only through this experience can we access our highest physical potential.

To prove this very bold point—that the elusive Zone is readily available within all of us and *can* be called up intentionally—we must look into the origins of exercise and sport.

Try your normal workout while breathing through your nose. If you find it more difficult than usual and can't get enough oxygen, this indicates that you do not have maximum respiratory efficiency, and that you need this program! You can reach your full respiratory potential when you learn how to draw on it.

BACK TO THE FUTURE

If we went far enough back in time, we would see that the purpose of exercise was not to build muscle, lose weight, win races, or receive gold medals. To the ancient Greeks, for example, exercise was a vital part of daily life. The historian Xenophon said, "No citizen has any right to be an amateur in the matter of physical training; it is part of his profession as a citizen to keep himself in good condition." He added that it is "a disgrace for a man to grow old without seeing the beauty and the strength of which his body is capable."

This attitude had a deeper, spiritual basis, explained by the great Greek philosophers Plato and Aristotle. Plato, throughout his writings, emphasized the importance of exercise for developing the spiritual side of life. His ideal was harmonious perfection of both the body and the mind, or soul, and exercise was one of the methods he advocated. Aristotle also favored exercise and emphasized a theme that I will return to often in this book: that exercise should be moderate rather than excessive or insufficient, and that it should be undertaken in accordance with one's individual physical capacity.

Today, historians point out that the original martial arts did not consist solely of kicks, blocks, and punches. Their real purpose was to be found in the *spiritual* side, an aspect largely missing in modern American dojos. Even members of the U.S. karate team lament the absence of a spiritual base.

The history of the martial arts is sketchy in places, but most historians now agree that its roots in China were actually seeded from the even older Vedic culture of India. About fourteen hundred years ago an Indian monk named Bodhidharma journeyed from India over the Himalayas to bring the teachings of Buddha to China. He stopped to teach at the Shaolin Monastery in the Honan Province of central China. Tradition regards his teachings at Shaolin as the origin of the martial arts in China. This traditional lore gained credibility recently when two books attributed to Bodhidharma were discovered in the temple walls.

According to legend, Bodhidharma—who later became known in Japan as Daruma—taught a form of Buddhism for developing mind and body that is now known as Zen. He told the monks of Shaolin that he would teach them techniques to develop the necessary physical and spiritual strength to master the Way of Buddha, but he soon found that they were physically weak and unable to keep up with his training.

The focus of their life in the monastery had been on the inner aspect of life—the mind, or soul—with little attention to the health and strength of the body. Bodhidharma taught them that although Buddha's message was about the soul, body and soul are really inseparable. You cannot train one without the other.

The physical techniques that Bodhidharma taught were not for the purpose of overcoming opponents but for the integrated development of body, mind, and spirit. Using these methods, which are recorded in the ancient *Ekkin Sutras*, the Shaolin monks became renowned for their physical and spiritual strength, courage, and fortitude.

The message of Zen Buddhism, brought first to China and then to Japan from the Vedic civilization of India, was that enlightenment was not meant to be enjoyed only in silent, disembodied contemplation. It was a way of life, to be lived at all times, or, as the famous Zen saying goes, "while carrying water and chopping wood."

Bodhidharma's work at the Shaolin temples led to the development of Kung Fu and Tai Chi. Kung Fu is the more aggressive form, which displays the dynamic "yang" aspect of nature, and Tai Chi reflects the more peaceful and silent "yin" component. Both of these qualities must be developed and expressed during exercise in order to cultivate regular experience of the Zone.

In martial arts, or in any other sport, the only way man can harness the power and the strength of nature and the universe is to mimic nature's way. Wherever nature exists, this formula also exists: dynamic action along with perfect silence. The dead of winter is balanced by the activity of summer. The more dynamic the activity, the more dramatic the contrast of opposites. The bigger the hurricane, the bigger its eye.

Exercise is a proven approach to life's ultimate goal, which modern Zen master D. T. Suzuki called "motionless realization." Tennis great Billie Jean King described it in her autobiography: "I transport myself to a place beyond the turmoil of the court to a place of total peace and calm." She was *on* the court but beyond the *turmoil* of the court. She was in the Zone, where the most dynamic physical activity coexists with mental composure, peace, and calm.

The legendary Ted Williams, who coined the phrase "the Zone," said he could see the seams of the baseball as it came whirling up to the plate at 100 miles per hour!

Williams had no doubt that he had seen a 100-mph fastball with the close-up clarity of a slow-motion instant replay, yet "experts" claim that it is optically impossible. The 4-minute mile was once considered impossible, as were the 500-pound lift and many other feats that today are accomplished by many. I read recently that experts now predict a 3:30 mile by the year 2054, one hundred years after Roger Bannister's boundary-breaking achievement. Records fall every day. So, what is "impossible"?

New records generally do not leap far above previous ones, yet no one can predict final limits. As soon as a record is called "unbeatable," someone inevitably comes along who is capable of going faster, higher, farther. It is said that fish are 80 to 90 percent efficient in the water, while a world-class swimmer is only 8 to 9 percent efficient. Does this mean that we will never be truly efficient in the water, or that our potential gains are unlimited?

IS THE SKY THE LIMIT?

Ninety miles south of Phoenix, Arizona, live the Tarahumara Indians, a native Mexican tribe with an unfathomable skill in running. The Tarahumara run from their first steps to their last; it is their way of life. These remarkable people can run down deer and horses; they can run 50 to 100 miles in a day with ease, and up to 150 miles seemingly without effort. They have been known to run 40 to 50 miles at a time, taking only the briefest of breaks. Even more striking, they are said to improve with age, and the young look up to their grandfathers as the runners with the greatest skill.

> ONCE A TOURIST DROVE BY A RUNNING TARAHUMARA AND ASKED IF HE WOULD LIKE A LIFT. THE TARAHUMARA SAID, "NO, THANKS, I'M IN A HURRY."

A few years ago, a group of North American researchers visited the Tarahumara to study their feats. They staged a 26-mile run—a marathon, a run the researchers considered most grueling and demanding. The Indians laughed at the distance, regarding it as child's play.

The test took the Indians over rugged, extremely mountainous terrain in the scorching heat of the Mexican desert. The runners averaged 6 miles per hour including breaks; they took no food or water. At the end, they stood calmly near the finish line, breathing effortlessly as the researchers examined them in disbelief. Pulse rates averaged about 130 beats per minute, and blood pressure, which had been low at the start, was even lower at the end of the run.

The scientists concluded that what they had witnessed was not humanly possible! Yet the Tarahumara were decidedly human, possessing no "super gene" or any other unique physical quality.

This kind of accomplishment should not be considered mystical or magical. Throughout history, man has harnessed similar powers. There are tribes in the Andes mountains of South America whose accomplishments in running are similar to those of the Tarahumara. Holy men in the Himalayas live virtually on roots in freezing weather at fifteen thousand feet the year round. The Hunza of Pakistan are known for their extraordinary longevity. Yogis and Zen masters have displayed breath suspension and lowered metabolism while performing amazing deeds of strength and endurance.

We usually assume that such phenomena occur only among monks or martial arts masters who have abandoned our modern ways in favor of austerity. But human potential is unlimited and can be achieved by anyone who desires to do so.

Certainly the message of Bodhidharma contains a resounding vote for the unlimited potential of the human body. Modern researchers agree. According to neuroscientists, humans use less than .01 percent of our potential brain power. Translated into economic terms, we are surviving on $1 while $10,000 sit in the bank. A state-of-the-art computer with the same number of information bits as there are neurons in the human brain would fill a 100-story building the size of Texas.

Using conservative estimates, there are 100 trillion neuron junctions in the brain. (Some scientists are now saying that there are closer to two to the trillionth power connections among brain cells.) This means that there are more possible mental states than there are atoms in the universe— which makes it seem even more unlikely that anything should be impossible for us.

Mind-body reactions take place at phenomenal speeds. Messages from the brain to the body and back are measured in thousandths and ten-thousandths of a second. Evidence even exists that every one of our thoughts affects every one of our cells *instantaneously.*

The hardware for maximum integration of mind and body is built in. If we could access even a little bit more of it, athletic performance would soar far beyond what we believe are our normal limits. Considering the potential that lies within us, it is more remarkable that we are ever *out* of the Zone than that we are only occasionally in it.

TRAINING TIP NO. 2
COUNT YOUR STEPS

Go for a walk and count how many steps you can take per one full inhale and exhale through your nose. Keep trying to increase the number of steps per one complete breath. Anything over 18 steps indicates a good start toward total respiratory efficiency.

THE ILLEGITIMATE ZONE

There are two different experiences of the Zone. One is born of integration and harmony between mind and body, the other from a breakdown between the two. Many instances of "runner's high" occur after or toward the end of long endurance events. The Western States 100 Mile Endurance Run is known for producing such experiences. After enduring 70 to 80 miles of canyon heat, followed by high-altitude climbs, the body reaches its limits. The mind, however, is still set on its goal: to cross the finish line, no matter the cost.

When exhaustion occurs and the body is in pain—severe overheating; painful knees, ankles, and shins; aching lungs; and so on—the body begins to produce painkillers to help the person endure the ordeal. These painkillers, in the form of endorphins, enkephalons, and other morphinelike substances, are generated to combat the physical punishment inflicted on the body by a mind that is out of touch with what is happening on the physical level. The runner feels high, but his performance has disintegrated.

As the flood of endorphins is released into the bloodstream, it does more than kill the pain; as the mind swims in the pool of morphine, it becomes numb to the body. The result in some cases is complete dissociation of the mind from the body.

During the Western States 100 Mile Endurance Run in 1983, I was a pacer for one of the seeded runners, Bill McKean. After Bill broke his ankle, I pulled another runner from the bottom of a canyon at the 45-mile mark. Exhausted and delirious, he had collapsed and couldn't take another step, yet he said he had been feeling "fantastic" until his legs gave out and he collapsed.

How did he go from feeling so good to so bad, so fast? Painkilling endorphins gave him a false sense of euphoria, which masked the body's extreme fatigue. Because his mind was disconnected from his body, he could not muster the simple coordination needed to stand up and walk.

As the man's exaltation wore off, unbearable pain set in. I watched him flip from an unintelligible babble to uncontrollable tears as we dragged him to safety five miles out of the canyon. One might label it a runner's high, but it's not the legitimate Zone athletes seek, where the mind and body are inseparable.

ENTER THE ZONE

The euphoric experience that athletes call the Zone or exercise high is now, at best, random. It comes when it comes—or it doesn't come at all. When athletes lock in to it, exceptional performance seems automatic. Sports psychologist Bruce Ogilvie says that when they are in the Zone, "these athletes are able to relinquish a conscious awareness, and to focus in an internal way. It's a harmony of mind-body experience, a lack of interference. It's the essence of focusing, the art of the flow."

Nancy Kalil, the number-one ranked U.S. women's handball champion, wrote of her experiences in the Zone:

> I began playing handball in 1981. Handball is a game that develops both sides of one's body—the left and right sides must be developed and coordinated. As an athlete I had the strength and coordination, yet the mind-body connection was not balanced. There was a period when I became more involved in the mental aspect of the game, yet there was always something missing.
>
> I continued to excel in handball, winning national titles, and have remained in the top four among women since 1985.
>
> The 1991–92 season was my best, as I became the #1 ranked U.S. woman. Although I accomplished this, I realized that there was still something missing—the total mind-body connection, how to be in peak performance when I needed it, not just when it happened randomly. Not just training and hoping I'd peak when the tournaments were scheduled. Not just playing great during preliminary matches, only to "not have it together" during the semifinals or finals.
>
> In July 1992, while taking a break from handball, I learned of John Douillard's Invincible Athletics course, and began training using its principles.
>
> As I first began to apply the techniques, I felt as though I was hardly working out. I was enjoying myself too much, and not straining myself: this couldn't be right, I thought! But to my amazement, within a few weeks my body began to recondition itself naturally. I was able to do

more, while keeping in my optimal training zone (50 percent of maximum heart rate), and I was stress-free.

Where I notice the greatest difference is in my actual handball game. As I began to become in tune with my mind and body—through the breathing techniques, heart rate monitoring, and focused attention, becoming absorbed within myself—my handball game jumped to a whole new level. What I have practiced over and over to do on the handball court for the past five or six years all of a sudden began to happen. I am covering the court, forty feet long, effortlessly and easily from back to front, with a speed I've never known. I'm playing two-hour matches and still feeling fresh and energetic.

In the past, I've been known as a defensive player, conditioned to keep the volley going and waiting for my opponent to make a mistake. Now, with my performance at a new level, and playing in the Zone each time, I have become a very offensive player, hitting shots I always dreamed about but rarely did. It still feels funny to be playing so well while staying so relaxed and full of energy, being calm and almost moving at a slow pace in between volleys. Even during the volleys the speed seems slow and relaxed, although in reality the ball and I are moving very quickly. I am amazed at how I am getting to the ball so quickly and effortlessly.

The opponents I play on a regular basis are also amazed. I play men (there are few women players in my immediate area) and the strength and quickness factors are apparent. I've always played men who are better than I, so I can improve my game. I am now consistently either beating them, or almost beating them, staying neck-and-neck during the match. They have all commented on how much I've improved since I incorporated the Invincible Athletics principles into my life.

Even my husband, who is on the men's pro tour in handball, used to easily beat me 21–0. He says he now has to push harder when we play. The volleys are longer, and I win a number of them. My husband, who also started the techniques, has noticed benefits in his own play, most notably a heightened desire to work out. The motivation has been higher, and the workouts more fun.

Although scientists and sports psychologists insist that the Zone experience cannot be generated at will, I've seen case after case of enhanced performance, many similar to Nancy's, and heard many descriptions of being in the Zone, as a result of using the techniques in this book.

Until recently, scientists had been unable to measure the elusive runner's high, to see what it's made of, so to speak. But a growing body of scientific information and a preliminary study (Travis, et al., 1993) seem to be breaking new ground.

ALPHA POWER

We took ten athletes who had been using our techniques for at least twelve weeks and compared their mental and physical performance during conventional exercise and Invincible Athletics. The preliminary findings were unprecedented.

Using Invincible Athletics, the athletes achieved a psychomotor state that differed sharply from that reached through conventional techniques. This state had both the subjective and objective qualities of ease and comfort that athletes commonly say characterize their experience of the Zone. Their EEGs indicated that their minds were in a state of relaxation, and their breath rates, heart rates, and perceived exertion were lower throughout a workout when compared to conventional exercise. Yet their actual level of performance was the same or higher.

In graph B (see page 16), you see the typical brain wave pattern expected during exercise as measured on the EEG. These brain waves, known as beta, are common to all activity with the eyes open, such as conversation, eating, walking, or exercise.

Graph A shows a pattern of brain waves that is obviously more coherent. At first glance, if I asked you, "What style of functioning would you rather have, A or B?" you would likely say that graph A seems more appealing.

The brain waves depicted in graph A are predominantly alpha. They reflect a state of mind that is more relaxed and composed, as compared to graph B, which portrays a mind full of active thoughts. Alpha is usually found during sleep, deep states of relaxation, biofeedback, and meditation.

What is so unusual about the alpha bursts seen in graph A is that they were produced during exercise. Yet they are characteristic of a style of functioning in which thoughts are minimal, and mind and body are relaxed. This seems to be the neurophysiological correlate of what athletes sometimes call the "mindless state," where everything just happens and you're not thinking about it.

In sports, particularly in competition, there is no time to think. If the right action or reaction, the right move, doesn't just flow, it's too late. That is why athletes practice so often. If you do it a thousand times, hopefully there will be no distracting thoughts in the game.

Tim Flannery of the San Diego Padres said, "When I'm locked in, I feel like a giant eye. I don't feel my hands, I don't feel my stride, I don't know where my shoulders are. All I do is just see the ball and everything else just happens." Flannery is obviously not describing an analytical or "mindful" state but an automatic and highly coordinated flow between mind and body. This is the kind of experience that is predicted when alpha bursts are lively in the brain. (Previous research has indicated that 20 percent of the

Graph A

Alpha Brain Wave Activity During Invincible Athletics Exercise

C_3P_3
P_3O_1
F_7T_3
T_3T_5
T_4T_6
F_8T_4
P_4O_2
C_4P_4

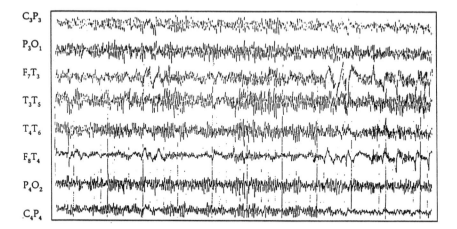

Alpha activity 11 minutes into "Listening Phase" (during bicycle ergometer submaximal stress test)

Graph B

Beta Brain Wave Activity During Conventional Exercise

C_3P_3
P_3O_1
F_7T_3
T_3T_5
T_4T_6
F_8T_4
P_4O_2

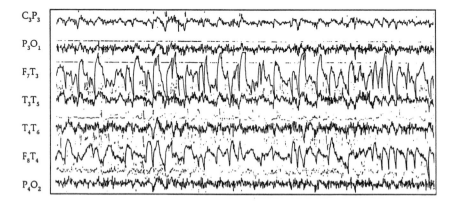

Beta activity seen 18 minutes into conventional bicycle ergometer submaximal stress test (comparable in time to 11 minutes of "Listening Phase")

*large waves in F_7T_3, F_8T_4 are due to eye movements

population seems incapable of producing alpha waves. Although the number of subjects we have studied is still quite small, we have seen alpha bursts in all of them. A heightened state of ease and comfort appears to be possible for everyone.)

Glance again at the graphs and consider this: Both graphs portray brain waves produced during exercise by the same person, at the exact same workload, on the same exercise bike, during the same standard exercise stress test. There is only one difference. The second time—graph A—he was using the principles in this book.

Here science opens a window on the familiar formula for the Zone: dynamic action and composed silence coexisting, as the eye of the hurricane coexists with the wind.

We did an exhaustive search of past research, looking for the production of alpha waves during aerobic exercise with the eyes open. As far as we can tell, ours is an unprecedented finding.

Graph C

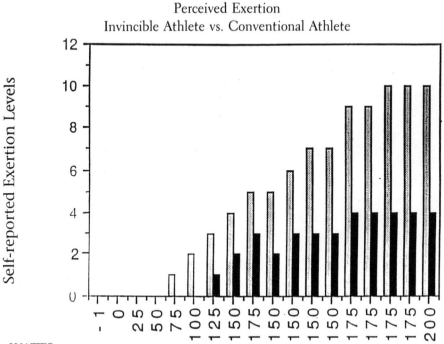

Perceived Exertion
Invincible Athlete vs. Conventional Athlete

WATTS
(resistance increasing over time during bicycle ergometer submaximal stress test)

□ Conventional Athlete
■ Invincible Athlete

Of course, more research is needed to confirm our findings, but it seems reasonable to assume that the exercise high, the Zone, which embodies the experiences that occur when alpha waves are present, can now be the expected result during exercise. This means that the Zone is reproducible. You don't have to wait and hope for it to come, you can create it.

When the brain is in alpha, reflecting a quiet mind while the body is dynamic, the athlete will naturally slip into the Zone, and the performance will be from the inside out.

When the brain is in beta, the mind is active, the body is active, and the competition becomes enough of a distraction to disintegrate the mind from the body. The flow between body and mind is restricted, and enjoyment vanishes.

When our research subjects were compared on the Borg Scale of Perceived Exertion, as seen on graph C, these conventional exercise methods produced significantly more sense of strain. As the workload built up, the athletes' subjective experience of exertion increased proportionately, so that at maximum workload, the subjects felt the maximum strain. The Invincible Athletes experienced far less perceived exertion. At the maximum workload, one of our subjects experienced just 50 percent of the exertion he felt with conventional methods.

When exercise is experienced as strain, it is no wonder that so few people—only about 10 to 15 percent of the American population, according to a government survey—participate in a regular exercise program.

TRAINING TIP NO. 3
LET COMFORT BE YOUR GUIDE

Begin your exercising, gradually increasing the pace while monitoring the subjective experience of comfort. Note exactly where during the workout comfort becomes discomfort—heavy breathing, heart pounding, pain, or strain. For more details see chapters 13 and 14.

BODY, MIND, AND BOW

The great warriors of ancient times were said to experience sleep and inner alertness simultaneously. Even while asleep they would remain completely aware of their environment. This ability to remain alert while asleep made them immune to surprise attacks during the night.

Their inner wakefulness was accomplished through certain meditative practices for developing the highest mental and physical capacities. These practices were reserved for the warrior class and for the rulers, whose superior development was considered essential for a peaceful balance in society.

By cultivating calmness along with dynamism through their training methods, the warriors gained the physical precision and mental composure needed to excel in the pandemonium of combat. Their extraordinary psychophysiological development gave them a reputation for being invincible. Who would attack a nation whose great warriors were invulnerable to surprise attack and too skilled to defeat in open battle? This strength acted as a natural deterrent, and—so say the legends—their nations lived in peace.

Today our national defense is also said to depend on strength, only now strength is believed to lie in the most potent offense. In this system, the country that is the largest manufacturer of weapons is the most feared and therefore the least likely to be attacked. While we sport weapons of external destruction, the ancient warriors drew their invincibility from within. By mastering the forces of nature through discipline and training, they established a state of composure that remained undisturbed even amid the rigors of battle. This is the formula that athletes seek in their quest for the Zone.

Among the physical and mental techniques employed to develop the superior warrior, the art of archery was the foremost. The ancient warriors of China and Japan recognized the power of the bow, although the most ancient reference to the military use of the bow appears in India's Dhanur Veda. (*Dhanur* means "bow"; *Veda* means "knowledge" or "truth"; hence, the "Pure Knowledge of the Bow.") The texts of Dhanur Veda expound the means of developing action in harmony with nature.

In our search for studies showing the production of alpha waves during exercise, although we located no cases of alpha during aerobic exercise, we did find one study that showed that during the practice of archery, a high percentage of individuals were found in a state of alpha. This substantiated what the ancient cultures knew to be true.

The correct shooting of an arrow from a bow requires the ability to maintain mental composure and physical calm. Pulling back the bowstring requires great strength. The body's muscles must be in a state of dynamic contraction, yet they must become perfectly still as they bring the arrow to rest on the string. The slightest movement of the bow, when drawn, will exponentially distort the flight of the arrow. Perfect physical silence must exist along with the dynamic power and strength needed to carry the arrow with precision and accuracy.

The mind of the archer must also be composed and still while at the same time dynamically focused on the target. This mental silence and composure must not be disturbed any more than the physical stillness. Any mental excitation, any unnecessary or inappropriate thoughts, will distract the mind from what the body is doing and break down the fine coordination essential for this harmony of mind, body, and sport.

According to the Vedas, the power of the universe is reflected in archery during the split-second release of the bowstring. As the arrow is released, the muscles are sprung into a heightened state of activity, then quickly relax. The release of a 60-pound bowstring creates a dynamic physical transformation from muscular action to muscular relaxation. At the same time, the mind releases its intense focus on the target. As the mind lets go, the focus is transformed into silence, where there is no focus, just a heightened state of awareness. At this instant, there are absolutely no thoughts, just a mind suspended in alert awareness as the arrow races to its target.

During this instant, when the mind had let go of its focus and the body had relaxed its muscular contraction, the archer slips into the Zone.

Everything comes to rest. But it is a dynamic rest, awake, alert, ready to move again with great power. It is like slipping for a moment into the hurricane's eye, but using it as a command post to direct the force of the hurricane at will.

On the battlefield depicted in the epic poem *Mahabharata*, Krishna revealed the secret of victory to the great archer Arjuna. He said, *Yogastha kuru karmani*—first established yourself in Being, then perform action. ("Established in Being" defines *Yoga* as literally "union," the permanent, living coexistence of inner silence with outer activity.) Establish first a composed and calm mind and body, then you can create a hurricane. Billie Jean King called it "a perfect combination of violent action taking place in an atmosphere of total tranquillity."

TRAINING TIP NO. 4
SILENCE IN ACTION

Take notice while playing a particular sport—for example, when you shoot a basketball. Note the immense focus during the shot, followed by an immediate mind-body release right after the ball leaves your fingers. For a second, the mind is totally free of thoughts and the body is totally relaxed. It's the same silence ancient warriors sought in the release of the bow on the battlefield. Find this silence in your tennis shot, soccer kick, or any other skill-related activity.

SILENT GLORY

Patsy Neal was captain of the U.S. women's team in the 1964 World Basketball Tournament. In high school, Ms. Neal set the Georgia State women's basketball single-game scoring record with a fabulous 64-point performance. She later competed in the Pan American Games and played on the U.S. All-Star Team against women stars from Russia, France, and Germany. She also taught college health and physical education courses for nineteen years and has published four books on sports. In her book *Sport and Identity* she related her experience of being in the Zone when she won the 1957 Free-Throw Championship at the National AAU Basketball Tournament:

When I shot my free-throws in the finals, I was probably the calmest I have ever been in my life. I didn't even see or hear the crowd. It was only me, the ball, and the basket. The number of baskets I made really had no importance to me at the time. The only thing that really mattered was what I felt. But even so, I would have found it hard to miss even if I had wanted to. My motions were beyond my conscious control. . . . If it were in my power to maintain what I was experiencing at that point in time, I would have given up everything in my possession in preference to that sensation. But it was beyond my will . . . beyond my own understanding . . . beyond me. Yet, I was *it*.

That evening, I hit 48 out of 50 free-throws to win the 1957 Free-Throw Championship. The only thing that surprised me was the fact that two of the shots missed. I felt in such a state of perfection that it seemed only right that my performance would have been perfect. Even now, when I think of the Free-Throw Championship, I don't think about the fact that I won it . . . I think of what I *was* that evening. . . .

There have been other moments in my life when I have touched on this unlimited source of power—where things *happened* in spite of me. But never once have I been able to consciously *will* it to happen. I have been open to it because I know it's *there*. . . . But the occasions are so rare—perhaps this adds to the preciousness of it.

As a result of that experience, I know that spirit and bodily movements can be correlated. As they intertwine, one seems to hang between the real world and another world of miracles. One accomplishes things one never dreamed of doing. One walks beyond the usual physical powers and goes *into* the power of the universe, finding streams and sensations that seem to have no beginning or end within the self.

2

WINNING FROM INSIDE OUT

> In the 1928 men's single sculls, the Australian champion was unexpectedly delayed by a family of ducks. After pausing to let them pass in front of him, in single file, he went on to win the event by five lengths.

I once heard a beautiful story about the spirit of competition. An English naval officer was marooned on a remote island in the South Pacific. He had befriended a native man to whom he was constantly trying to prove his superiority and the superiority of his culture. For the Englishman, everything was a contest—from who could build a better fire to who could design a more functional hut. This puzzled the native, for whom life was fun, like a game. He simply could not fathom the Englishman's intensity.

One day the Englishman, in typical fashion, threw a challenge to the native. Pointing out a spot about half a mile down the beautiful sandy beach, he announced, "We will have a competition from here to that distant point."

The native agreed. The Englishman, always taking charge of things, set up the conditions: "We will train in our own style, privately, for two weeks. On the fourteenth day, we will compete."

When the day arrived, they took their places on the starting line, and the Englishman fired his pistol in the air to set them off. With his usual intensity, pushing himself to the limit of his physical ability and grimacing with the strain, he drove himself through the sand until, gasping for breath, he lunged for the finish line. Exhausted and soaked in sweat, he turned to see how his opponent was doing.

To his joy and amazement, the native was only about halfway to the finish line. The Englishman watched him float gracefully along the shoreline with long, comfortable strides, a smile on his handsome face. When he finally pranced across the finish line he found the Englishman jumping up and down and shouting, "I won! I won!"

The native looked at the Englishman in disbelief. "What? *You* won? No, *I* won. *I* was the most beautiful!"

The story makes you wonder: Who had the better idea? Is it better to win at any cost or simply to enjoy the game? Taking first place is only one perspective on what it means to be a winner. For the native, being beautiful was the real competition. Maybe the ancient Greeks were right to emphasize physical exercise for the cultivation of the self, rather than for the conquest of an opponent. The modern-day credo of "No pain, no gain" and Vince Lombardi's "Winning isn't everything; it's the only thing" just may be due for revision.

INNER LIGHTS OR SPOTLIGHTS?

We are conditioned to think that to win, to be the best, is the only legitimate goal. An Olympic gold medal, parlayed into Coke commercials and TV appearances, is the sign of the greatest achievement. A silver medalist—second best in the world, and not a small accomplishment—is considered a risky investment by the marketing wizards who exploit the achievements of world-class athletes. But as Colleen Cannon, a world-class triathlete, said to me, "I think the real race we're involved in here is the *human* race. The important thing is not whether you win in San Jose on Saturday, but the process you're going through as an individual—how you develop as a human being."

A couple of years ago I worked with Steve Bennet, a Pan American Games world champion in karate. One of the kindest, most soft-spoken guys I'd ever met, Steve told me that during his training as a young boy his coach had brainwashed him into never entertaining the possibility of defeat. Thus, Steve became obsessed with winning. Karate was for defeating the opposition, and nothing more. Even as he trained his childhood away, he complained continually to his coach, "I'm tired. I'm tired." This was viewed as a sign of weakness. He was simply forced to train harder, and learned to keep his mouth shut.

The pressure on him to win became so great that he would panic before competitions. He developed insomnia and severe anxiety, which later manifested itself as aggressive behavior with his family. Before a match he would become uncontrollably nervous. First his hands would sweat, then his whole body. His heart would begin to race, he would start to tremble, then he would finally burst into the ring in a frenzied state born of nervous exhaustion.

Yes, Steve became a winner—but by the age of 24 he had collapsed both physically and mentally. He could barely walk, would hyperventilate at the smallest stress, and was unable to drive a car because his legs shook uncontrollably. He was forced to take tranquilizers and was told that he would need to take them for the rest of his life.

Driven by his coach, Steve almost gave his life not to let his coach down. Steve derived little enjoyment or satisfaction from his efforts. And deep inside, he always knew he was destroying himself. Yet, he found himself going through the painful motions of training and competition only because he had a gift—he could win.

Steve somehow managed to become a world champion even while taking tranquilizers, thanks to his enormous determination and physical endurance. He is now off all medications and has devoted his life to teaching the true meaning of karate and sports and the deeper purpose of competition.

Competition is not for the sole purpose of defeating the opposition and becoming the winner. After all, who can remember last year's champions? For all its flash, this type of victory is short-lived. The more lasting victory has to be an inner one.

Inner victory comes from the knowledge that you have done your best. It is a feeling of respect for your achievements and for those of your fellow athletes. It is the essence of the word *Aidos*, the ancient Greek athletic ideal, which includes modesty, respect, moral dignity, and good sportsmanship, coupled with valor and the "joy of battle," the joy of competition itself.

We all grew up believing that we can be happy, even elated, if we win, but if we lose, we have to be miserable and dejected. At the end of the World Series or the NCAA play-offs, the cameras routinely pan back and forth from the jubilant winners, leaping and shouting, to the dejected losers, sitting on the bench with lowered heads. This has a terrible effect, particularly on our children, who model this behavior and thus learn to trade anything in order to win.

Buy why should this be? Why shouldn't we enjoy the game, the action, the sheer joy of being our best?

I introduced my training principles to a small-town high school soccer team. At the time, they barely had enough kids to field a team. Earlier in the year, their coach had sent me a note about one of their games. They had lost 8–0, "but the interesting thing was that our kids were still able to enjoy the match. In fact, despite the fact that they were getting creamed, they were having a noticeably good time, to such an extent that the winning team began to get upset. How could these kids still be enjoying themselves in the midst of being shut out?

"As the match ended, our kids got together in what looked like a victory huddle, then went to congratulate the winners. The winning team was blown away at this unusual display of sportsmanship, and they asked our kids, 'How can you be so happy? We just shut you out 8–0.' Our boys said that they were happy because they felt that their playing was good, that they could see themselves getting better with each game. It was fun, and they simply loved to play soccer.

"This only served to anger the winners even more; in fact they challenged our little team to a rematch—in hopes, I suppose, of finally humiliating them and making them feel 'the agony of defeat.' "

This soccer team lost the match but won the game. They took home the inner prize because they found joy in the *process*, the path to the goal, rather than having their satisfaction depend on the game's outcome. If the process itself is fulfilling, winning will always be the experience, regardless of the final score. External victories will come and go, but internal victories are here to stay.

As we've seen, to the ancient Greeks, and to the originators of the martial arts, the inner competition was regarded as the highest. Only there could a person be a true champion. Seen in this light, the purpose of competition is to display the athlete's skill. The opposition is there as a distraction, to try to take the athlete away from himself, to tempt him to focus on the challenger instead of on himself and his performance. Distracted, the athlete loses the mind-body coordination needed to win from inside out.

Does this sound strange? For a moment, imagine yourself on a tennis court. You've been playing very well into the final set, calling the shots, making your opponent play your kind of game. Then suddenly you find yourself playing your opponent's game. He begins dictating the strategy, the shots, and, ultimately, the outcome. A match you thought you were in control of suddenly slips through your hands because your opponent distracted you from yourself and your game.

Steve Briggs, a tennis instructor and former competitor on the pro tennis tour, put it this way: "In tennis you're going head to head with another person. So to a certain extent you have to pay attention to where they're going to serve or hit the next shot. But if you think too much about what they're going to do, then what *you're* going to do becomes subordinate to their strategy, and then you lose. You have to strike a balance between being absorbed in what you want to do, flowing in your own zone, and a sense or intuition of how your opponent is planning to play you."

This is the difference between making all perfect shots in practice, when you are completely relaxed, and then going on the match court and wondering where all those great shots went. The trick is to maintain the composure and ease of practice even during the most stressful competition, so that you never lose yourself to the fleeting promise of an outward victory.

Winning from the inside out means being more dedicated to the cumulative development of mind-body coordination than to momentary victories. And the way to gain this development is to focus more on the *process* of what you are doing than on the outward goal of winning.

BLINDERS TO VICTORY

Racehorses are made to wear blinders to keep them from being distracted on their path around the track. Maybe if we could wear some kind of psychological blinders to keep us from being distracted from our path, we would be more successful.

Focusing on the process or path is important for three reasons. First, because it develops mind-body coordination, it leads to regular experience of the Zone during exercise. The primary cause of the Zone experience is increased mind-body integration, the harmonious cooperation of mind and body. Second, the degree of mind-body coordination you develop through exercise is *yours*—that is, it stays with you all the time, so that you begin to carry that peak experience into your life. Then winning becomes a daily experience, not just a memory of one day's glory. Third, focusing on the process actually brings the greatest success. If you are distracted by what your opponent is doing, you are not focusing on what *you* are doing. Only by doing your best, playing your own game, can you excel.

It is necessary to set goals, and it is good to set them high, but one of the most important principles you can ever learn is this: To *accomplish* the goal, you have to let go of it. You have to forget about it and focus on the path. You can't keep looking over your shoulder to see how the other guy is doing; you've got to run your best race and let the chips fall where they may.

I can remember my swim coach urging me not to keep raising my head to see where I was going, but to focus more on what I was doing. Process was valued as the means to the most successful end. When Carl Lewis finally beat LeRoy Burrell after ten straight defeats and set a new world record in the 100-meter dash, he said, "I didn't look at him, I just did my own thing. I didn't look at him until I hit the tape."

Ben Hogan, one of the top golfers of all time, was famous for his high-intensity focus on the golf course. Many times Hogan was criticized for what appeared to be antisocial behavior but in fact was just total immersion in his golf game. One story reports him having an 18-foot putt to sink to win a tournament. As he was taking the putter back to stroke the ball, a train came roaring by at the edge of the course and blew its whistle. The crowd gasped in concern at the disturbance, but Hogan, seemingly unaffected, sank the putt and clinched the tournament.

In an interview afterward, a reporter asked, "Mr. Hogan, what did you think when that train came by and blew its whistle? Didn't it break your concentration?" Hogan looked up in surprise. "What train?" he said.

Hogan was so intently focused on his game, so established within himself, that the distraction only drove him deeper inside and heightened his concentration. This focus helped Hogan win more tournaments than most professionals even dream of, and he is still regarded as one of the premier golfers who ever lived.

I trained the coaches and members of the 1991 Iowa state high school singles and team championship tennis team. Their coach, Lawrence Ayer, told me this story about a doubles match on the road to the state title:

"The kids were up against a much bigger school and a pair of much more talented players. But they played extremely well, and in fact it was one of the closest matches during the entire state tournament, a real down-to-the-wire, neck-and-neck thriller. In a tie-breaker in the final set, the kids lost the match.

"Then an amazing thing happened, witnessed by everyone in the stands. Our kids walked to the net to shake hands with the new state doubles champs, congratulated them, and then proceeded to have a very calm five-minute conversation while standing at the net! The coaches from the other school came up to me and said, 'Do you see that? I've never seen that kind of sportsmanship from a high school kid in my life!' And it's true. The usual reaction to losing the state championship by a point or two would be to throw a racket, kick the fence, or some display of emotional frustration."

Coach Ayer had seen this style of process-oriented play from his kids all year, but he hadn't realized how unusual it was until he was approached by the other coaches. That proved to him that we can be reconditioned to enjoy the process, the path, rather than be obsessed with winning the number-one slot.

"The funny thing," he concluded, "was that these two kids had the feeling of victory regardless of the final score. Although they lost the Iowa State doubles title, when the whole tournament was over the team's cumulative points were high enough for them to win the overall 1991 Iowa State tennis team championship. The Fairfield, Iowa, Maharishi School tennis team went on to win the state doubles title in 1992 and 1993 using these principles."

TRAINING TIP NO. 5
DON'T KEEP SCORE

The next time you practice tennis or any other competitive sport, experiment with not keeping score. Compare the experience of enjoyment, skill, and satisfaction during scorekeeping and non-scorekeeping competition. The score is important, but it should not dictate how you play the game. Focusing on the score attaches you to the result. Focusing on the process lets you access your greatest skill and increases your fun.

Researchers at the University of Texas in Austin compared goal-oriented and process-oriented people in the workplace and made some surprising discoveries. The goal-oriented group was competitive. Their main concern was to be the best, to win, to make the most money, to get the promotions, to receive all the visible signs of success. They felt themselves in competition with everyone else in the office, and they not only strove to perform at their highest level but often pushed and maneuvered to win at all costs.

The people in the process-oriented group genuinely enjoyed their jobs and were more concerned with mastering job skills and doing their work well than with promotions and financial reward. As long as their work provided personal satisfaction, they were content.

According to the prevailing wisdom of our culture, the first group—the more aggressive and competitive people—should be more successful than their "laid-back" counterparts, but that is not what the Texas study found. The process-oriented people received more promotions and raises, earned higher salaries, took fewer sick days, and made greater contributions to their companies than did the goal-oriented group. They were better employees from a company standpoint, and they were happier people. They even had a history of higher grade-point averages when they were in school.

We can see the same contrast in the world of exercise and athletics. Here again, the more goal-oriented, competitive people are not always the ones who end up with the winning season. Whenever an individual focuses away from the process, and only toward achieving an outward goal—a trophy, some numbers on a watch, an image in a mirror—the mind stops listening to the body.

The body may be feeling, "I'm tired" or "That's too hard right now," but the mind will be saying, "I've got to keep going," or "I've got to win," or "I need to beat my last time." The mind becomes blind to the needs of the body, and this breaks the coordination between the two. Yet, mind-body coordination is the essential ingredient for maximizing both performance and *enjoyment* of the performance.

I'm not suggesting that there is something wrong with having goals, whether for personal fitness or for competitive achievement. It is natural to have a goal in mind when you exercise, whether it is to lose a few pounds, get your cardiovascular system in better condition, tone up your muscles, or break the world record in the high jump. It's important to set a goal so that you know your direction and the intended result. But if attaining the goal becomes the *only* reason you exercise or train, then you are looking for trouble.

THE AGONY OF DEFEAT

What happens if you come up short and miss the goal? Suppose you lose only 8 pounds instead of 10, or pull a hamstring and can't compete in the marathon? If the training itself isn't enjoyable, if all the dieting and working out is worth the effort only if you win, and yet you're not able to achieve your goal, where does that leave you? The whole experience becomes a frustrating ordeal, and you become a "failure."

That is the case for the vast majority of athletes. When the winners are interviewed on TV, still trying to catch their breath and with sweat running down their faces, they always say, "All the hard work was worth it." When Mary Lou Retton, the 1984 Olympic gold-medal gymnast, was asked to comment on all the intensity and misery of training in hopes of enjoying glory and fame, her response was a not-too-surprising "You don't hear many complaints from the winners."

The unpleasant reality is that for every winner, there are thousands of so-called losers. Most aspiring athletes simply never make it—at least in terms of the lofty goals they set for themselves. Through all the months and years of preparations, they have a dream that sustains them, but they are setting themselves up for a huge disappointment. If they do not enjoy the daily training but are doing it solely for the expected fruits of victory, the eventual fruit may be bitter indeed.

For professional athletes, that disappointment can be devastating. It is well known that many athletes have a difficult time integrating into "ordinary life" after retiring from their professional careers. Psychological problems and eating disorders are common among them; some still have nightmares about their grueling training even ten or more years later.

THE THREE GOALS OF EXERCISE

When I studied in India I asked some scholars what the purpose of exercise was according to the Vedic texts. Their response was unanimous and makes perfect sense. Exercise has three main functions.

1. To rejuvenate the body and cultivate the mind
2. To remove stress
3. To develop mind-body coordination

REJUVENATION

I once trained a runner from a popular Seattle runners' club. After working with me for six months, he told me that he had never imagined he could actually feel good and fresh after a 10-mile run. The concept of rejuvenation had never even occurred to him.

"I used to feel totally drained, both mentally and physically, after my regular 10-mile runs," he said. "Now, even though I'm running the same distance at about the same pace, I actually feel energized."

He said he had had a hard time accepting the fact that it was okay to feel good after a workout. "When I used to meet with the other people in the runners' club, all we ever talked about was our injuries, how many miles we had logged each week, and how grueling it was. I don't think anyone wants to hear how easy my training has become and how much fun I'm having, so for now I'm just keeping quiet about it."

That refreshed feeling after a workout is just what you should experience, too. Pushing yourself to exhaustion puts a strain on your body that, as I will explain in chapter 3, builds up and can eventually create serious health problems.

STRESS REDUCTION

Everyone knows that exercise can alleviate tensions and reduce stress. But here's the key question: How much exercise helps to *remove* stress, and how much actually *creates more?*

Many people think that if a little exercise is a good thing, a lot must be better. However, according to Kathy Waller, assistant professor of medical technology at Ohio State University, if you exercise too much you may be suppressing your immune system rather than enhancing it. In an article in *Clinical Laboratory Science,* Waller reviewed dozens of studies on the effect of exercise on the immune system. The studies showed that moderate exercise does give our immunity a slight boost. However, serious athletes such as marathon runners may actually get more colds and infections than the average person. "The optimum level of exercise that enhances but does not suppress immune function *is not known*," Professor Waller said.

Exercise is a two-edged sword. The proper amount can keep you healthy or even help to cure you; too much can make you sick or even kill you.

You may remember Jim Fixx, the running guru of the 1970s who wrote *The Complete Book of Running*. Fixx exemplified the "mind over matter" approach to training. Before he started running, he was an obese, sedentary drinker and smoker and had a high genetic risk of cardiovascular disease. Running became his panacea. He became obsessed with exercise, actively promoted it, and helped to create a fitness craze that swept across America.

Fixx set himself a goal of running 10 miles a day, every day, rain or shine, no matter how he felt. He became addicted to it. The result was that the same thing that made him well eventually killed him.

He ignored early-warning signs of overtraining, fatigue, even exhaustion. In June 1984, when he was still in his early fifties, Jim Fixx dropped dead after a 10-mile run—a run that he never should have taken. It was a hot and humid day; he hadn't eaten; he was tired from a long car drive. And he was no longer a healthy man. Jim had pushed himself so hard that he reached the limit of stress that his body could endure, but his mind drove him beyond that point, and he simply broke down.

An autopsy revealed that during the eight weeks preceding his death, he had suffered three heart attacks. Somehow he had managed to disregard even those severe warning signals. He told no one about it, not even his girlfriend. His mind had decided that no matter what his body wanted, he simply *had* to put in his 10 miles.

The lesson from this story is that we must know how much exercise is good for us, and how much more can be harmful. We must know how to listen and what to listen for. In chapter 4 you will learn that each body type is different and requires different kinds, amounts, and intensities of exercise. Within those broader categories, every single person is unique and has different needs and capacities. It's essential that each person learn not only to assess his or her exercise needs and limits but to pay attention when the body starts to say, "I've had enough."

Doctors and trainers are catching on to this. The experts used to recommend the exercise minimum of 75 percent of one's maximum heart rate for a healthy individual. Now the minimum is down to 60 percent to achieve cardiovascular benefits. Aerobics used to be highly recommended; now the experts are urging us to use *low-impact* aerobics, which put less stress on the body.

The most common recommendation today to prevent overtraining is to exercise at a pace at which you could comfortably hold a conversation. The principle is sound: You can't chat with someone when you're gasping for breath and your heart is pounding in your ears, and you shouldn't push yourself to exercise at that level of strain. However, this advice should not be taken literally, for you cannot listen to your body's signals during a workout or a run while engaged in conversation. In short, you cannot possibly listen to your body while listening to somebody else's voice.

If you stay within your personal limits of ease and comfort—as I will teach you to do in the Three Phase Workout in chapters 13 and 14—your exercise program will always help you reduce your stress level and will never cause you strain or fatigue.

Too much of a good thing can make you sick. But the reverse is also true. If too much exercise has caused problems, the *right amount* can make you well.

Kale Sorenson, a former U.S. rugby team member, is a big-boned, easy-going type whose career was curtailed by what is known as exercise-induced asthma. The more he exercised, the more his asthma flared up.

When I saw him ten years after his doctors had pronounced a life sentence of "no exercise," I asked him to run with me.

He said, "No, I really can't run, my asthma would act up and I'd be wheezing for days."

I said, "Come on, we'll take it easy." I told him that the same thing that had caused his asthma would cure it, if it was the right amount. "You just need to know how much exercise will rejuvenate you rather than break you down."

We went through the workout for his body type—the same workout described later in this book—and then we began to run.

Kale was in shock. Very excited, he said, "This is the first time in five years I've been able to run without taking medication or losing my breath."

Exercise is a very powerful tool to either bring balance or create imbalance. The correct amount will blaze the trail to balance.

TRAINING TIP NO. 6
WHEN TO REST

Determine your average heart rate first thing in the morning. (Take your wake-up pulse several days in a row.) If the heart rate increases or decreases 10 or more beats per minute above or below the average, rest that day. Exercise less, don't overschedule, and as much as possible, take it easy until the heart rate returns to normal. (See chapter 9 for more details.)

MIND-BODY COORDINATION

The third major reason to exercise is to improve coordination between mind and body. Clearly, any athletic performance depends on mind-body integration. Perception, reaction, and movement are complex interactions between the body and the mind. The main factor that determines how well the whole system works is communication.

Stress and fatigue in the mind-body system break down coordination. The stressed body simply can't respond as quickly and effectively to the commands of the mind. And unless the mind is calm and stress-free, it may not pick up signals from the body.

Stress makes perception foggy, reactions slow, and coordination sloppy. That explains why the goal of exercise must be to *reduce* stress, not to increase it. When the first two purposes of exercise have been accomplished—when the system is rejuvenated and freed of stress—the stage is automatically set for improved mind-body coordination.

David Hemery set a world record in the 400-meter hurdles during the 1968 Olympics. He won the race not by a few inches or a few feet but by a truly amazing 44-yard margin. Afterward, he said, "Only a couple of times in my life have I felt in such condition that my mind and body worked almost as one. This was one of those times. My limbs reacted as my mind was thinking. . . . Instead of forcing and working my legs, they responded with the speed and in the motion that was being asked of them."

If the mind and body could work together at full capacity, human potential would extend far beyond our present vision of what is normal and possible. We could do anything. While conventional exercise methods break down mind-body coordination, the principles outlined in this book are designed to enhance it.

THE PROCESS-ORIENTED ATHLETE

Whatever the mind is doing, the body must do also; whatever the body is doing, the mind must do also. That was Ben Hogan's experience when he was so absorbed in his putt that he didn't even hear the train blasting its whistle. It's the concentration that every great athlete knows is essential to the highest achievement.

And it's exactly what most people *don't* do these days. If you walk into a health club today you'll hear blaring music and see rows of men and women on stationary bikes, rowing machines, treadmills, or stair climbers, in front of a big-screen TV. Many are wearing headphones; some are reading newspapers or magazines. All the minds are busy reading, watching TV, or listening to music, while the bodies are engaged in a physical activity supposedly designed to produce better mind-body coordination!

The golden rule to a successful fitness program is that the mind and body must never be divided. The "experts" say that such "exercise aids" as music and magazines are great for fighting the boredom of exercise. But exercise is boring only when it is done incorrectly. When exercise is done properly, it integrates mind and body; at that point, exercise stops being something you *have* to do and becomes something you *want* to do. It becomes more than just enjoyable—it becomes exhilarating.

No matter what your exercise goals are, you will love striving toward them when they become secondary to the process of achievement itself. Then you will become a process-oriented athlete.

The one common denominator in working to achieve any goal, large or small, is that there must be a path to it. The goal of the program in this book is to make the path to fitness so appealing that you would happily trade the goal for the path. But don't worry—you won't have to. Through this program, the path becomes as enjoyable as the achievement, and at the same time the program helps you to upgrade your accomplishments.

Total focus on the path will bring the fun back into exercise, physical education, and training, will improve your performance, and will put you in the Zone every time you exercise.

TRAINING TIP NO. 7
NOSE BREATHING

Experiment during your next exercise session or training workout. Breathe through your nose, and let the slow, steady rhythm of your breath set the pace. If nose breathing becomes labored, or if you have to breathe through your mouth, then slow down your pace and reestablish the comfortable nasal breath. In time, your pace will improve and your breath will stay stable. (See part III for details.)

3

FALSE STARTS

The physical education system in this country is in crisis. When a lack-luster economy takes its toll on school budgets across the country, P.E. is the first class to go. Secondary-school P.E. is no longer required in every state, and eight states have abandoned the program altogether. Illinois is the only state left that conducts physical education courses daily in its public schools.

Arnold Schwarzenegger, former chairman of the President's Council on Physical Fitness and Sports, says that budget cuts should not affect P.E. "It doesn't cost money to do push-ups or sit-ups, I never paid a dime to do a pull-up in my life," he said. And he is right.

Educators say the kids aren't interested; parents blame the school boards for withholding funds. Meanwhile, the kids walk the malls and hang out on the streets out of boredom, while their physical health and fitness suffer. "The hearts and lungs of kids today don't work as well as they used to," says fitness expert Ken Cooper, M.D. "It takes them a minute and a half longer to run a mile today than it did ten years ago."

Children watch an average of twenty to twenty-two hours of TV each week. Rather than exercise, they sit in front of computers or pour quarters into video games for entertainment. Because of this, many people blame the media and Nintendo games for the physical apathy of our youth, but a progressive Indiana middle school proved otherwise.

Plainfield Middle School initiated a revolutionary program to combat the so-called lack of interest in school sports. Their theory was that kids failed to sign up for sports not due to apathy but because of the humiliation in trying out and being "cut" from the team. So the school implemented a "no-cut" system: If kids show up for tryouts, they make the team.

When the risk of rejection and failure was removed, team rosters doubled and tripled. Tryouts for cross-country went from 13 to 78 under the no-cut system. The track team increased from 67 to 120 members. Overnight, more than half the children at Plainfield Middle School were involved in some extracurricular activities. Empty lockers were filled and team buses became overcrowded when talent and skill became secondary to having fun.

Everyone figured that the no-cut system was a noble concept that would be good for the kids' self-esteem. When it came to competition, expectations were reserved. But to the amazement of students, teachers, and skeptical parents, the team won eight local championships and were county champs in wrestling, cross-country, and swimming.

This pilot program demonstrated without any doubt that the problem with our physical education system does not lie in lack of student interest. Kids love exercise and turn out in droves when they know they will not be humiliated or rejected.

I know the feeling well. I can still feel the anxiety I experienced on the morning of my Little League tryouts. It was the day to put it all on the line. Was I going up to the majors to face curve balls and become one of the elite, or was I doomed to another year in the minors, to play with everybody's little brother?

There I was, 8 years old, facing a test that could change the course of my entire life. The risks were high; rejection and failure loomed. Parents were wrapped up in the success of their children, and for us kids, our best friends on that day became our enemies. Although I may not have had the words for it, I knew that my reputation and self-worth were at stake.

I remember being so nervous when it was my turn to field grounders. The first one miraculously got caught in my mitt. I was so charged up from catching it that when I threw it to first base I launched it over both the first baseman's head as well as the fence. The rest of the tryouts went okay, but I couldn't get that wild throw out of my head. I thought for sure I was not going to make the major league. That weekend I remember being glued to the phone waiting to hear if I made it. Finally the phone rang for me; it was Mr. Maloney, the manager of the Tigers. He said he wanted me to play for him in the major leagues. He said he needed a strong arm on the team and that I had impressed him in tryouts. When I hung up, I couldn't believe it—I was a major leaguer. Maybe he was getting a hot dog or something when I threw the ball over the fence, but I wasn't about to ask any questions. I made it.

When I think about it, yeah, I made it, but what a stress. It probably took ten years off my life and the memories are permanently etched into my brain. When I wake up on some April mornings, the smell of the cool and crisp air floods my mind with the memories of my very stressful Little League tryouts. I was one of the lucky ones, but what about those who didn't make it?

By age 9, children in traditional schools in the United States begin dropping out of organized sports. By age 13, most boys, and an even greater majority of girls, are no longer participating in organized sports *or any other form of regular physical activity*. But, as the experiment at Plainfield Middle School so clearly shows, this reflects not a lack of interest but a basic instinct for survival. This is the age when self-esteem is just developing, and most kids are not willing to risk it climbing the ropes or trying out for cheerleading.

Critics of the no-cut system say we must prepare our kids for the failures and rejections that await them in their adult lives, and that if we sugarcoat their childhood experiences, their false sense of reality will be harmful to them as adults. I disagree. I don't doubt that dealing with a little rejection is good, but a well-known survey indicates that kids are already getting more than their fair share. This study compared the ratio of criticisms to compliments directed from teachers to students and from parents to their children. In the average secondary school, teachers dish out eighteen criticisms for every compliment. What's worse is that when those children go home, their parents don't reverse the trend; they deliver twelve criticisms for every precious word of praise. When you tally the number of parent and teacher rejections, it's no wonder that the majority of kids don't try out for sports. It's just too risky.

The Plainfield coach told a story that made me appreciate the no-cut system even more. Just before a basketball game an eighth-grade cheerleader, one of seventy-three, came to him and said, "I'm going to high school next year, and I know I won't make the cheerleading squad there. There are a lot of girls who are better at it than I am. But at least I got to have the experience. It's something I can remember all my life."

EVERYBODY'S FAVORITE CLASS?

When I went to school, one class was far and away my favorite. I thought it was the same for every redblooded American kid. Wasn't gym everyone's favorite? You could run around, play games, be outside—and best of all, you weren't confined to the timeless boredom of a classroom.

I didn't realize then that for some kids, P.E. presented the toughest and most humiliating experiences of their entire school careers. I remember there were kids who were present for math in first period but regularly skipped P.E. in second period. I felt sorry for them. "Their moms must have scheduled an eye doctor's appointment," I reasoned. "But why couldn't they have made it during algebra or chemistry? Anything but gym!"

START A NO-CUT SYSTEM
IN YOUR SCHOOL

You can do this for sports, theater, music, and all other extracurricular activities that require a tryout. Petition your school board, through the PTA (use Plainfield Middle School as a precedent). An across-the-board no-cut system may not be practical initially, due to lack of space, uniforms, or funds for busing. These obstacles can be overcome by creating separate "home" and "away" teams, or starting with only certain teams and activities. When the kids' interest has been aroused, the funding will come, either privately or publicly. For the sake of our children, just get started.

Eventually it dawned on me that some kids were actually failing P.E. due to their absences. It wasn't doctors' appointments that were keeping these kids out of gym. They were staying away because they didn't like it—or, even worse, because they were afraid of it.

Such absenteeism afflicts more children than you might think. A Louis Harris poll disclosed that *upward of 50 percent of Americans experience their first major failure in life as a sports failure.* Just think back for a minute. Maybe you were pretty good at some sports, but what about the others? I always had trouble climbing the ropes. When I was 14 my body type was such that I was simply heavier than my muscles were strong. I could get up the ropes, but it was no picnic.

But what about the kids who just couldn't make it? Or couldn't manage even one pull-up? What about the heavier kids who couldn't make it around the track in the minimum time required for a passing grade, or the wiry kids who looked at football as an opportunity to get destroyed?

Just imagine the humiliation involved in being the last one picked for a team week after week, year after year. What kind of self-esteem gets built up by being labeled "uncoordinated" by your peers? I remember the panic I felt when teams were being chosen in gym. Imagine standing there trying not to feel ashamed while the captains pick everyone but you. Then, when there's no one else left and you *have* to go to a team, everyone groans just to let you know for certain that you're not wanted. You get stuck in right field or assigned to the glorious duty of "hike and block" each week during football season.

In an academic class, if you get an F on a test at least it's between you and the teacher. The whole world doesn't know it. But when you can't climb the ropes, hit the baseball, or slog your way even once around the track, it's a public event. No wonder that as adults 85 percent of us do not exercise regularly.

All this was brought home to me very vividly one recent afternoon. I was visiting a private school on the West Coast to talk to the coaches about my Invincible Athletics program. A little girl named Sharon, who knew why I was there, came up to me right after her gym class. She was about 10 years old and had just finished struggling around the track in a test for the 1-mile run. Her beautiful round face was beet red, and sweat was dripping off her nose. She was totally exhausted and depressed.

"Dr. Douillard," she said, "can you write me an excuse to get out of gym class?"

"Don't you like gym?" I asked her.

"I hate it."

"Why? Isn't it fun?"

"It's no fun at all."

"Isn't there anything about it that you like?"

"No. I'm not good at anything."

Sharon was the Babe Ruth type—round-faced and lovely, with big bones and a large frame. With her natural strength and coordination, there were many sports she could excel in and enjoy.

As she went on to tell me what had happened out on the track, she began to cry. "Everyone was running as fast as they could. The coaches were yelling at us and blowing their whistles, telling us to go faster. I was hurting so bad, and trying as hard as I could, but I just couldn't go any faster. I finished in 11 minutes and 30 seconds."

I knew that in order to get a passing grade, the kids had to run the mile in 10 minutes. I knew that for someone Sharon's age and body type, it was a tall order. Fifty percent of American schoolgirls can't do it.

"It's just not fair," she said, wiping away her tears. "I tried my very best." And then she added the clincher: "And all the other kids were watching. I was the last one."

My heart went out to her. I knew she was sincere, and that the kind of exercise she was being asked to do was only going to make her hate exercise for the rest of her life. However, I knew I couldn't write her a note. So I went to talk to her coach, who was watching his fifth-grade class organize a softball game.

"Take a look at those kids," I said. "Look at all the different sizes and shapes out there. Each one has different strengths and talents. Some might make great gymnasts, while others could become defensive linemen in the NFL. Wouldn't it be nice to guide them, early in their lives, toward sports they'll do well in? Then they'll enjoy themselves instead of feeling tortured, and there's a good chance they'll continue being physically active later on."

I pointed out that there are three basic body types. First are the smaller-framed people, with active minds and restless bodies. These people talk a lot, ask a lot of questions, and can't seem to sit still. They are quick, light, and agile, and they make good sprinters, but they're not very muscular and don't have a lot of endurance.

THIS BODY TYPE IS KNOWN AS VATA. THROUGHOUT THE BOOK, IT WILL BE REFERRED TO WITH THIS SYMBOL: 🦢 (FOR COMPLETE BODY-TYPE DESCRIPTIONS AND A QUESTIONNAIRE TO DETERMINE YOUR TYPE, SEE CHAPTER 4.)

Next are the Dennis the Menace types. They are fiery, aggressive, competitive, and vocal, and they tend to assume the leadership role whether anyone wants them to or not! They are usually strong and medium-framed. They are well coordinated and don't have trouble with sports.

THIS BODY TYPE IS KNOWN AS PITTA. THROUGHOUT THE BOOK, IT WILL BE REFERRED TO WITH THIS SYMBOL: 🔥

Last but not least are the Babe Ruth types, who are physically gifted but very slow-going by nature. They often need motivation to become more active. They are usually on the husky side, like Sharon, and won't break any records in the rope climb or the 100-yard dash. Children of this type are strong and have high endurance; they can hit, kick, and throw a ball a country mile, but at 10 years of age they're unlikely to finish the mile in under 10 minutes. These basic types combine to make a total of ten types which we will discuss in chapter 4.

THIS BODY TYPE IS KNOWN AS KAPHA. THROUGHOUT THE BOOK, IT WILL BE REFERRED TO WITH THIS SYMBOL: 🌸

"Once you recognize these differences," I said to the coach, "it becomes clear that to test them all the same way just won't work." I told him that Dr. Kenneth Cooper, the aerobics expert, argues that the standards set by the President's Council on Physical Fitness and Sports are inadequate. "They are far too oriented toward athletics," says Cooper, "testing sports-related skills such as softball throw, rather than being *health* related." If body typing was added to the testing design, Fitness Testing Week wouldn't send chills down all those innocent young spines.

"If Sharon keeps getting tested and graded as a runner," I said, "a number of things will happen: First, she will fail the class. Second, she will feel humiliated by the experience. Third, she will reject exercise entirely, and even while she's a child she will become drastically out of shape. Fourth, her childhood humiliation and failure will stay with her into her adult life, and will contribute to how she accepts challenges. These are the 'wonder years'—if we don't feed these kids with the proper physical, mental, and emotional nutrition, problems will surely surface later on.

"All that's necessary to keep Sharon from having to endure this scenario is to help her discover the kind of exercise that's easy and natural for her and makes her happy."

I'm glad to say that my arguments persuaded the physical education teachers at Sharon's school to investigate the principles outlined in this book. The teachers and students learned how to determine body types and how to select the appropriate exercise programs and sports for each constitutional type.

About a year later, I received a phone call from Sharon's mother. She told me—with some amazement and a lot of pride—that Sharon was going to compete in the regional championships as a race walker. She had a newfound interest in sports, and her mother was thrilled that she was exploring new territory and becoming a more well-rounded person—and maybe even an athlete.

Several weeks later, when I visited the school again, Sharon told me excitedly about her competition and that her favorite class in school was now gym. It was hard to imagine that this was the same little girl who a year ago had tearfully begged me for a note excusing her from gym class.

BRING BACK THE FUN

Fear of rejection and failure is one reason why kids drop out of sports and physical education programs. Another reason is that these programs simply are not much fun.

Professor Alois Mader of the University of Sport Sciences in Cologne,

Germany, attributed the success of the championship Kenyan running team to their unwritten philosophy: "Run every day from youth on. And run so you will enjoy it the next day. Everything else will follow automatically." Or, in the words of former Pittsburgh Pirates star Willie Stargell, now a member of baseball's Hall of Fame: "The secret of my success is that I don't go out to work; I go out to play."

This pinpoints the problem with our conventional approach to exercise. The basic idea of today's "workout" (even the word denotes that it is work, not fun) is to push yourself until you feel strained and exhausted. Only when the limits of discomfort are reached can the workout properly end. The key to this "wisdom" is discomfort. You must experience discomfort or your effort will be fruitless.

Kenyan runners, instead of pushing themselves until they are uncomfortable, use comfort and enjoyment as the key to their success. With enjoyment as their bottom line, performance unfolds gracefully. Loving what they do gives them a built-in desire to train. Their outstanding achievements are more a side effect of enjoyment than the result of an obsession to win.

It seems to me that when we were children, we exercised just that way. We didn't do it to lose weight or to break records, whether our own or somebody else's. It was just a lot of fun.

In my neighborhood, depending on the season, fun was defined on the baseball diamond or the basketball court. There was nothing better than afternoons of pick-up softball, or, when we were younger, evenings playing kick-the-can or hide-and-seek. An innocent enthusiasm motivated us. There were no requirements or restrictions; it was free, and it was for everyone.

As we grew older, the whole thing became more complicated. The pleasure that originally drove us merged with more serious aspirations. And as the enjoyment disappeared, so did most of the kids. Surveys show the following reasons why kids drop out of sports:

· Too much drilling in practice and not enough fun time
· Emotional stress from excessive performance demands
· A feeling of constant failure, largely due to negative feedback from coaches
· Not getting to play enough in the games

The turning point may have come when the adults got involved and developed "organized sports." It seemed organized enough without them, but nevertheless teams were established and serious competition began. Winning became the prime motivator. Frustrated dads became coaches, and "perform under pressure or be replaced" became the law.

It was a new world, a world in which kids were forced to play an adults' game. Fun became a memory of childhood, and exercise became hard work. The natural enthusiasm for physical activity degenerated into boring workouts. "Fight the boredom" articles appeared in the newly emerging fitness magazines, as people became more and more sedentary.

It's hard to believe that something so enjoyable could become so uninviting. Maybe if we dropped the name *workout* and brought the fun back into physical exercise, children would grow up liking it, and adults would end up doing it.

HEALTH OR FITNESS?

The vast majority of physical education is conducted the same way it was ten years ago, yet the health and fitness of our children have deteriorated significantly. Part of the blame goes to the President's Council on Physical Fitness and Sports, which prescribed a set of criteria for fitness that is supposedly universal but is actually modeled on one body type.

Dr. Kenneth Cooper has labeled the Council's tests "unfit for kids' consumption," and many fitness groups and physical education departments have stopped using them. The coaches with tunnel vision who abide by the Council's tests and hold to the conventional "no pain, no gain" principles remain determined to push their children around the track and up the ropes, with no regard to individual makeup. They are convinced that the kids need to be coerced to bring out their personal greatness, whether the kids like it or not!

This single-model standard, which most children can't live up to, has stripped the fun out of exercise and left kids too intimidated even to try to be physically fit. As a result, America's new generation is seriously out of shape.

• 11 million American kids from ages 6 to 17 are overweight, and 50 percent don't get enough exercise to develop healthy hearts and lungs.

• According to the standards of the Amateur Athletic Association, 68 percent of kids ages 6 to 17 have below-average cardiovascular fitness, flexibility, and abdominal and upper-body strength. This is down 11 percent since 1981.

• Forty percent of our 5- to 8-year-olds are overweight and have increased cholesterol, high blood pressure, and other coronary risk factors.

What about the children who make it—the ones who are tough enough, or naturally gifted enough, to perform and succeed under the duress of the current system? These are the kids like Steve Briggs, the karate champion

I described in chapter 2, kids who, when pushed, try harder and harder to please the crowd, the coach, and their parents, going all-out to win.

A New England study reported on the health and fitness of kids who were state-champion high school athletes. The study focused on a large school that was a consistent producer of champions in many sports. The top athletes were given a standard health-related physical fitness test, designed by the American Alliance of Health, Physical Education, Recreation, and Dance (AAHPERD). The results were surprising. Nearly all the 16-, 17-, and 18-year-old state champions failed. Despite their athletic prowess, they could not pass a health-oriented examination of fitness.

This rather shocking finding is actually consistent with a growing body of scientific evidence indicating that due to overtraining, athletes suffer from a number of serious health problems, including a compromised immune system. There appears to be a large number of former professional athletes with chronic career-ending conditions, such as Epstein-Barr disease (also known as chronic fatigue syndrome), exercise-induced asthma and bronchitis, and chronic pneumonia. When Magic Johnson shocked the world with his announcement that he was HIV positive, his doctors recommended that he leave basketball to safeguard his immune system from the demands of intensive training.

When I had the opportunity to spend a few weeks teaching in Russia, Dr. Yuri Belous, the chairman of the former USSR Committee on Physical Culture and Sports, was lamenting the chronic illnesses of his country's top athletes. "As these athletes get closer to competition," he said, "they become more susceptible to illness. They are pushed so hard that their bodies give in, and they get sick."

The line between peak performance and illness due to overtraining is nearly invisible, and top athletes frequently stumble across it.

Training Tip No. 8
Start 'Em Young

Train your children to breathe through their noses. While they sleep, if they are mouth breathing or snoring, gently close their lips and tip their heads forward to a more chin-down attitude. This will make nose breathing imperative. According to the science of Yoga, nose breathing is the best prevention one can take against infection. The mucous membranes in the nose regulate temperature and humidity and filter impurities before they reach the bronchioles and lungs. Mouth breathing allows the air to enter the lungs unfiltered and dry and is the reported cause of many cold and catarrhal afflictions. In Yoga Ramacharaka's book *Hatha Yoga*, he cites a scientific report that sailors who slept with their mouths open were more likely to contract contagious diseases. During a smallpox epidemic, all related deaths were reported to be of mouth breathers; not a single nose breather succumbed. No animal except man breathes through the mouth while sleeping or exercising. (The mechanics and benefits of nose breathing are fully described in chapter 10.)

The facts are sad but true. Children are fatter, less fit, and less interested in exercise today than they were a decade ago. High school champions can't pass health-related fitness exams. Overtrained athletes are suffering from injuries and weakened immune systems. About $4 billion is spent each year to treat 5 million running injuries, and an estimated 70 percent of all runners will incur an injury at some time during their running "career." One expert commented, "The way some people treat their bodies, you would think they were opposed to good health."

The problems do not stop there. The estimated life span of an NFL football player is a shocking 56 years, 19 years below the national average. Sports hero "Pistol Pete" Maravich and running guru Jim Fixx died suddenly from heart attacks during exercise, and collegiate basketball star Hank Gathers and Olympic volleyball great Flo Hyman were victims of "exercise-related sudden death."

These problems do not pertain only to elite and professional athletes. More than 200,000 deaths are reported each year from heart attacks during or immediately after exercise. I'm sure the 30 million unfit Americans are in no hurry to strap on their running shoes when they hear these frightening statistics!

And yet we all know that exercise is basically good for us. When the body is inactive it loses flexibility, muscle strength, and aerobic capacity. People who are sedentary are at greater risk for many diseases. A widely acclaimed landmark study by the Cooper Institute of Aerobic Research indicated that men and women in a low fitness status are more than twice as likely to die from cancer, cardiovascular disease, and all causes combined than are those in the moderate fitness group. Other research has shown that moderate exercise gives a boost to the body's immune system and reduces the incidence of many serious medical conditions such as diabetes, hypertension, colon and breast cancers, obesity, and osteoporosis.

In October 1992, the American Heart Association (AHA) added physical inactivity to its list of major risk factors for heart disease. This placed lack of exercise in the same category as smoking, high blood pressure, and high cholesterol levels. "We are not born with this disease," said Dr. Gerald

Fletcher, chairman of the AHA committee that wrote the position statement. "We really develop this disease because of our lifestyle."

Despite this information, 64 percent of the adult population is overweight, and 50 percent of American women over age 60 are not able to lift ten pounds. This means that half of our 60-year-old grandmothers can't lift their infant grandchildren.

This is not to say that once you're over 60, it's too late to get in shape. Quite the contrary. Studies have shown that even men and women in their nineties can increase their strength by 300 percent in just six to eight weeks through a program of moderate exercise. The ability of elderly people to gain muscle strength is proportionately as great as it is in young, vibrant adults. The potential is there, and remains there until a person's last breath.

THE CONVENTIONAL WISDOM

The essence of the conventional approach to exercise is that to increase performance, the body must be taken to its physiological limit, even pushed to the point of exhaustion, then allowed to recover, only to be led out to the gym or the track the next day and stressed in the same way. A familiar example of the stress-and-recover model is the approach to building muscle. The first step is to apply a stressor to a muscle. Bench-press repetitions and bicep curls overload the muscles and literally break down the cells. Then, with rest, the body bounces back, rebuilding itself to be stronger.

Proponents of the stress-and-recover method gather support from the work of Dr. Hans Selye, pioneering theorist on stress. Selye held that exposure to some degree of stress stimulates the body's "adaptive response." If we subject the body to stress, it learns to compensate, raising its performance level to meet the stress.

One of the difficulties with putting this theory into practice is that it is hard to find the appropriate amount of stress. Too much overwhelms the body so that it can't adapt, but not enough results in no improvement.

Exercise training techniques based on the stress-and-recover model certainly work. World records continue to be broken. But all too often they work at the expense of the athlete's health, both in the present and in the future. As the weeks and months of training go by, a huge debt of fatigue and stress can build up in both body and mind. This stress takes all the fun out of exercising and training, reduces mind-body coordination, and often results in injury and illness.

In my primary sport, triathlon, athletes are known for phenomenal feats of endurance. What is little known is that many triathletes suffer from lowered resistance levels and frequently have colds, flus, fevers, stomachaches, and sore throats. Nearly all spend inordinate amounts of time sleeping to recover from their stressful pursuits.

This problem goes back to ancient times. The Greek physician Galen wrote two thousand years ago that athletes "overexert every day at their exercises, and force feed themselves. Their sleep, too, is immoderate." He quoted the physician Hippocrates, who said, "Excess is the enemy of nature," and complained that "athletes pay no attention to these or others of his wonderful sayings which they transgress, and their practices are in direct opposition to doctrines of good health." Galen even pointed out that athletes develop fitness for their sport, "but as soon as they retire from competition, degeneration sets it. Some soon die, some live longer but do not reach old age."

In competitive circles, the formula for victory begins with enduring the punishment of training. Grueling training regimens are considered necessary to force the body to accommodate to the overzealous desires of the athlete's mind—or, worse, the coach's mind.

A former Canadian cross-country ski champion vividly recalled how her coach was set on driving her to exhaustion or championship, whichever came first. When I met Cynthia Moore, she told me that she had chronic pneumonia, which had ended her athletic career:

"I had my first bout of pneumonia in my junior year in college. I was so totally exhausted that I literally slept through my classes. Then I'd go all out every afternoon in ski practice. I can still see my coach hitting his whistle on his clipboard and shouting at me to go faster."

Like all modern athletes, Cynthia was trained to obey the demands of her coach, no matter how overbearing. To do so, she had to disregard her deep fatigue. She desperately needed rest, but didn't get enough of it and became chronically ill. In order to continue competing, she became dependent on antibiotics; eventually they stopped working, and she had to drop out of the sport she loved and in which she excelled.

Cynthia's coach was just doing his job, guiding her in the best way he knew within the limits of conventional methods. But the result was that after four years of college competition in cross-country skiing, Cynthia graduated with a permanent case of chronic lung congestion and remains at constant risk of lung infection.

Unfortunately, Cynthia's story is a common one, involving tens of thousands of young athletes. Although their skills are in different sports, they all experience overtraining, injuries, chronic illnesses, and shattered dreams.

In the 1992 Summer Olympic Games in Barcelona, chronic overtraining gained national publicity when Kim Zmescal, the 16-year-old American Olympic gold-medal hopeful, experienced the emotional disappointment of defeat during the gymnastics competition. The question, "Are we pushing our athletes too hard?" appeared in the headlines of many sports sections and news magazines.

Zmescal's famed coach, Bela Karolyi, was censored for his very tough coaching style, and some of his former protégées went public with their feelings about him. Chelle Stack, an Olympian from the Seoul Games, was quoted in *Newsweek*: "I didn't realize how much hatred I had toward him." Others reported having nightmares about Karolyi and his training style years after they had stopped working with him.

Karolyi is not a bad coach. He has produced more world champions than any other coach in the history of gymnastics. He is not only good, he is the best. But he is a victim of conventional wisdom. He pushes his students to their limits in the same way as the Russians and East Germans do. The same philosophy prevails in the NFL, the NBA, the NHL, and in just about all other professional athletic organizations.

STEROIDS: MAGIC BULLETS OR SILVER BULLETS?

If the conventional system were truly working and athletes were satisfied with their training methods, would they be attracted to artificial means of enhancing performance, especially means that have been proven dangerous? I don't think so. The fact is that they are not satisfied, and that is why they desperately seek alternatives.

Until now, all the alternatives that have been tried—visualization, biofeedback, sports psychology, hypnosis, and so on—remain within the boundaries of the stress-and-recover model. But the strain on the body caused by following this method of training accumulates. Recently, many techniques have been developed to help athletes recover from exercise stress. However, no one has addressed the real problem: the stress itself.

Forcing the body to adapt and compensate to meet stressful physical demands over a prolonged period of time will ultimately break down the body and inhibit maximum performance. When this point is reached, the athlete is faced with a choice between accepting his or her limitations or extending the stress-and-recover cycle artificially.

To accept limitations goes against the grain of human nature, which is always to seek higher achievement, and therefore few athletes choose this option. The vast majority either push themselves into exhaustion, injury, and illness or choose a second alternative: steroids.

Steroids may seem a wonderful solution to the drawbacks of stress-and-recover training. They allow the athlete to stress him- or herself two to three times as much and to recover two to three times more quickly. Using these drugs, athletes can train at least twice as hard, recover faster, and exceed their previous performance levels. The catch is that steroids pose an enormous health threat.

Many first-class athletes, including Olympic sprinter Ben Johnson and the late Lyle Alzado, and scores of former Soviet and East German athletes, have taken the risk and have paid the price. Alzado, the L.A. Raiders' all-pro defensive end who died in 1992, claimed that steroids had caused his incurable brain cancer. Although medical authorities could not confirm a cause-and-effect relationship, he remained sure of it until his death.

Alzado claimed that 75 to 90 percent of professional football players used performance enhancers such as steroids. The NFL has issued more conservative estimates but admits that the proportion of drug users is high. Following the lead of their professional role models, an estimated 7 to 18 percent of male high school athletes—over a quarter million adolescents—now use steroids, according to the Department of Health and Human Services. Some high schools report steroid use by male high school athletes as high as 30 to 40 percent, according to James Puffer, M.D., of the U.S. Olympic Committee.

Gene Upshaw, executive director of the NFL Players' Association, voiced his inside perspective: "Teams draft a kid who looks like he could be a player. But when they get the player at minicamp, they see that he is smaller and not as strong as they thought. They tell him he's got to be bigger and stronger before he reports to training camp. He's got eight weeks to do it. There are only so many steaks, potatoes, and milk shakes you can eat in eight weeks. If the player is up against a time frame, he'll do what he has to do to get the results."

Chronic abuse of steroids is more serious than we think, and the danger extends beyond the very real health hazards in the present and down the road. An even greater peril lies in our acceptance of the idea that it is worth doing anything to accomplish the goal of winning. "I was so wild about winning," said Alzado. "It's all I cared about, winning, winning. All I thought about."

Steroids are simply an expedient, a shortcut to success in a culture dominated by the need to win. Dr. Gabe Mirkin, who wrote *The Sportsmedicine Book*, polled more than 100 top runners. He asked them: "If I could give you a pill that would make you an Olympic champion—and also kill you in a year—would you take it?" Amazingly, more than half the athletes responded that they would take the magic pill. For them, the goal of winning was more important than life itself. Clearly something is very wrong here.

First place has become the only place worth occupying. Child and adult athletes alike feel driven to capture the crown and glory of victory at any cost. The compulsion to achieve the goal has made the process of getting there unimportant. Any means are justified in order to achieve the coveted end. But magic bullets turn into lethal silver bullets when top athletes like Lyle Alzado and Ben Johnson are willing to risk everything—career, reputation, personal integrity, even life itself—to be Number One.

The all-too-common illusion in American society is that reaching the goal, whether it be wealth, winning, or the accumulation of worldly possessions, will bring happiness. In this mad and misguided pursuit of happiness, many fall prey to the mirage of victory.

This kind of victory involves attaining something outside ourselves, be it a medal or a Mercedes. The lure of such victory is great and glittering with promise. But that victory fades as quickly as the leaves on the laurel wreath, placed on the heads of winners in the original Olympics many centuries ago in Greece.

MADDEN'S MIRACLE

In her early teens, Joanne Madden sustained a back injury. Although it was diagnosed as only a minor strain, her pain persisted. For years, despite CAT scans, bone scans, and visits to various specialists and therapists, her pain went undiagnosed and unsuccessfully treated. By the age of 18 she was in constant agony and had developed a permanent limp. Having hobbled from one doctor's office to another, and frustrated with her predicament, she decided to take matters into her own hands: She started a moderate weight-training program in hopes of regaining her strength.

Sooner than she expected, she noticed improvements. As her strength returned, her pain lessened. Soon she was free of both the pain and the limp and found herself fantasizing about a career in body building.

Very quickly she turned the fantasy into reality, and, once again, success came sooner than expected. Within two years of her weight-training debut, Joanne was crowned Ms. Maine and Ms. Natural New England. Then she took second place in the Ms. America body-building contest, in which she competed against many women who were using steroids and other performance enhancers. Again frustrated, she founded the Maine Alliance of Drug Free Athletes, to help clean up the sport of body building and send out a powerful message against the use of steroids.

Driven to excel in her sport both for personal reasons and as an example in the fight against steroid use, Joanne trained harder and harder. She continually pushed herself to exhaustion, and, as she put it, "Even though my mind wanted to be with my family, when we were together, my body wasn't there, I was exhausted." She was convinced that she "had to train in a certain way, and do certain stressful things like everyone else, because if I didn't do them, I wasn't going to make it, I wasn't going to make the grade."

It wasn't long before her exhaustion turned into pain. With chronically pulled shoulder and neck muscles, she had to use local anesthetics to continue her training. After months of enduring this strain, she reinjured her back. Totally frustrated, she was back where she had started. The very thing that had cured her was now hurting her and threatening her career.

In desperation, and realizing that she was overtrained, she eased up on her workouts. "I would try whatever convention seemed reasonable," she said. "There were rest days or light sessions, when I'd cut back in order to offset the hard training days. I sandwiched periods of extensive rest between contests, so my body could recover. I'd never increase my weekly training by more than 10 percent. I'd cross-train, use intervals, and follow tapering and peaking schedules. But frankly, I still felt I was walking a fine line between not enough work and too much.

"Acute pain became the main sign of a problem. When I felt unbearable pain, I stopped what I was doing and eased off. Plain discomfort, soreness, and fatigue were fine. In fact, they were the expected result. I used ice, heat, or massage to keep me going. The truth is that overtraining doesn't dawn on you until it happens, and then it's too late."

At this point, Joanne attended my Invincible Athletics seminar, where I told her she could still be a competitive body builder but without the conventional strain. "It doesn't have to hurt," I said. She began using my techniques and six months later wrote this:

> When I finally let go of all that strain, it was scary. I thought, "Maybe you'll fail completely." But what I was rewarded with was this unboundedness, and a very responsive physiology. Without that stress, what happened immediately was that everything seemed possible, including being able to lift higher weights, fuller muscles, no fatigue, and the ability to feel the muscle in the correct form, every time, instead of hitting that once out of every three workouts.
>
> It was such a delightful process to let go and be greeted by the reality that the body is totally mutable . . . that you have an input into it as long as you're willing to coordinate your body's impulses with your mind's impulses and not too vigorously demand things from the body without listening to the body.
>
> I feel like I'm walking on clouds now when I go to the gym and see all the people in the trenches absolutely killing themselves. I've been there, so I have deep compassion for them. I can see that this Kapha type is not

doing enough over here; the Vata type is absolutely killing himself by doing sets of 6,000 repetitions, thinking that he's going to build muscle mass doing it. And that Pitta over there could get somewhere if she'd put her awareness on the weights, and not on trying to beat her partner by going up in weight.

Just this knowledge of body types changes everything. So much could be corrected with this knowledge alone. When people come to me for feedback on their training, they'll say, "I've read this, I've been training like this, and picked this up from so-and-so, what do you think?" So much of the information needs to be dismissed straightaway because it doesn't consider that this person is one body type, and the program they're talking about is very good for another type, but not for them. This is something that is immediately useful, a revelation in training.

Knowing my Ayurvedic body type has allowed me to choose the right exercises for me, which cross-training sports to do, the best times of day to exercise, and how long and how intensely I should work out. The dietary and other guidelines and practices that supplement the workouts make this program unbelievably comprehensive.

What this program is really about is showing the dynamics of outer and inner harmony, about making visible the integration of body and mind. Training becomes an inner experience, more quiet and settled, yet outwardly it's very, very dynamic and lively.

The message here is provocative. There is really a great contrast, a kind of paradox at the deepest level of all athletics—inner silence and spontaneous outer dynamism coexist, and the outer depends on the inner. With this simple shift of attention, body building takes on the worthy stature of its name—building the body, the whole body, constructing its infinite potential, no longer at the expense of the body but with wholeness as its reward.

This program gets the mind working for you, and provides a system of techniques, of objective and subjective monitors, that keeps the body coordinated with the mind. The quintessential point is not only to develop the connection between mind and body, but to learn to use it. The ultimate lesson is that the greatest knowledge comes from inside. I affectionately call the program "enlightening the dumbbells."

Let's look at some of Joanne's results. When she wrote to me, her resting heart rate had decreased from the mid-60s to the low 40s, and her heart recovery rate was quicker than ever before. Her breathing was smooth, relaxed, and slow during workouts, averaging under 10 breaths per minute. Her muscle definition and mass increased, as did her flexibility. She now could train intensively without exhaustion, restlessness, or injury.

The pain, spasms, and soreness that once affected her trapezius and shoulder muscles during certain exercises have disappeared, "as if something has healed or reworked itself." The back problems are gone. In fact, there is no longer any pain in any aspect of training, "no more chronically sore elbows, wrists, or knees. And the sore joints held almost universally as a sign of accomplishment during contest preparation by body builders are completely gone."

With the changes she has made in her diet, there are no more mega-doses of vitamins, no extreme protein consumption, no radical shifts in eating depending on how close she is to competition, and no more required eating six times a day. In addition, when she goes home she's refreshed and enjoys her life with her family. In terms of performance, Joanne has placed in every contest she has entered since beginning the program, and she carries a new air of confidence, relaxation, and happiness when she's on stage. She sums up the process in a phrase: "It's absolutely easy."

The concept of "less is more," although still quite controversial, is commanding a respectful look from the experts. For example, the swimming team at Ball State University was plagued with fatigue and poor performance. Dr. David Costill, a leading researcher on overtraining, recommended that the team reduce its training time from two hours a day to one hour a day, thereby cutting 1,000 yards of training each week. The team went from last place in the conference to third.

In part II we will lay the foundations for the consistent achievement of the exercise high and for the practices that will teach you (in part III) how to do less and accomplish more. The first step, as Joanne said, is to know your body type. From there, as the saying goes, "Well begun is half done."

The principles and techniques described in part II are based on knowledge from the Vedic tradition of India, which inspired Bodhidharma, the father of Zen Buddhism and the first teacher of the martial arts. This knowledge is taken specifically from the timeless science of life called Maharishi Ayur-Ved.

The program begins with determining your constitutional type, so that you can plan your exercise or training program to perfectly match your physical needs and capacities. This is what you will learn in chapter 4.

PART TWO

4

DISCOVER YOUR BODY TYPE

The first requirement for developing a successful exercise program from the inside out, and for achieving the Zone, is to know your nature, your individual mind-body type. Do you burn regular or leaded, do you burn hot or cold, do you run fast or with endurance, do you more easily gain weight or lose it? Are you a heavy sleeper or a light one? Are you the life of the party or do you prefer solitude? Do you excel in team sports or as an individual?

In this chapter I will describe the three primary body types, each with its own likes, dislikes, strengths, and weaknesses. According to Maharishi Ayur-Ved, these constitutional types are so fundamental to your identity that they are considered to define your individual *nature*.

To illustrate the concept of body types, let's look on the football field, where a diverse group of men display their special talents based on their physical uniqueness. Players of different sizes and shapes dominate various areas of the field. There are big, heavyset linemen, long, lanky ends and wide receivers, and stocky linebackers. The quarterbacks seem to be a blend of all the others. Maybe that's why they can lead their troops into battle: They've got a little of everyone inside them.

To try to make these very different sorts of men play every position well would be ridiculous. Imagine a 300-pound tackle chugging out for a pass, or a 180-pound tight end crouching on the line of scrimmage, facing a 300-pound opponent! This would be much like the President's Council on Physical Fitness and Sports testing children based on the strengths and talents of one body type, when in reality we are all different and should be tested on our individual areas of strength.

Dr. Claude Bouchard of Laval University in Quebec City, perhaps the world's leading sports geneticist, came to a remarkable conclusion regarding individual uniqueness. Based on his research, he concluded that if you gathered a random group of nontrained, out-of-shape people, put them all on the identical training program, and measured their progress, the results would be far from uniform. Some would progress rapidly, some slowly, and others not at all.

The cause for this vast difference in trainability, Dr. Bouchard believes, is 75 percent genetic—i.e., people are intrinsically different. Our genetic makeup is expressed by our individual body type. The different constitutional types will respond to, enjoy, and benefit from different sports and types of exercise. Our unique mind-body types give us each unique requirements for health and fitness.

CODES OF INTELLIGENCE

A look back to our days in grade school will further clarify the constitutional types.

The first type is epitomized by a fifth-grade girl named Erica. (See Figure 1.) Compared to the other kids, Erica is a little on the skinny side, but she maintains her cool image by being quick, both physically and mentally. Because of Erica's restless nature, her teacher constantly has to ask her to settle down and be quiet.

Erica's body type is known in Sanskrit—the language of the ancient Vedic civilization—as Vata, which means air and movement. Air by nature moves, and that's what predominates in Erica's body type. She moves quickly, thinks quickly, and forgets quickly. She also has a hard time focusing on one project for any length of time, because her mind is constantly leaping from one thing to another.

Of the three learning styles now recognized by most educators, Erica learns best auditorily, rather than visually or kinesthetically (through movement). She usually does well in school, excelling in English, grammar, and social studies. This is because our present educational system strongly favors the Vata body type, and so almost all information is delivered verbally.

Erica tends to be a little nervous or even anxious at times, but her natural mental and physical quickness will ultimately prove to be her greatest asset.

Erica's classmate Katie belongs to the type that learns best visually.

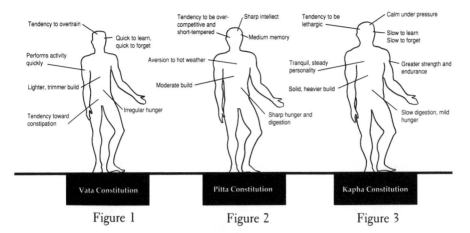

| Vata Constitution | Pitta Constitution | Kapha Constitution |

Figure 1   Figure 2   Figure 3

This type is known as Pitta, which means fiery. (See Figure 2.) Katie excels in schoolwork, particularly in more visually oriented subjects such as math and science. Her adorable face is covered with freckles, and she sports two long and slightly curly red pigtails.

Katie is extremely competitive and is quick to take command and lead the class if necessary. Her fiery mind tends to drive her body hard, and she is something of a perfectionist. This trait often makes her the best at whatever she chooses to do, but on the negative side, it sometimes makes her overly demanding of herself. If she doesn't win or come out on top it really gets her down. In the summer, Katie's face turns bright red when she gets overheated, which occurs often because the Pitta body type carries a lot of heat by nature.

The third basic type (see Figure 3) couldn't be more accurately reflected than in their classmate Tom. One of the bigger boys in the class, Tom is a Kapha type. By nature he is slow to learn, but once he "gets" it, he's got it for life. He is just the opposite of Erica, who takes in information quickly but can't remember it for long.

Tom learns best kinesthetically. But most of his classes are taught visually, using textbooks, videos, and blackboards, or auditorily, with lectures and discussions, so he has a hard time in school. However, he excels in geometry and geography, which allow him to learn kinesthetically from pictures and shapes. Tom is a late bloomer and soon will be able to command any field of activity.

Tom's demeanor is calm and tranquil. He moves slowly and methodically but with no wasted effort. In our fast-paced society, Tom runs the risk of being labeled slow or even dyslexic, but he has as much or more natural talent and ability than do the other two types—he is just different.

Physically, Tom has great endurance and strength, but he is short on agility. He is not the type to be a world-class rope climber, but his natural strength makes him popular when choosing up sides for football, and he will probably bat clean-up on the baseball team.

These three basic body types reflect the three fundamental governing principles of nature—Vata, Pitta, and Kapha. At conception, we are all given some amount of each quality, and the proportion that we have—which qualities dominate our makeup—determines our type. However, it is much more than just a body type; it is a true psychophysiological, constitutional, and mind-body type. It influences how you think, spend money, eat, sleep, and much more, as well as the size and shape of your body. However, to simplify matters, in this book we will just call it your body type.

🦋 CHARACTERISTICS OF VATA TYPE

- Light, thinner build
- Performs activity quickly
- Tendency toward dry skin
- Aversion to cold weather
- Irregular hunger and digestion
- Quick to grasp new information, also quick to forget
- Tendency toward worry
- Tendency toward constipation
- Tendency toward light and interrupted sleep

🖋 CHARACTERISTICS OF PITTA TYPE

- Moderate build
- Performs activity with medium speed
- Aversion to hot weather
- Prefers cold food and drinks
- Extreme hunger and quick digestion
- Can't skip meals
- Medium time to grasp new information
- Medium memory
- Tendency toward reddish hair and complexion, moles, freckles
- Good public speakers

- Tendency toward irritability and anger
- Enterprising and sharp in character

♀ CHARACTERISTICS OF KAPHA TYPE

- Solid, heavier build
- Greater strength and endurance
- Slow and methodical in activity
- Oily, smooth skin
- Slow digestion, mild hunger
- Tranquil, steady personality
- Slow to grasp new information, slow to forget
- Slow to become excited or irritated
- Sleep is heavy and long
- Hair is plentiful, thick, and wavy

Once you determine your body type, your unique combination of Vata, Pitta, and Kapha, you will know your fundamental requirements for action in harmony with nature. Knowledge of your body type gives you an owner's manual, which describes your maintenance schedule and performance records. Without this knowledge, optimal functioning may sometimes occur, but it will be random. With it, you will have clear guidelines for what sport is most suitable, how much exercise is good and how much more can be harmful, when to exercise and when to rest, and what to eat to fuel optimal performance.

To better understand this concept, let's connect the body types back to their source in nature. According to most ancient systems of medicine, the basic component parts of nature are the *five elements*—space, air, fire, water, and earth. (See Figure 4.)

As you can see, Vata is derived from the combination of space and air. In nature, Vata controls wind, cold, and the dry qualities that are most dramatically expressed in the fall and winter, known as the Vata season. In the body, Vata is responsible for all movement, such as breathing, blood circulation, and the movement of food through the digestive tract. Vata also controls the nervous system.

Pitta is made up primarily of the element fire, with a smaller amount of water—probably to keep the pot from burning! The qualities of Pitta are

The Five Elements

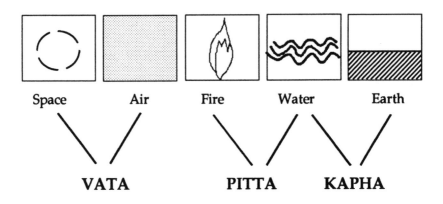

Figure 4

expressed in nature most during the hot months of summer—the Pitta season. In the body, Pitta is responsible for digestion and metabolism. Its forte is transforming one thing into another, such as converting food into energy.

The Kapha body type, which is slow and methodical in nature, is composed of the heavier elements, earth and water. In nature, the rainy qualities of spring make it the Kapha season. In the body, Kapha is responsible for structural stability and water balance. Kapha individuals may have trouble with water retention and congestion and as a result are more susceptible to allergies; in addition, they are the type most likely to be overweight.

BODY-TYPE QUESTIONNAIRE

The next step in determining your individual nature is to fill out the following questionnaire. It will give you a preliminary indication of your body type and help you to design the most appropriate exercise program.

The questionnaire contains four sections: Mental Profile, Behavioral Profile, Physical Profile, and Athletic Profile. Each is important to complete the picture of your constitution.

The questionnaire is divided into three columns for each of the primary body types, Vata, Pitta, and Kapha. For each item (sleep patterns, appetite, endurance, concentration ability, and so on), circle the answer that most accurately describes your long-term nature. If two answers apply, circle both. If none applies, leave it blank. Then tally each column. The column with the most marks is your primary type; the column with the second largest number of marks is your secondary type. For example, if you score 15 Vata, 24 Pitta, and 4 Kapha, your body type is Pitta-Vata, a combination of Pitta and Vata with a predominance of Pitta.

Take the time now to fill out the questionnaire, and then we will analyze the results.

Note: If this is a library book, please be kind to future readers and either keep your score on a separate sheet of paper or write so lightly in pencil that you can erase your marks after you tally your score.

MENTAL PROFILE

	Vata	Pitta	Kapha
Mental activity	quick mind, restless	sharp intellect, aggressive	calm, steady, stable
Memory	short-term best	good general memory	long-term best
Thoughts	constantly changing	fairly steady	steady
Concentration	short-term focus best	better than average mental concentration	focus for long time
Grasping power	quick grasping power	medium grasp power	takes longer to grasp new information
Dreams	fearful, flying, running, jumping	anger, fiery, violent	water, clouds, relationship, romance
Sleep	interrupted, light	sound, medium length	sound, heavy, long
Talk	fast, sometimes missing words	fast, sharp, clear-cut	slow, clear, sweet
Voice	high pitch	medium pitch	low pitch

Mental Subtotal _____ _____ _____

BEHAVIORAL PROFILE

	☙	♦	♀
Eat	quickly	medium speed	slowly
Hunger	irregular	sharp, needs food	can easily miss meals
Food and drink	prefer warm	prefer cold	prefer dry and warm
Moods	changes quickly	slowly changing	steady, nonchanging
Sex drive	variable-low	moderate	strong
Weather	aversion to cold	aversion to hot	aversion to damp, cool
React to stress	excite quickly	medium	slow to get excited
Financial	doesn't save, spends quickly	saves but big spender	saves regularly, accumulates wealth
Friendships	tends toward short-term friendships	tends to be a loner (friends related to occupation)	tends toward more long-lasting friendships
Behavioral Subtotal	_____	_____	_____

PHYSICAL PROFILE

	☙	♦	♀
Hair amount	average	thinning	thick
Hair type	dry	medium	oily
Hair color	light brown	red/auburn	dark brown/black
Skin	dry/rough	soft/medium oily	oily, moist, cool
Skin temperature	cold hands/feet	warm	cool
Complexion	darker	pink-red	pale-white
Eyes	small	medium	large
Whites of eyes	blue/brown	yellow or red	white glossy
Size of teeth	very large or very small	small-medium	medium-large
Weight	Thin, hard to gain	medium weight	heavy, easy to gain
Elimination	dry, hard, thin, constipation	many, soft to normal	heavy, slow, thick regular
Resting pulse rate Men	70–90	60–70	50–60

Women	80–100	70–80	60–70
Veins and tendons	very prominent	fairly prominent	well covered

Physical Subtotal _____   _____   _____

ATHLETIC PROFILE

Exercise tolerance	low	medium	high
Endurance	fair	good	excellent
Strength	fair	better than average	excellent
Speed	very good	good	not so fast
Competition	doesn't like competitive pressure	excellent (driven) competitor	easily deals with competitive stress
Walking speed	fast	average	slow and steady
Muscle tone	lean, low body fat	medium w/good definition	bulk w/higher fat percentage
Runs like	deer	tiger	bear
Body size	small frame, lean or long	medium frame	large frame, fleshy
Reaction time	quick	average	slow

Athletic Subtotal _____   _____   _____

TOTALS

Mental _____   _____   _____

Behavioral _____   _____   _____

Physical _____   _____   _____

Athletic

Your Mind-Body

Type _____   _____   _____

Vata   Pitta   Kapha

INTERPRETING THE RESULTS

This is a complete body-typing system that analyzes your constitution in terms of mental, emotional, physical, and behavioral patterns. Through this comprehensive analysis we can get a true picture of the psychophysiological nature of each individual.

Let's look at a few examples. Let's say your score is 3 Vata, 30 Pitta, and

6 Kapha. Your body type is Pitta. Because Pitta is the primary influence in your body, you would follow all the Pitta programs described later in this book. For maximum health and success, you would choose Pitta sports, Pitta diet, and a Pitta fitness program.

If your score on the Body-Type Questionnaire was 3 Vata, 18 Pitta, and 21 Kapha, your body type has a predominance of two qualities, Kapha and Pitta, making you a Kapha-Pitta body type. If your score was 18 Vata, 5 Pitta, and 21 Kapha, you would be a Kapha-Vata, with the emphasis on Kapha because it is slightly more dominant.

The last possible configuration is when all three qualities are close to equal. For example, if your score was 14 Vata, 15 Pitta, and 13 Kapha, you have a fairly equal distribution of Vata, Pitta, and Kapha. This is called *Sama* type "the same."

If your body type is a combination of two or three qualities, you will create your exercise program (described in detail in later chapters) based on the nature of your predominant body type plus where you are in the cycles of the seasons. If you are a Pitta-Vata, for example, you would favor exercise patterns for Pitta types in the summer months and the Vata program in the autumn and winter months.

I will make this easy for you to determine by including, at the end of each chapter in our program (Diet, Sport Selection, and Three Phase Workout), a chart showing all the body types and the three primary seasons. By looking up your body type and the current season on the chart, you will be able to create a balanced program that is suitable to your individual nature and in sync with the larger, more powerful seasonal cycles of nature.

There are ten basic body types, based on the possible combinations of the three qualities:

Vata
Pitta
Kapha
Vata-Pitta
Pitta-Vata
Pitta-Kapha
Kapha-Pitta
Vata-Kapha
Kapha-Vata
Vata-Pitta-Kapha

Throughout the remainder of the book, I will provide recommendations for each of these ten types to help you develop the most suitable mind-body fitness program based on your individual nature.

IF YOUR SCORE DOESN'T SEEM RIGHT . . .

There are two reasons why the results of the Body-Type Questionnaire might be confusing or seem not to be a true representation of your body type. The first is due to the subjective nature of the test. Sometimes we just don't see ourselves clearly, or, due to a long-standing habit of trying to do well on tests, we put down the answers that reflect how we would *like* to be rather than how we really are.

To clear up any confusion, I suggest that you ask your spouse or a close friend or relative who knows you very well either to ask you the questions or to go over the answers with you. Getting an objective view can help us see ourselves more realistically.

The second reason why the questionnaire might not accurately reflect your body type is that you could have a temporary imbalance in your system. For example, you may be primarily Pitta-Kapha, but if your Vata is aggravated (maybe due to staying up late or keeping an erratic schedule), you may have Vata-like symptoms such as anxiety, insomnia, constipation, and so on. If your answers to some of the questions were based on a state of imbalance rather than on your true constitution, it would skew the results of the questionnaire. Try to answer the questions based on your long-term characteristics, not necessarily on how things are at this moment.

When an individual is in balance, this does not mean that Vata, Pitta, and Kapha are equal. It simply means that your body type is functioning in harmony with its nature and its environment. Balance in the body promotes normal, healthy bodily function.

❦ **Balanced Vata** promotes:

Mental alertness
Proper formation of body tissues
Normal elimination
Sound sleep
Strong immunity
Sense of exhilaration

❦ **Balanced Pitta** promotes:

Normal heat and thirst mechanisms
Strong digestion
Lustrous complexion
Sharp intellect
Contentment

♀ Balanced Kapha promotes:

Muscular strength
Vitality and stamina
Strong immunity
Affection, generosity, courage, dignity
Stability of mind
Healthy, normal joints

When the body drifts out of balance, the harmony of mind and body is lost and symptoms of disease can result.

♗ Imbalance in Vata creates:

Dry or rough skin
Insomnia
Constipation
Fatigue
Tension headaches
Intolerance of cold
Degenerative arthritis
Underweight
Anxiety
Worry

♀ Imbalance in Pitta creates:

Rashes
Inflammatory skin conditions
Peptic ulcers
Heartburn
Visual problems
Excessive body heat
Premature graying or baldness
Hostility
Irritability

♀ Imbalance in Kapha creates

Oily skin
Slow digestion
Sinus congestion
Nasal allergies
Asthma

Obesity
Cysts and other growths
Possessiveness
Apathy

Understanding your body type and using all aspects of this mind-body system in your exercise program can play a major role in restoring balanced functioning, in harmony with your true nature and the cycles and rhythms of the natural environment. The topic of treating imbalances is beyond the scope of this book. For more information, or for the location of a certified Maharishi Ayur-Ved physician in your area, call (508) 365-4549.

5

THE LAW OF THE LAND

The next step in the process of reproducing and living in the Zone is to understand the very powerful daily and seasonal cycles of nature. With knowledge of these cycles added to an understanding of our body type, we can begin to flow with nature's intelligence.

Understanding nature's intelligence can be infinitely complex or infinitely simple. While man tends to complicate matters, animals simplify them. Birds don't sit in their nests in October deliberating whether they should fly south. They just do it. They have no choice, as their survival is dependent on their adherence to daily and seasonal cycles. We humans, on the other hand, endowed with the ability to choose, will plan and debate for weeks or months before deciding to fly south and winter in Florida. We can also choose to function—and to exercise—in harmony with these cycles, or we can swim against the current and suffer the consequences.

The warriors of ancient societies recognized the enormous power of nature and strove to keep their training and their personal lives aligned with these natural cycles. They derived their formula for living in the Zone—silence along with dynamism—directly from nature. They saw that the silence of winter provides the basis for the dynamism of summer; that without rest there would be no activity; without the eye there would be no hurricane. This deep understanding of nature and how to live in accordance with its cycles and laws allowed these warriors to harness its unlimited power.

LEASING LIFE MONTH TO MONTH

Every year we watch the seasons change. We see bright green forests come to life in a pageant of autumn color; then, within weeks, the leaves are gone and the trees hang out a sign, "closed for the season." Birds migrate across oceans and continents, whales travel tens of thousands of miles, and flowers bloom as if on cue at the first hint of spring. How does all this happen?

It is remarkable that season after season, century after century, Mother Nature and her offspring live on in perfect harmony. But we humans seem so out of touch with the environment that supports our existence. We believe we can remain unaffected when the dead of winter transforms into the budding life of spring. Somehow, we think that all we have to do is take off a sweater or open a window, and we're all set.

In truth, however, we are every bit as connected to the seasonal cycles of nature as are all living creatures, but we have detached ourselves from these cycles with such things as heated houses, air-conditioned cars, and electric lights. I'm not suggesting that these conveniences are in any way bad. They provide comforts that humans, through their accomplishments, rightfully deserve. But when they tempt us to lose our connection to the natural world in which we live, that is cause for concern.

Exercise offers us a unique opportunity to help link us back to nature. In this chapter we will explore our relationship to the seasonal cycles. In chapter 6, we will learn how we can further optimize our performance by getting in tune with nature's daily rhythms.

♀ NATURE'S NEW YEAR

The first season in nature is spring, which runs approximately from March through June. This marks nature's new year, when everything begins to grow and come alive after the long, dormant winter. This is the time for spring training, the perfect time to pick up the pace after the quiet, restful winter. The cool, moist air is just what the doctor ordered for seeds to germinate, eggs to hatch, and rivers to run. The onset of spring is the catalyst for everything in nature to wake up and start mating, growing, hatching, and housing its young. After the long winter's rest, nature is alive and bursting with energy.

Just as nature starts off with springtime, so do we. The first twelve years of life are considered our springtime. These are Kapha years, marked by the same qualities that predominate during spring. It is a time of growth and development, for children as well as nature.

Spring is also a season of moisture, when rains come, snow melts, and the ground becomes soggy and muddy. As nature becomes wet and congested, children, during their Kapha years of maximum growth, frequently complain of colds, congestion, ear infections, and upper respiratory conditions. During the Kapha time of year, children experience even more trouble with congestion and allergies, and child asthmatics have to be particularly careful during this season, known appropriately as "allergy season."

THE THREE SEASONS AND CORRESPONDING BODY TYPES

SEASON—FALL AND WINTER	EXERCISE REQUIREMENTS
November through February (cold, windy, and dry) Vata qualities are increasing.	Don't need as much exercise.

SEASON—SUMMER	
July through October (basically hot) Pitta qualities are increasing.	Avoid overheating during exercise.

SEASON—SPRING	
March through June (wet and cool) Kapha qualities are increasing.	Need more vigorous exercise.

A Kapha child, in the Kapha years of life, in Kapha season, will almost certainly exhibit signs of accumulated Kapha qualities. In addition to congestion and allergies, the child may be lethargic, tired, complacent, and show signs of what we call "mental viscosity," or dullness. This is the time when many Kapha children get labeled as slow or even dyslexic.

There is a good chance that these Babe Ruth types may turn out to be late bloomers, who do not begin to fully express their God-given talents until they grow out of the Kapha period of life. At that point, their health may also improve dramatically. This knowledge can be a great relief to parents of Kapha children who have been diagnosed as slow learners or who suffer from chronic congestive disorders.

Remember Sharon, the young girl mentioned in chapter 3 who could not run a mile in under 10 minutes. She found great success in race walking, a sport that utilized her natural Kapha strength and endurance. Understanding her Kapha constitution, the grain of her own nature, helped her to appreciate herself for who she was. Now a basketball player, she said of her team, "It's just perfect how all the Vata and Pitta kids, who run real fast, stay outside the basket dribbling and passing, while us bigger Kapha kids stay underneath for lay-ups and rebounds."

During spring, the heavy, damp, slow, congestive season, Kapha qualities tend to increase in our bodies as they increase in the environment. People who possess more Kapha in their body type will find that their allergies act up and they tend to gain weight and feel tired and lethargic. Therefore, they need more vigorous exercise in spring. Understanding this natural tendency of the Kapha body type to accumulate Kapha in the spring can play a key role in maintaining a balance of mind, body, and nature.

✦ HERE COMES THE SUN

As the cool air of spring begins to warm, the moist Kapha qualities burn off. The sun stays in the sky longer, and the heat of the summer begins to build. Summer—which lasts from June through September—is known as Pitta season. It serves as a warning light for Pitta types, in whose bodies heat is a predominant quality. Heat builds up in everyone, but Pittas have to be especially careful not to overheat during the more active summer months, or they will find themselves boiling over. Pure Pitta types, who are blessed with hot and fiery personalities, usually find the summer months uncomfortable and should take care not to participate in sports on hot afternoons.

During summer, nature kicks into full bloom. The seeds sown in Kapha season now reach for the sky to get closer to the magic of the summer sun. The sun rises earlier and earlier and sets later and later as summer peaks. Most animals, after their long winter's rest, are ready for these long days.

Most of us don't realize it, but we are closely connected to these cycles. We all tend to get more sleep, or at least to need more sleep, in the dark winter months, and to sleep less in the summer. An extreme example is northern Alaska, where the sun is up all summer—"the land of the midnight sun"—and down all winter. There, residents typically stay awake virtually all summer, enjoying the cherished sunlight, and catch up on their rest during winter.

If you are a camper, you know that when you are in the wilderness it is customary to settle down and go to sleep soon after dark and to wake up with the sun. Out in nature, we find ourselves living in tune with nature's cycles; ordinarily we simply ignore them.

As we reach adulthood we enter the more active and productive Pitta phase. In the Kapha phase of childhood, the heavy, moist, congestive qualities provide the perfect medium for growth. Seeds germinate best in the same springlike environment. When summer hits, nature is in full gear, and the heat of the sun is the necessary catalyst for further development.

In the middle part of life, we are also in full gear. These are our most dynamic and creative years. The heat of the sun, which activates nature in summer, launches us into the most active phase of our lives. These years should be the most physically and mentally productive of our lives. It seems unnatural that many of our best athletes retire in their twenties, before they even enter the prime of their lives.

☙ HUMAN HIBERNATION

The third and final season lasts from October through February. What we call autumn and winter are combined in one long season traditionally known as Vata season. Similar characteristics are visible in Vata season and in people with Vata constitutions. Vata by nature is quick, cold, rough, dry, and constantly changing. People with Vata body types tend to have cold hands and feet. Their movements are described as being "quick as a rabbit," as compared to the very Kapha-like elephant. Their moods and routines are constantly changing, and their skin easily becomes dry.

As the environment becomes drier in the fall and winter, dryness accumulates in our bodies. Many of us notice, for example, that our skin and sinuses become dryer in the winter months.

Toward the end of summer, the accumulated heat of the Pitta season is dramatically expressed by the crimson, orange, and bright yellow fall foliage. This heat ignites the trees into a bright spectacle of autumn color, then leaves them burned up and dried out. The crisp leaves of autumn are the first sign of the oncoming very dry winter season.

An analogous process takes place in our bodies. As the Pitta heat accumulates in the late summer months, it also builds up inside us. This heat rises in the body and dries out the sinuses and upper respiratory tract. The oncoming Vata season increases the dryness. The result, in many people, is "hay fever."

Hay fever occurs when the sinuses become dry and lose their ability to protect against irritants such as ragweed pollen. To flush out pollen irritants and combat the dryness, the body produces a flow of mucus. The mucus is the allergic response; the fever is the rising Pitta in the head and sinuses.

The symptoms of hay fever—congestion and excessive mucus—may appear to stem from a Kapha aggravation, as children in the Kapha phase of life frequently suffer from congestion and catarrhal disorders. But Kapha is not the culprit here.

The Vata season moves on toward the depths of winter. The air gets very cold and even drier, but, like the fascinating Vata personality, the season is ever-changing. One day it's raining, the next day snow falls from a gray sky, and then comes a week of warm, balmy southern air.

As the cold, dry air persists, Vata builds up. The skin can get very dry and chapped, while internally we may also dry out, and constipation can become a problem. The joints may become dry and begin to ache. The nervous system in Vata season can also respond to the influence of the cold, dry weather and become overexcited, resulting in nervousness and anxious behavior.

For these reasons, people with a lot of Vata in their constitution generally don't do very well in colder climates. They should exercise indoors or in warmer climates whenever possible. If they must exercise outdoors, proper dress is very important. (Although there are many high-tech waterproof synthetic fabrics, I recommend that whenever possible you wear 100 percent natural fabrics such as silk, cotton, and wool.)

When we reach older age, we enter the Vata phase of our lives. Some people resort to cosmetic surgeons to combat the wrinkling, drying, and sagging caused largely by the influence of Vata. Florida and other Sunbelt states are thriving as retirement communities because Vata types are more comfortable in a warmer climate. As their bones become dry and their bodies get thinner, elderly people find natural relief in warm environments.

In nature, the Vata season is a resting phase, and therefore we naturally need less exercise. Animals hibernate, leaves fall, lakes freeze, and nature's age-old annual life cycle comes to an end. All the laws of nature go into temporary retirement, in preparation for the onset of spring and the annual renewal of life, the celebration of nature's new year.

It is all so perfectly balanced and harmonious, effective in sustaining life millennium after millennium. Nature wisely alternates phases of rest and activity—silence and dynamism. The hibernating rest of winter is the silence from which all the growth and dynamism of life sprouts. Without it, all life would collapse.

Both nature's formula for sustaining life and our formula for reaching the exercise high depend on the coexistence of the opposite values of dynamism and silence. Nature regulates the seasonal, monthly, and daily cycles to maintain and coordinate balance, while we, with our inherent ability to choose, can create balance and harmony by living our lives with reference to, and respect for, natural law.

For us to experience this balance, we must enjoy appropriate cycles of rest and activity in our daily life. To harness and reproduce the longevity, infinite potential, and effortless functioning of nature, we must mimic its way. We must exercise in harmony with these very powerful cycles of nature.

6

THE HUMAN TIME MACHINE

Man has spent centuries trying to design the perfect timepiece. High-tech and handmade precision watches battle it out for the largest market share. But not long ago, we survived quite well without the aid of timepieces. And the birds in the forest still seem to know exactly when to eat, sleep, and wake up, without the intrusive use of clocks, wristwatches, or alarms.

In this chapter I will introduce you to an internal clock that is every bit as accurate and valuable as the fanciest man-made timepieces.

All of nature's creatures, including human beings, operate according to daily diurnal or circadian rhythms—patterns of physiological functioning that repeat every 24 hours. Birds wake up with the sun and go to sleep when it sets. Many flowers open their petals in the daylight and close up again at dusk. In humans, specific biochemical patterns recur regularly and predictably, day after day. For example, cortisol, which is produced by the body and released into the bloodstream to help you deal with the stress of daily life, increases in the early morning hours and decreases in the evening. When you sleep, blood pressure, heart rate, and body temperature drop, then rise again in the morning. We are intimately connected to the daily clock of Mother Nature. The invention of the alarm clock was necessary only because of our disregard for this connection.

The most ancient description of the relationship of human beings to the environment is found in the principles of Maharishi Ayur-Ved, more than five thousand years old. It is clearly stated that the same master clock that commands the seasons to come and go and the rooster to crow regulates the timing of our internal biological functioning.

In chapter 5 we saw that each season possesses characteristic qualities. In response to these qualities, nature performs different sets of coordinated activities. It wouldn't make sense if the birds flew *north* for winter, or the salmon swam *downstream* when their internal clocks told them it was time to spawn. Nor would it make sense for us to wear heavy clothes and eat hot, spicy foods in summer, or wear bathing suits and have a diet of ice cream and salads in winter. It is helpful to regulate our lives in accordance with this Ayurvedic clock, because we feel better and function more effectively when we "go with the flow" rather than oppose it.

Similar patterns flow through each day. The qualities of Vata, Pitta, and Kapha are highlighted at different times during the 24-hour cycle. If we respond to these rhythms, we can put the power of nature behind our actions. Therefore, I recommend that you make an effort to restructure your life in accordance with these natural patterns. I believe that once you try it, you will maintain it because you will *want* to—not because you "should" or because I recommend it. All the principles in this book are based on the science of life, not on the science of pain and struggle. Like the exercise high, life when "in the flow" is easier and more enjoyable.

The best way to evaluate this aspect of the program is to try it for one week, then decide whether to continue it based on how you feel.

NATURE'S CLOCK

6:00 A.M.–10:00 A.M. KAPHA TIME

(As we view this clock, we will assume that 6:00 A.M. is sunrise and 6:00 P.M. is sunset.)

Did you ever notice that first thing in the morning you might feel somewhat heavy or sluggish, and if you go back to sleep or lie around in bed you feel even more lazy, drowsy, and stiff? And that if you sleep very late, the whole day can take on a kind of cloudy and dull quality? The reason for this is that every minute after the sun rises, Kapha increases both in the environment and in your body. The longer you continue to do a Kapha-like activity such as lying in bed or sleeping after sunrise, the more you are likely to experience the heavy, dull, and lethargic qualities of Kapha.

To combat the heaviness of Kapha, morning is the best time to engage in physical activity. Morning is also when the natural structural strengths of Kapha are more pronounced. Dancers and ballerinas, for example, generally have a light, Vata-type constitution, rather than the natural structural strength and resiliency of Kapha types. Intensive training can easily overstress their lighter frames and lead to injury. Therefore, as a preventive measure, I recommend that this type train in the early morning hours, when Kapha and the structural resiliency in the body are more abundant. Give your body a chance to become accustomed to exercise in the morning and see if it doesn't make a difference.

The nature of Kapha is heavy and slow, qualities that predominate in the morning hours. Physical activity, whether gardening, walking, cleaning the house, or training for a marathon, will help to counteract the tendency toward heaviness and take advantage of the structural strength of the Kapha time of day. Studies have shown that 75 percent of Americans who have a regular morning exercise program are still exercising a year later, versus only 25 percent who work out at their lunch break or after work.

♦ 10:00 A.M.–2:00 P.M. PITTA TIME

When the sun climbs to the middle of the sky we enter the Pitta period, the hottest part of the day. Now the sun is kindling the digestive fire to stimulate the most efficient digestion. At this time, especially for Pitta types, exercise should be minimal. Rather, this it the time to eat! It is said that the only time of day in which human beings can properly digest a large meal, which we all need for energy during a long and hectic day, is between 10:00 A.M. and 2:00 P.M., when the digestive fire of Pitta burns most brightly.

Most athletes think that the traditional precompetition carbo-loading meal must be eaten the night before the competition, and that it must be huge. The longer the race, they conclude, the bigger the carbo-loading dinner. But just once, try having your carbo-loading meal at lunch the day before the race, followed by a light dinner, and see how you feel; note whether you have less endurance or more. I'll bet you switch to that routine. (More on this, including menus and recipes for carbo-loading meals for each body type, in chapter 7.)

Dave Carlson, who has competed in every ironman triathlon since 1980, told me that he often felt heavy and dull on race-day morning, after eating a huge dinner loaded with carbohydrates the night before. He usually had to run off the heaviness that apparently came from overeating the night before. Dave decided to try having a large carbo-loading lunch and a light dinner, as I recommended. He woke up feeling "noticeably more fresh, feeling light, and ready to race." He actually raced better and felt he had more energy and endurance stores from the preceding day's large lunch. During that ironman, he recalled needing to eat only half the food he carried on his bike to nourish himself for the run.

Eating in this way is not just for athletes. It has been a way of life for thousands of years. Today in Europe and Asia many shops still close for an hour and a half or more so that everyone can go home for lunch. Families meet every day to eat together. Their entire day revolves around the midday meal.

Of course, it isn't practical for us always to eat a large midday meal. If competitions are scheduled, we must adjust. The point here is to know when the best time is, and then whenever possible to schedule your training around a big lunch.

To prove the value of this to yourself, have a typical large evening meal one night, and when you wake up the next morning, observe how you feel and write it down. Later that day, have a big lunch and light dinner (or no dinner at all, depending on your hunger), and the next morning compare how you feel.

Any food taken after the sun goes down means that digestion will be compromised. I'm sure that is why restaurants are filled with senior citizens at 4:00 P.M. My grandfather, who is 84 years old, tells me emphatically, "If you want to take me to dinner, get me there by five o'clock or I won't go." If he does eat late, he pays for it with indigestion later that night, and pain, stiffness, and lethargy the morning after.

I've decided not to wait until I'm 70 or 80, when I'm forced to structure good eating habits out of necessity! I do my best to eat on the schedule of our ancestors, one which many people in farm communities in this country still adhere to. I figure that if I keep my digestion strong, when I'm 80 I won't be restricted to certain foods and certain times to eat. I still enjoy the pleasure of an occasional evening out at a terrific restaurant—but if you break the rules of eating every day of your life for thirty or forty years, you will eventually pay the price for it.

Although we were originally designed to digest and assimilate food better in the middle of the day, in our society lunch hour has become a time to do errands, grab a quick bite, and rush back to work. This prevents us from properly nourishing our bodies. If food is eaten in haste and followed immediately by exercise or activity, digestion and assimilation are impaired. We don't receive sufficient nourishment from our food, so, consequently, a few hours later we feel hungry. That's why, around 3:00 or 4:00 P.M., a lot of people feel a late afternoon "sugar low" and head for the Coke machine and the Snickers and Twinkies. Unfortunately, these sugar-laden snacks can sometimes trigger compulsive eating disorders. To avoid this, eat a large, balanced lunch at noon.

A couple of years ago a man named Richard Barnes came to me weighing 408 pounds. He said, "John, I've really got to lose this weight." A former top athlete, he had been active until quite recently, playing golf and softball. But his excessive weight was affecting his knees and joints, and he had gotten to the point where he just couldn't do the things he loved. He had finally realized that carrying so much weight was *structurally* dangerous (not to speak of the danger to his general health), and he came to me committed to doing something about it.

I told him I wanted him to do only one thing: "Eat only one meal a day, and eat it at noon. And make it *huge*. Have a Thanksgiving feast every day, if you like. If you find yourself hungry at dinnertime, that means you didn't eat enough for lunch."

Richard looked at me as if I were crazy.

I said, "I'm serious. If you feel hungry at night, it's because you didn't properly nourish yourself at noon." I told him it didn't matter what he ate, as long as it was balanced and healthy. More important was how and when he ate. " 'When' means midday, during Pitta time, and 'how' means eat slowly and really taste your food. Don't watch TV or open your mail. Remember the golden rule: 'Whatever the mind is doing, the body must do,' and vice versa.

"Think about it. If the mind is busy reading a book, talking on the phone, or driving a car, while the body is trying to eat, then the food, which is designed to nourish mind or body, is actually disintegrating the mind from the body. The result will be compromised digestion, and either indigestion or lack of vitality."

I told him that after eating, to improve the digestion process, he should take a 5- to 10-minute rest, lying on his left side, followed by a 5- to 10-minute walk. This was probably the purpose behind the habit of taking a siesta after lunch, a custom in many cultures.

"Breakfast is optional," I said to Richard. "If you need it, have it early and very light, preferably just some fruit."

He called me after the first week and said he had lost 10 pounds. "More amazing than that, I'm not hungry at night—or any other time of day, for that matter. I've found myself eating late at night in front of the TV, more out of habit than because I was hungry."

The next week he lost 3 pounds, then 7, then 10, totaling 30 pounds in the first month. The second month he lost another 20, and after three months had lost a total of 68 pounds, without any dieting or strain.

Here's the reason why the "big meal at noon" plan is so effective: You can eat more food pound for pound in the middle of the day, when the body can most efficiently digest it, and still lose weight. On the other hand, you can ration yourself throughout the day, eat less food, and still gain weight, because digestion is less efficient later on.

I put Richard on an extreme program, restricting him from dinner. For the person without a serious weight problem, dinner is an optional meal, depending on hunger. The one rule to keep in mind is that dinner, if taken, should always be light. Any food eaten after the sun goes down will be processed by a weaker digestive system. Please note that this is the best schedule for *adults*, who have stopped growing. Parents, it's best to feed your children at least three times a day, doing your best to serve dinner before sunset.

When I bring up this point in my seminars, someone always says, "If I eat a big lunch, I fall asleep at two in the afternoon." The answer to this is: If you put gas in your car and your car stalls five miles down the road, you would conclude that there was something wrong either with the gas or with the car. If you eat a big meal and subsequently fall asleep, then there is probably something wrong with the food, with how you ate it, or with your digestion.

When I was studying in India, I frequently ate with the Ayurvedic doctors. They would often have only one meal a day, around noon, and it would be a feast. I remember the first time I ate one of those huge meals and wondered how in the world I was going to stay awake in the afternoon lecture. The doctors told me not to worry. "We will all go to our rooms for a 10- to 15-minute rest, and take it on the left side, and then we'll meet and walk to the lecture hall." To my surprise, I found myself alert and clear during the entire afternoon lecture, which actually carried on until 9:00 P.M.! After the lecture, I asked the doctors what I should do about eating dinner. When they asked if I was really hungry, I realized that I was not. Their advice: "Don't eat!"

I then realized how out of touch I was with myself. Being a typical Westerner, I had also smiled to myself over the idea of resting *on the left side*—what possible reason could there be for that? But recent research has confirmed the benefits of lying on the left side, particularly in cases of acid indigestion and heartburn. The stomach actually hangs to the left, and when we lie in that position for a time, food can be processed more efficiently.

When you eat your main meal at lunchtime, in a relaxed way, with a little rest and a walk afterward, you can feast and still confidently engage in mental activity during the rest of the afternoon without getting tired.

🕑 2:00 P.M.–6:00 P.M. VATA TIME

Since Vata controls the nervous system and is primarily responsible for mental activity, it makes perfect sense that the Vata time of day follows the Pitta period. The brain uses about 80 percent of the body's glycogen (energy) supplies. The tanks are filled during the large meal at Pitta time, allowing the brain to be sufficiently fueled during the Vata time. Sleepiness at this time is an indication of some imbalance, probably due to lack of proper nutrition at lunch.

When researchers in the former Soviet Union found declining muscle strength and electrical activity in their athletes during the period from 2:00 to 6:00 P.M., they scheduled their power-lifting contests and workouts away from this Vata time of day. During Vata time, the body is naturally primed for the most efficient mental activity. Of course, physical activity can also be performed, but this is not the best time of day for it.

Vata types, who are the most susceptible to the injuries and stress of overtraining, should take particular care to refrain from exercise during this time whenever possible. As mentioned earlier, their lighter frames will last longer and thrive if they do most of their exercise during the Kapha time of day.

6:00 p.m.–10:00 p.m. KAPHA TIME

Every minute after the sun sets, Kapha qualities increase in the environment. The evening Kapha period marks the start of the second 12-hour cycle, which repeats day in and day out. For all body types, this is the second best time to exercise. It is favorable for the same reasons as it is healthy in the morning Kapha hours. However, I recommend exercising only from around 6:00 to 7:00 p.m., just after sunset and during the early part of the Kapha phase, so the stimulation you feel won't mask the feeling of tiredness later in the evening and keep you up all night.

Sunset triggers the heavy, shock-resistant Kapha qualities, making exercise appropriate. However, nature's purpose for this second Kapha period is not to spur more activity but to bring on a resting phase. When the sun sets, the birds go to sleep, as do all of nature's nonnocturnal creatures. Human beings are not nocturnal, as we know from our internal circadian rhythms, the rise and fall of body temperatures, the increase and decrease of cortisol levels, and hundreds of other adjustments in the body.

If you observe yourself dispassionately between 7:00 and 9:00 p.m., you will notice a feeling of lethargy and sleepiness overtaking you. You may find yourself dozing off in front of the TV or nodding over a book or the evening newspaper. This is not a sign of exhaustion but a natural response to the cycles of nature. The qualities of Kapha are increasing, putting the animals to sleep and inviting us to do the same.

Most of us perceive this tired feeling in the early evening, but how many of us actually go to bed? We have been conditioned to think that bedtime is between ten and midnight, and the thought of going to bed at eight or nine o'clock seems ridiculous. Yet, that is when our bodies start to feel the natural impulse to sleep. There's an old saying, "Eat when hungry; sleep when sleepy." It's not that revolutionary a notion—the animals in the forest have been doing it since the beginning of time.

10:00 p.m.–2:00 a.m. PITTA TIME

Did you ever wonder why you get a burst of energy in the late evening hours? You were falling asleep on the couch between seven and eight o'clock, but full of energy after ten. This is the Pitta time of night. If you did not fall asleep during the Kapha time, and are still awake between 10:00 p.m. and 2:00 a.m., you will find yourself starting projects, reading books, studying, and appreciating a seemingly very productive time of day.

Since Pitta represents the digestive fire, you may find yourself quite hungry and indulge in a substantial midnight snack.

Many people with a lot of Pitta in their constitutions have this kind of experience regularly and label themselves "night people." I remember that when I was in school, if I tried to study between 7:00 and 8:00 P.M., I'd fall asleep. Through trial and error I realized that I was better off waiting until 10:00 to start studying, and then burning the candle till 2:00 A.M. while the energy was flowing.

Now, looking back, I wonder how smart I really was. Other, more connected students would sleep from 8:00 P.M. to 4:00 A.M. and get four good hours of study before the test. I always admired this behavior but was concerned that if I went to bed at 8:00 P.M. I would sleep till 7:00 A.M., then take the test unprepared, without any study time under my belt.

The Pitta time of night is designed as an "internal cleansing cycle," when the body has a chance to rejuvenate. If you are up watching late-night TV, having midnight snacks, studying for midterms, or working on a project, you are missing out on this internal cleansing cycle. It won't hurt once in a while, but again—if this is your habit every day for thirty or forty years, it will accumulate and eventually break down the body.

Research has shown conclusively that the health of policemen and firemen who work late-night shifts suffers substantially—physically, emotionally, and psychologically. Of course, the body is very adaptable, and this schedule may seem fine for a time. But it definitely goes against the grain of nature, and sooner or later the cumulative effects of working at night will catch up.

In our society most households—and restaurants—plan their day around a big, heavy dinner, usually between 6:00 and 10:00 P.M., during the Kapha time. The problem with this is that our digestive fires left town at 2:00 P.M., the end of the Pitta cycle. So, when we eat this big meal at night, no one is home to digest it. The Kapha influence has absolutely no digestive skills. Its purpose is to put everyone to sleep.

When the Pitta influence rolls in at around 10:00 P.M., the burden of digesting this big meal naturally falls on Pitta. But this Pitta time is the internal cleansing cycle designed to clean house and prepare the system for the next day. Digestion isn't really its "thing," either.

If the food isn't digested, it will cause a bigger problem later, so, reluctantly, the nighttime Pitta digests it. But the damage has already been done. The food has been sitting for several hours, largely undigested. Then, the internal cleansing routine was replaced with an ineffective digestive process. The result is usually felt in the morning, in the form of heaviness, dullness, and lethargy.

If you eat late, you will wake up late, stiff, and dull. You will also tend to stay up late; many people say that they can't go to sleep after a big dinner and remain awake till midnight just to digest. This throws off the entire cycle.

When I told this to a group in Los Angeles and went so far as to say, "There really is no such thing as a nocturnal human," I sensed a lot of resistance in the room. (Maybe it was because the freeway had been jammed with eight lanes of bumper-to-bumper traffic at 1:00 A.M. near the airport the night before!) Some people are quite set in their ways, and the idea that what has worked for them for thirty years actually goes against their own nature is not easy for them to accept.

One man said that he goes to bed at midnight and wakes up at 4:00 A.M. and has been doing this for thirty years. "And I feel just great," he said, challenging me to tell him that there was something wrong with it! I said, "Try an experiment. Just notice if you feel any tiredness around 8:00 P.M. If so, go to sleep immediately, and sleep until your eyes naturally open."

Three weeks later he called me to say that he had tried it, and for the first time in his life he didn't have a desire or a need for his three or four cups of coffee in the morning to propel him through the Kapha time of day. He also didn't have the afternoon "sugar low" that he had considered a life sentence.

A woman in the audience that weekend was also a self-proclaimed nocturnal human. What's more, she told the group, both of her children were also "night people," and had been that way even when she was carrying them in her womb! She had felt them kick and turn more at night, and she was convinced that certain people are night people, and that was that!

I felt myself at a loss. How could I call in to question her innate maternal instincts? At that point a man stood up in the back of the hall and said, "I recently returned from a camping trip with forty people from all walks of life. There were Vata, Pitta, and Kapha types, and just about every combination. It was a wilderness survival trip, where food was rationed and we had no flashlights or lanterns. This got us all more plugged in to the cycles of nature.

"On that trip, *everyone* was fast asleep within an hour after the sun set, and everyone was up with or before the sun. No one had any trouble falling asleep at eight o'clock at night and being up at dawn. There were no 'night people' in *that* group!

"I think," he concluded, "that when you take away all our modern distractions and put yourself back into nature, you will see that we are all intimately connected to nature's cycles, and that none of us are really nocturnal creatures."

2:00 A.M.–6:00 A.M. VATA TIME

In the summertime in the Northern Hemisphere a variety of birds arrive from all over the world to mate and to raise their young. Some of them, with perhaps more of a Vata nature, wake up as early as 3:30 A.M., while the rest sequentially chime in to the morning musical in accord with their individual natures. If they were like humans, the Pitta birds would wake up next, followed at long last by the Kapha birds. Even though they all seem to need somewhat different amounts of sleep, they all wake up at some point in the Vata time of morning, and all are awake in plenty of time to watch the sun rise.

You too may sometimes wake up in those early morning hours—but how often do you actually get out of bed? You might wake up, look at the clock and see that it's 5:00 A.M. and still dark outside, and immediately go back to sleep. The good news is that you were connected enough, tuned in enough to nature, to wake up. The bad news is that you were too exhausted to stay up.

Have you ever noticed that when you wake up in the morning, you are stiffer and less flexible than you were when you went to bed the night before? If you go to bed in the Kapha time of night and wake up naturally in the Vata time of morning, before sunrise, you will wake up every morning as limber and flexible as you were the night before. Imagine increasing your flexibility and becoming more limber every day, instead of waking up every morning stiff and achy, having to get the gears moving before you feel loose enough to touch your toes.

A ONE-WEEK SAMPLE ROUTINE

To get a proper taste of this routine, pick a week in which you will not have any evening activities. Remember, this is a trial for only one week, it's not for the rest of your life—unless you decide to continue because you like it.

First, try to carve out at least 45 minutes in the middle of the day for a nice, big, relaxing meal. Be sure to eat it at a comfortable pace, and make the food your priority rather than the TV or a magazine. Afterward, rest for 5 to 10 minutes, lying down, preferably on your left side. After that, take an easy walk for another 5 to 10 minutes.

Then go about your business, doing your best to reserve most of your mental activity for the Vata time of day, between 2:00 and 6:00 P.M. After the sun sets, have some light exercise, followed by a light dinner. Around 7:00 or 8:00 P.M., get ready for bed and then lie down with a book and begin reading. As the heavy, slow qualities of Kapha increase in the environment, you will begin to notice those same qualities in yourself. When you feel sleepy, put down the book, turn off the light, and go to sleep.

This early bedtime is a crucial part of the test period, because most of

THE DAILY CYCLE

☿ KAPHA TIME—6:00 A.M.–10:00 A.M.

Best time for physical activity for all body types. Don't sleep past sunrise.

♀ PITTA TIME—10:00 A.M.–2:00 P.M.

Best time to eat the largest meal of the day. Worst time to exercise for Pitta types.

☿ VATA TIME—2:00 P.M.–6:00 P.M.

Best time for mental activity. Muscular strength is reduced; therefore this is the worst time of day to exercise, especially for Vata types.

☿ KAPHA TIME—6:00 P.M.–10:00 P.M.

From 6 to 7 is the second best time to exercise for all body types. From 7 to 10, when tiredness comes, go to sleep.

♀ PITTA TIME—10:00 P.M.–2:00 A.M.

The internal cleansing time. Not for midnight snacks or late-night projects. The most important time to sleep.

☿ VATA TIME—2:00 A.M.–6:00 A.M.

Best time to wake up.

Remember: Kapha types can exercise at any time of day because of their natural resiliency and need for exercise. These times are only guidelines. The most important rule is that exercise must be comfortable.

---

us are conditioned to stay up into the internal cleansing cycle of nighttime Pitta. For most people, the tiredness of Kapha comes somewhere between 6:00 and 10:00 P.M., and if we're not listening for it, or in a position to act on it, we will get swept up by the fire of Pitta, lose the desire for sleep, and get caught in activity. So, as early as it may seem, act on that drowsiness when it comes, and go to sleep.

You will then sleep during the internal cleansing time and naturally wake up somewhere in the Vata time of day. The exact time doesn't matter. If you follow this plan, you will have gotten plenty of sleep during the Kapha and Pitta times of night and naturally awaken at the time most suited for your body type.

After only a week or so on this schedule, you will begin to notice that you are as flexible in the early morning hours as you used to be only in the afternoon and evening.

Compare the difference when getting ten hours of sleep. One day go to

---

EARLY TO BED AND EARLY TO RISE MAKES YOU HEALTHY, WEALTHY,
AND WISE. NOT A BAD PAYOFF FOR GOING WITH THE FLOW!

---

bed at 12:00 A.M. and get up at 10:00 A.M. and see how you feel in the morning—probably a little dull and stiff. The next night go to bed at 8:00 P.M. and get up at up at 6:00 A.M. and see how you feel. Both nights you got ten hours of sleep but I'll bet the second morning you felt more refreshed and less stiff. The amount of sleep you get is not the only question; when you get it can be just as important.

If you are hungry, prepare a light breakfast. During or soon after sunrise is the best time to engage in your heaviest physical activity. If you are not an exerciser, then do your gardening or go for a walk. Whenever possible, try to structure your day so that your more physical tasks are performed in the morning Kapha hours. With an early, light breakfast followed by some exercise, you will find that by the midday Pitta time you will be famished and ready to sit down and really enjoy a large, warm, cooked meal!

Now the mind has been properly fueled for intellectual endeavors, most easily performed during the lively Vata time. When the Kapha time rolls around again, you will find it easier to fall asleep.

The following material sums it up clearly.

BEST TIME TO EXERCISE—BY BODY TYPE

YOUR MIND-BODY TYPE	6 A.M.-10 A.M.	10 A.M.-2 P.M.	2 P.M.-6 P.M.	6 P.M.-10 P.M.	10 P.M.-2 A.M.	2 A.M.-6 A.M.
Vata	***	*	0	*	0	0
Pitta	***	0	*	*	0	0
Kapha	***	**	*	**	0	0
Vata-Pitta	***	*	0	**	0	0
Pitta-Vata	***	0	*	**	0	0
Vata-Kapha	***	**	0	**	0	0
Kapha-Vata	***	**	*	**	0	0
Pitta-Kapha	***	*	*	**	0	0
Kapha-Pitta	***	*	*	**	0	0
Sama (VPK)	***	**	0	**	0	0

KEY:

BEST = ***   OK = *

GOOD = **   AVOID = O

Find your body type on vertical axis, find the time of day on horizontal axis, and cross-reference the best time to exercise.

7

FUELING THE MIND,
FEEDING THE BODY

When I first went into practice, I often worked nonstop from 9:00 A.M. to 5:00 P.M. I never thought much about it; it seemed normal and the only way to accomplish all the work that was scheduled for the day.

When a touring Maharishi Ayur-Ved physician was visiting my city I was quick to sign up for a consultation. During the medical screening by the Western nurse before my interview with the doctor, she mentioned that my blood pressure was a little high.

"How high?" I asked.

"It's 135 over 90," she responded.

I immediately went into total denial. "Would you mind repeating the test?" I asked. I was certain she had made a mistake. But it came out the same.

After three new blood pressure cuffs and six tests on each arm, I conceded to the depressing fact that I had high blood pressure. In school, less than a year before, my pressure had been a very healthy 110 over 70 something. I just couldn't believe I had the beginning states of hypertension.

I walked listlessly into the doctor's office. An Indian doctor with a broken English accent greeted me, looked at my chart—probably noticing the high blood pressure—and proceeded to take my pulse. This pulse reading was not to measure my heart rate. It was his primary form of diagnosis. Pulse diagnosis detects imbalances in Vata, Pitta, and Kapha, and one trained in this method of diagnosis can help the patient prevent disease by treating the imbalances that are the underlying cause of problems.

He paused for a moment after taking my pulse and said, "What do you usually eat for lunch?"

I proudly pleaded guilty, telling him that I had a very busy practice and that the half-hour I responsibly scheduled was always swallowed up by one thing or another. "More often than not," I said, "I have to skip my lunch. When I do get a chance to eat, it's usually on the run."

He looked at me calmly and said, "That is why you have high blood pressure."

"What? What does eating lunch have to do with blood pressure?"

"Everything. Schedule yourself one hour for lunch. Go home and have a nice big warm cooked meal. Make it the largest meal of the day. And you will never have high blood pressure again."

I was skeptical, but I gave it a try. To my surprise and amazement, my blood pressure went down, and now, almost ten years later, it is still unusually low. Even after I took a recent exercise stress test, my pressure logged in at 118 over 80.

Behavioral stress was making me a candidate for early hypertension. If I had continued to jam through the day without taking time to nourish myself properly (as we discussed in chapter 6), I'm certain I would be being medicated for high blood pressure by now. The advice I received—and my willingness to follow it—is prevention in the truest sense of the word. I have made similar recommendations during hundreds of consultations and watched the fright of hypertension quickly disappear as the cause was attended to.

In this chapter I will discuss the most appropriate foods for each body type during each season. But please remember: You can eat the best food on God's green earth, but if you consistently eat in haste, at the wrong time, or at varying times each day, the process simply won't work. How and when you eat are just as important as what you eat. The familiar saying "You are what you eat" can be updated to include, "You are *how* you eat."

If you eat fast and on the run, you will become nervous and feel constantly pressed for time. The pace of the entire day can be set by the pace of the midday meal. If lunch is eaten in haste, just to get rid of the hunger pain and go on to the next activity, the whole day will feel rushed. This has become the American way of life—"too much to do, not enough time to do it." In our haste, we have forgotten the importance of eating.

If we didn't eat, we would die. On the survival priority list, eating stands right behind drinking. How many of us can say that eating and drinking are activities given our respect and attention? Our lives depend on them, yet we take them for granted. And for athletes, proper nutrition is essential for peak performance. If eating could be given its due time and considered as important as a job, exercise, and raising a family, I believe we would see many fewer stress-related problems such as anxiety, hypertension, and eating disorders, to name just a few.

Remember, when you feed your body, you also nourish your mind and balance your emotions. As Bodhidharma instructed the sedentary Shaolin temple monks, you cannot separate the body from the mind, and you must train them as one.

Since ancient times, the high cultures of the world have regarded eating a sacred activity. Mealtime was considered an opportunity for us to communicate with the intelligence of nature through our sense of taste. The art of eating began and ended with the appreciation of food as an expression of nature's intelligence. Food, its preparation, and the act of eating were highly prized for their role in the preservation and upliftment of nature's most precious gift of all, human life.

THE SPICE OF LIFE

Predating the Four Basic Food Groups and the Minimum Recommended Daily Allowances of modern science was a more basic understanding of nutrition.

In nature, it is rare to find an undernourished animal species, unless of course man has stripped away its natural food sources. How is it that animals in the jungle and forest know exactly what to eat and what not to eat? They have no pamphlets or handy pocket guides to nutrition and diet. Each species's parents provided some basic guidance to kick-start the new generation, but for the most part, it's trial and error. They respond either favorably or unfavorably to the taste of certain roots, plants, or berries. Nature in her wisdom has set things up so that what *tastes* good to them and is available *is* good for them. Over time, they learn, via their sense of taste, which foods will nourish them.

In some survival training schools, individuals are sent out into the wilderness for days or weeks at a time. A common experience is that the plants and berries labeled "safe" in the classroom sessions are scarcely to be found: The animals got there first, and the survivalists are forced to taste and analyze each bite to determine the safety and nutritional value.

If all the grocery stores and supermarkets closed and we were forced to survive in the wilderness, we would eventually map out the good and bad sources of nutrition. Some herbs, leaves, etc., would become known as nourishing; some we would learn to leave alone. Others would be found to have great therapeutic value. Soon a science of natural nutrition would be discovered, as knowledge of these healing and nourishing foods got passed on from generation to generation, expanding and becoming refined over the centuries.

This science already exists. It is known as Maharishi Ayur-Ved. It classifies foods according to the "six tastes"—sweet, sour, salty, pungent, bitter, and astringent. It adds to these the qualities of heavy/light, dry/oily, and hot/cold. This time-tested nutritional map, along with the knowledge of each individual body type and the associated seasons (Vata/winter; Pitta/summer; Kapha/spring), provides the most comprehensive and natural means of nutrition available today.

This chapter will help you to find the seasonal roots and berries best suited to your body type.

THE SIX TASTES

Sweet	Sugar, milk, butter, rice, breads, pasta
Sour	Yogurt, lemon, cheese
Salty	Salt
Pungent	Spicy foods, ginger, hot peppers, cumin
Bitter	Green leafy vegetables, turmeric
Astringent	Beans, lentils, pomegranate

HOW THE SIX TASTES AFFECT VATA, PITTA, AND KAPHA

Decrease Vata:	Sweet, sour, salty
Increase Vata:	Pungent, bitter, astringent
Decrease Pitta:	Sweet, bitter, astringent
Increase Pitta:	Pungent, sour, salty
Decrease Kapha:	Pungent, bitter, astringent
Increase Kapha:	Sweet, sour, salty

THE SIX QUALITIES

These six qualities are important in considering the effects of foods. Note that they come in pairs:

HEAVY AND LIGHT

Heavy—Wheat, beef, cheese
Light—Barley, chicken, skim milk

OILY AND DRY

Oily—Milk, soybeans, coconut
Dry—Honey, lentils, cabbage

HOT AND COLD (HEATS OR COOLS THE BODY)

Hot—Pepper, honey, eggs
Cold—Mint, sugar, milk

Connecting the six tastes, the qualities, and Vata, Pitta, and Kapha, we come up with the following:

Balances Vata		Aggravates Vata	
Sweet	Heavy	Pungent	Light
Sour	Oily	Bitter	Dry
Salty	Hot	Astringent	Cold

Balances Pitta		Aggravates Pitta	
Sweet	Cold	Pungent	Hot
Bitter	Heavy	Sour	Light
Astringent	Dry	Salty	Oily

Balances Kapha		Aggravates Kapha	
Pungent	Light	Sweet	Heavy
Bitter	Dry	Sour	Oily
Astringent	Hot	Salty	Cold

IN FAVOR OF FLAVOR

The simplest way to get acquainted with the foods most suited to each body type is via the six tastes. Although each taste has a specific effect on each type, it is recommended that all six be present at each meal.

Rasa, the Sanskrit word that means "taste," also translates as "emotions." Each of the six tastes carries with it a certain emotional tone or quality. For a meal to properly nourish body, mind, and emotions—to be psychophysiologically complete—it must provide an experience of all six tastes and their corresponding emotions.

Eighty percent of what we taste is actually smelled. The two senses are intimately related. The sense of smell has direct access to the limbic system of the brain, the seat of much of our emotional life. Tastes and smells are also directly connected to the hypothalamus, the master switchboard of the brain, which controls basic drives such as thirst and hunger and is responsible for neurochemical and hormonal regulation. In short, the entire functioning of the body, mind, and emotions is modulated via the senses of smell and taste. These are our most primitive senses. Animals still base their survival on them.

Billy Allen was a strict follower of a macrobiotic diet. He had had some blood sugar problems in the past and found safe haven within the austere macrobiotic regime. This diet, which worked wonders for Billy, is clinically respected for the treatment of certain conditions. Billy, however, took the diet to extremes and left out all sweets, one of the ingredients crucial for a good, lifelong diet.

The sweet taste, the missing element in Billy's diet, has its emotional correlate in the feelings of satisfaction, happiness, and pleasure. Billy had found a diet that gave him a balanced energy level throughout the day, without the highs and especially the lows associated with his blood sugar problem—but he was now complaining of bouts of depression.

This experience is common to many people who are on very strict or austere diets. Although they may have achieved a relatively symptom-free state, they often feel unhappy. They haven't eaten a sweet in years, and this usually shows in their disposition. They are often somewhat hard and tough emotionally, a natural result of depriving themselves of the one taste that immediately brings satisfaction and happiness.

Billy survived on leafy green vegetables (bitter) and lentils and grains (mostly astringent). These food tastes, when translated into their emotional correlates, created a bitter and withdrawn psychological profile. Billy had steered away from the rich, heavy, and sweet foods that provide balance for Vata, as well as for the nervous system and the pleasure centers in the brain, and had become chronically depressed.

Like Billy's macrobiotic diet, some modern diets that utilize a system of food combining (avoiding certain combinations and favoring others) and some restrictive diets definitely have a therapeutic value. They remove food stressors that overload some individuals' digestive systems, and render the person symptom-free, but not necessarily in balance. Even the most ardent food combiners would agree that if the body is in total balance, it should be able to digest proteins and sugars at the same meal (usually a no-no), and handle a meal consisting of the "four food groups" (fruits and vegetables; grains; meat and proteins; milk and dairy).

It is undeniably easier for the body to digest a meal consisting of a limited number of foods or food types (such as proteins, carbohydrates, fats, and so on). But limiting one's diet in this way often takes the pleasure out of eating and results in low compliance: People just don't stick with these diets very long. They may reap some benefits, but because of the lack of emotional satisfaction they get from their meals, they drift back to their old ways, vowing to "get back into it" later on.

A meal is not complete unless it contains all of the six tastes. If restrictive diets are needed for some time for therapeutic purposes, that is fine, but only as a temporary step on the way to attaining total balance.

THE SIX TASTES

SWEET

SWEET FOODS INCLUDE

SUGAR, HONEY
RICE
MILK, CREAM, BUTTER
WHEAT BREAD

SWEET FOODS (EXCEPT HONEY) INCREASE KAPHA
AND DECREASE PITTA AND VATA

The sweet taste, when taken in its natural form (such as rice, bread, or pasta) along with the other tastes, provides a "satisfaction factor." Without it, most people will leave the table feeling unsatisfied, although unable to pinpoint why. On the other hand, too much sweet taste can overstimulate the pleasure centers, leading to a feeling of complacency or lethargy, or to a loss of motivation.

Problems such as obesity and a variety of compulsive eating disorders can also occur as a result of overindulgence in the sweet taste. The sweet taste of food (often in the form of junk food) is frequently abused in the attempt to make up for the lack of satisfaction in one's life. Sweets are then inappropriately tried and found guilty for causing a multitude of food and sugar addictions.

The problem doesn't originate with the sweets. If we are not nourishing our minds, bodies, and emotions properly with all six tastes in each meal, we will become emotionally susceptible. The nutritional foundation needed to support balance in times of stress simply won't be there. As a result, wherever we have a weak link, whether emotional or physical, we will break down.

Studies have revealed an inordinate number of eating disorders among professional athletes and dancers. Professional women tennis players have been the focus of many such reports in recent years. In the population as a whole, approximately 1 percent of women between ages 13 and 30 suffer from bulimia and anorexia. But Julie Anthony, a former touring tennis pro who holds a Ph.D. in psychology, says percentages on the woman's pro tennis tour are much higher. "I wouldn't be surprised if around 30 percent of the women on the tour have some form of eating disorder. I know a number of women in the top twenty who do."

These women are placed under a huge amount of stress at a very young age. Tennis is an individual sport; you cannot fall back on the support system of a team environment. Winning carries the burden of being expected to win again. With this intense pressure, if the nutritional base is not sufficient, performance on and off the court will suffer.

The sweet taste balances both Vata and Pitta. It soothes and satisfies the Vata nervous system and quickly feeds the impatient and hungry Pitta by being absorbed into the blood faster than any other food group. But too much sweet taste will increase Kapha, producing added weight, congestion, and, eventually, lethargic behavior. For eating disorders, more attention should be put on balancing the meals with all six tastes, as well as eating at the right time of day.

SOUR

SOUR FOODS INCLUDE

LEMONS
CHEESE, YOGURT
TOMATOES, GRAPES, PLUMS, SOUR FRUITS
VINEGAR

SOUR FOODS INCREASE PITTA AND KAPHA
AND DECREASE VATA

The emotional correlate of the sour taste is easily seen on the face of any child after sucking on his or her first lemon! The experience is quite the opposite of the calm, soothing sweet taste. Sour is not warmly accepted by the body! Lemons, probably the thoroughbred of the sour taste, are rarely eaten alone; a little lemon juice provides a stimulating balance to a meal.

Sour foods, such as yogurt, cheeses, and sour fruits, are usually heavy in nature and therefore aggravate the heavy nature of the Kapha type. They have a balancing effect on the light Vata body type. Sour foods are usually a little harder for the body to digest and stimulate an increase of Pitta or digestive fire in order to properly break them down. This increase in digestive Pitta also fires up the mental/emotional Pitta and fuels the typically aggressive and competitive Pitta nature.

If the sour taste is taken in excess, particularly by a Pitta type, enjoyment of competition can be soured. The already intense Pitta desire to accomplish the goal and vanquish the opposition can be overshadowed by poor sportsmanship and being a "sourpuss."

SALT

SALTY FOODS INCREASE KAPHA AND PITTA AND DECREASE VATA

The stinging and burning of salt water on an open wound or in your eye reflect the heating nature of salt. In the same way as salt melts snow or ice on the road, it also heats up the body, increasing Pitta. Pure Pitta body types should take less salt in the summer months, when Pitta is predominant. Salt stimulates the digestive fire and is often used therapeutically when digestion is out of balance. When taken in excess, salt can aggravate Pitta, causing inflammatory skin disorders and difficulty in handling heat.

For decades, salt tablets were prescribed across the board for any extensive activity in the heat. Salt by nature attracts water to it. The rationale was that since we lost so much water through perspiration, salt replacement would safeguard the internal water supply, hence cooling the body, as well as balance the electrolytes (minerals needed for muscle contraction).

When salt is given in the right amount, this theory is correct. But what is the right amount? Today, multimillion-dollar laboratories are still trying to determine the perfect balance of sugars and salts for best performance in the heat. The problem with salt is that its properties of increasing Pitta (heat) are greater than the cooling properties derived from holding on to water. The net effect of taking in extra salt is usually to increase heat.

The effect of salt holding on to water is to increase Kapha or fluid in the body. This can upset the body's ability to handle water properly and create problems, such as hypertension, that have to be treated by diuretic drugs to help move the water out. It is for this reason that salt is restricted for people with hypertension.

Because of the water retention caused by salt, the body becomes heavier.

This balances the very light Vata type. The heat produced by the intake of salt is also helpful for balancing Vata, which is typically cold, and is particularly good for Vatas in the winter.

Emotionally, salt is much like sour. It stimulates the Pitta's driving, goal-oriented nature. When salt is taken in excess, the desire to accomplish, to win, to be the best can turn into imbalanced emotions of envy, jealousy, or resentment. When a person with a naturally aggressive Pitta mind seeks all his satisfaction from the achievement of outward goals, rather than from inside, he begins to judge himself and compare himself with others. As a result, he doesn't enjoy what he does and becomes envious or jealous of the accomplishments of others.

BITTER

BITTER FOODS INCLUDE

BITTER GREENS (ENDIVE, ROMAINE LETTUCE)
BITTER CUCUMBERS
TONIC WATER
SPINACH, OTHER LEAFY GREENS
TURMERIC, FENUGREEK

BITTER FOODS INCREASE VATA
AND DECREASE PITTA AND KAPHA

In our society, the taste of bitter is probably the most ignored and neglected of the six tastes. The vegetable kingdom is spilling over with bitter tastes, yet, despite the fact that we have all heard the "eat your vegetables" refrain for as long as we can remember, 22 percent of the population do not eat any vegetables. The American Heart and Cancer associations now recommend veggies for the prevention of disease and the maintenance of good health. All of the leafy green vegetables, such as spinach, Swiss chard, and romaine lettuce, and a variety of others sport the bitter taste.

These bitter foods are light in nature and therefore help to balance heavy Kapha types. They are also a cooling food group, which makes them good to eat, especially for Pitta types, in the summer—just when nature provides them in abundance. Aloe vera, which is bitter and cooling, is well known for its healing properties in treating skin rashes, inflammations, and fever. Any bitter foods or spices will have a similar effect.

Too much bitter taste can create excess lightness and therefore aggravate airy Vata types, who should probably eat less of them in the winter months.

Emotionally, the bitter taste is included in a balanced psychophysiological diet in order to balance the pleasure of the sweet taste. Too much pleasure without balance was said to have caused the downfall of the Roman empire by creating a complacent and ultimately decadent society! Bitter allows sweet to bring satisfaction and pleasure without becoming addictive. Bitter taste in excess will ultimately overcome sweet, happy feelings, leaving one at first bitter-sweet, and then just plain bitter.

PUNGENT

PUNGENT FOODS INCLUDE

CAYENNE, CHILI PEPPERS
ONIONS AND GARLIC
RADISHES
GINGER
SPICY FOODS IN GENERAL

PUNGENT FOODS INCREASE PITTA AND VATA
AND DECREASE KAPHA

Pungent foods, such as chili peppers, onions, and ginger, are hot and spicy. Their effect, as seen in people who sweat during a spicy Mexican meal, is to increase Pitta. These foods should be taken in moderation by Pitta types, especially during the summer months. The increased heat of summer coupled with Pitta-increasing pungent foods can send the Pitta body type into imbalance, leading to skin rashes, heartburn, and ulcers.

Emotionally, as discussed earlier, an excess of pungent foods will stoke the fires of Pitta, yielding quick tempers, irritability, aggressive behavior, and poor sportsmanship. Steroids have the same effect—they heat the body, aggravating Pitta. Abusers of steroids can often be identified by their aggression, anger, skin reactions, and inflamed, oversized muscles.

Pungent, spicy foods do have a beneficial effect in breaking up the congestion and mucus often seen in excess in Kapha types. You may have experienced the effect of a hot jalapeño pepper in clearing your sinuses. These foods can be of immediate benefit to the Kapha type who has a congestive bronchial condition or an asthmatic attack. Taken in moderation, they act as a preventative for Kaphas so that congestion doesn't build up.

ASTRINGENT

ASTRINGENT FOODS INCLUDE

BEANS
LENTILS
APPLES, PEARS, POMEGRANATES
CABBAGE, BROCCOLI, CAULIFLOWER
POTATOES

ASTRINGENT FOODS INCREASE VATA
AND DECREASE PITTA AND KAPHA

The astringent taste is not commonly recognized in our society. The taste has a puckering and drying effect inside the mouth. Pomegranates are probably the most easily recognizable astringent food. Astringent foods have a beneficial effect on drying out the wet and congestive nature of Kapha. These foods are good for Kapha types, particularly during the Kapha season (spring).

Astringent foods are also cooling by nature. When you scan the list of predominantly astringent foods, consider when they are harvested—typically at the end of summer, when the trees turn bright red and orange from the accumulated summer heat. These astringent, cooling foods—apples, pears, potatoes, as well as pomegranates—are ripe for the eating, to help dissipate excess heat. Nature intelligently provides an abundance of these foods just when we need them.

This formula applies to the other seasons as well. For example, nuts and sweet potatoes become naturally available just before winter, store well, and are good for Vata. Kapha-reducing foods, such as early-appearing green leafy vegetables, appear in the early spring, Kapha season.

Because of their light and drying effect, astringent foods, when taken in excess, will increase Vata. Most beans and lentils, for example, are known for their gas-producing qualities, the result of excess Vata. A person with a Vata constitution, complaining of constipation resulting from a dried-out colon, or experiencing abdominal gas, should avoid these dry and airy astringent foods. During the Vata season (fall/winter) Vata types should be particularly careful.

In excess, astringent foods will aggravate Vata and the nervous system.

The right amount of astringent can help to balance Kapha and Pitta, keeping them energetic and cool, respectively. Too much can trigger an overly withdrawn, shy, fearful, or phobic disposition, making it difficult for athletes to express themselves in front of a crowd or to do justice to their potential during competition. Rather than be balanced and "like ice" in the middle of a match, a person would tend to choke under pressure.

THE VEGGIE DEBATE

Yes, it's true: The classic Ayurvedic diet is vegetarian. Recent studies support the benefits of the vegetarian way. *The New England Journal of Medicine* reported in December 1990 that women who ate beef, pork, or lamb as a main dish every day had a two and a half times higher risk of developing colon cancer as compared to those who ate meat less than once a month. Those who ate chicken and fish did better than the heavy-meat eaters, but the conclusion was clear: For optimum health, eat less meat. Physicians now recommend that people who consume high quantities of animal fats replace them with grains and legumes, so that a higher percentage of their dishes are vegetarian.

For some people, the problem is not so much the amount of meat consumed as the lack of intake of fruits and vegetables, so that the diet is unbalanced. According to the *American Journal of Public Health*, only 9 percent of Americans eat the recommended servings of fruit and vegetables per day. Even more striking is the fact that on an average day, 45 percent do not eat any fruit or drink any fruit juice and 22 percent do not eat any vegetables.

Athletes often fear that without meat they will shrivel up and float away. But the fact is that we don't need animal protein, in the form of meat, either for strength or for survival. Many endurance athletes are currently switching to vegetarian diets and finding increased energy from the more pure and simple food sources. Brent Mayne, the Kansas City Royals catcher, followed a vegetarian diet along with a weight-training program during the 1991 off-season. Brent put on 20 pounds of muscle and moved out of contention for the "lightest catcher in the league" award.

The natural ability to gain or to lose weight is determined primarily by body type. This means that a person with a Vata body type should not expect to achieve the size and bulk of a Kapha (although steroids can "overcome" this, at great cost to life and health). Vata types actually make good body builders, partly because it benefits their leaner physiques to acquire more mass, size, and weight. They will, however, have a different look on the body-building platform from the oversized Kapha type.

Professional body builder Joanne Madden is a perfect example. Joanne is a Vata type who was injury prone and had structural problems with her body, both before she started exercising and early in her career, using conventional body-building principles. Weight training made a dramatic difference for her, giving her the bulk and size she needed for a stronger and more resilient musculoskeletal system. Soon, she put on enough muscle and size to compete successfully as a professional body builder.

Joanne is not the lone vegetarian in the world of body building. Some of the best in the business have built world-class physiques on a vegetarian diet. Mr. USA and 1992 national winner Chris Duffy and world champion Steve Brisbois are proponents of the vegetarian way. Probably the most impressive example is Bill Pearl. He is considered one of the greatest body builders in history, winning the Mr. Universe title four times and a 20-year vegetarian. It seems the image of vegetarians as scrawny wimps and bookworms is on the way out.

Another issue to consider is that consuming large amounts of meat can slowly kill you, while increasing your consumption of fruits and vegetables will slowly heal you. Meat is filled with all kinds of chemical preservatives and hormones that have been proven dangerous in high dosages. In 1989 the European Economic Community banned the import of beef from the United States because of the heavy use of growth hormones. A greater potential health concern is the relatively uncontrolled use of antibiotics commonly added to cattle and poultry feed. This, according to the Centers for Disease Control and Prevention could promote resistant strains of numerous infectious bacteria. Our seas are so polluted that the fish in our markets are often unfit for human consumption. Should we accept the reassurances of the meat industry that although high doses of the poisons found in meat and fish will kill us, small doses are okay? Or could it just be big business? If Americans stopped eating meat, the effect on the economy would be dramatic. Ninety percent of all crops grown in this country go to feed animals, most of which end up cooked.

The next question in our veggie debate is whether human beings were designed to eat meat in the first place. In nature, different animal species have different eating habits. Some are carnivores—strictly meat eaters. Others are herbivores, eating only vegetable foods. Then there are the fruit- and nut-picking frugivores. Last come the omnivores, who eat anything. Some people believe we are in this category, but a quick analysis of the teeth and digestive tracts of each species reveals man's true nature.

Carnivores, such as dogs and cats, have teeth or fangs for ripping meat and killing their prey. Their digestive tracts work very quickly and are very acidic, both to "cook" the raw meat quickly and to eliminate it quickly. Meat-eating animals require this kind of digestion in order to move the rapidly decaying and decomposing flesh through the system before it becomes toxic.

Animals in the omnivore group, such as bears, have teeth and digestive tracts identical to those of the meateaters. We, however, do not have teeth for ripping apart raw meat, nor do we have claws to tear it. In addition, our digestion is very slow, which causes meat to putrefy in our intestines and to infect our bodies with the resultant poisons.

Herbivores, such as cows, horses, and deer, graze in fields and forests all day long. They grind their food rather than chew it. This grinding is more effective than a chewing action in breaking down hard-to-digest leaves and grass.

Man's teeth are not like those of the pure herbivore, either. We have the capacity for both grinding and chewing, but we are not grazers. Our digestive systems are closer to the slow rate of the herbivores, but they have the advantage of a second stomach, which helps them digest the raw leaves and grasses that form their diet. Critics of vegetarianism cite this lack of a second stomach as "proof" that man is not designed to be a herbivore.

It's true that we are not designed to eat copious amounts of raw foods such as leaves and grasses. If we were, we would indeed have digestive systems similar to those of horses and cows. Maharishi Ayur-Ved recommends that the majority of our food be well cooked, although raw vegetables in small quantities and fruits and nuts are acceptable. If we do not cook plant foods properly, we cannot adequately digest large amounts of them. This clearly departs from the current recommendations of nutritionists regarding consumption of large amounts of raw foods.

I know that many raw-food advocates will take issue with this, but I must say from experience that very few people can stay on a predominantly raw-food diet for an extended length of time. Raw foods can have a wonderful cleansing and therapeutic effect, but it is difficult—and not really desirable—to eat them as a steady diet.

Raw vegetables, as mentioned earlier, represent mostly the bitter and astringent tastes, and a diet consisting primarily of raw vegetables, although better for Pitta and Kapha types, is sure to leave the mind, body, and emotions undernourished. People who eat primarily raw foods will be left with strong cravings for the four other psychophysiological tastes.

If you compared the digestion of man to that of other animals, it would appear that we were designed to be frugivores, much like the apes. Apes have the same standard equipment as we, and, unlike us, they have not been stripped of their natural instinctive dietary habits.

The ape has hands and fingers, as does man, which are remarkably useful for picking fruits, berries, and nuts. In nature, only certain foods come ready to eat off the vine; they constitute the primary diet of the frugivore apes and are most likely the best foods for humans.

Apes, like human beings, do not have the digestive power for a diet consisting primarily of raw leaves and grasses, although they will eat certain raw plants. Nor do they have the teeth or fast-acting, acidic digestive system needed to eat meat, whether cooked or raw. Apes have the same number of teeth as humans, of the kind needed for chewing and grinding, not ripping and killing. Their digestive tracts are almost exactly the same size as ours proportionally. The digestive power of both apes and humans comes from an acidic stomach, and both have alkaline saliva and waste products.

Therefore, the best (most natural) diet for humans appears to be fruits, nuts, and certain raw vegetables. With our ability to cook, we have the capacity to introduce a larger variety of foods into our diet, such as grains and cooked vegetables. Even cooked meats in small amounts are acceptable.

Science is beginning to confirm the pros of fruits and vegetables and the cons of meat eating. If it hadn't been such an economic and political issue, you can bet that the truth about meat would have made headlines years ago. Whatever you decide to eat, I hope you will take these remarks as food for thought! I urge you not to simply accept what is placed on the market shelves as being the best source of human nutrition, but to look more deeply into it.

This science of life has no shoulds or should nots. All I suggest is that you give yourself the chance to experience your natural needs, and then *you* decide if a particular diet, mealtime, or bedtime is suited to you. Any lifestyle, exercise, or diet that is forced upon us—even by ourselves— simply doesn't last. Give these principles a try—and then follow them if they make you feel better. (For more information about vegetarianism and athletics, read Peter Burwash's *Vegetarian Primer.*)

BODY-TYPE FUEL

Now it is time to lay out in detail the essentials of diet for Vata, Pitta, and Kapha body types. These diets are designed to provide a nutritional foundation for maximum performance and to *balance* your system.

For example, a Vata type needs to guard against eating too much Vata-increasing food, or he or she will become restless, spacy, nervous, or anxious. Pitta types, particularly in the heat of summer, must be careful not to indulge in Mexican dinners or other heating foods, or they run the risk of overheating on the athletic field. Kapha types have to be wary of taking in too many sweet, heavy foods, or they will find themselves overweight and/or lethargic and unmotivated. Therefore, these diets are sometimes referred to as Vata, Pitta, or Kapha *reducing* or *balancing* diets. For the sake of simplicity, I will refer to them simply as Vata, Pitta, or Kapha diets.

In deciding which foods to eat, take into consideration the season as well as your constitution. Pittas have to take extra care to eat cooling foods in summer; Vatas have to watch out for cooling, drying foods in winter; Kaphas need to exercise more care to keep away from moist, sweet, heavy foods in spring.

If, like many people, your body is a combination of two types, the seasonal influence becomes slightly more complicated. If you are a Pitta-Kapha, for example, favor the Pitta diet in summer and the Kapha diet in spring. For this body type, the winter months provide a natural balance. The cold of winter helps to keep the Pitta component cool, and the Kapha component is soothed by the winter dryness. During this season, nature provides her own prevention program, so it is not as crucial to follow any particular diet. If a Pitta-Kapha person desires to maintain a careful diet during winter, the Pitta diet would be best, since that is the dominant factor in this body type.

At the end of this chapter is a chart to help you determine at a glance which diet, in which season, is best for you. I assume that you have already discovered, using the questionnaire in chapter 4, what your body type is. If you haven't, please go back and do it now, as your body type will be the determining factor in how and when to apply the techniques in the remaining chapters of this book.

❧ THE VATA DIET

The Vata diet comprises the foods most suited to combat the dry, cold air of winter. Those with a Vata body type will find this diet most agreeable and often necessary for keeping balance. The foods of the Vata diet are generally warm, rich foods with the predominating tastes of sweet, sour, and salt. They contain a lot of oils to insulate against the dryness of Vata.

The Vata diet can actually serve as the best carbo-loading, precompetition endurance diet for most body types. The Vata diet is rich and heavy and therefore increases the Kapha qualities that fuel long-lasting energy reserves needed for endurance. However, if the competition requires quickness and mental alertness in short spurts, without the need for endurance, then create your diet strictly in accordance with the body type/season chart at the end of this chapter.

If you have a Vata constitution, the following list will help you determine the best foods to eat and which foods to minimize or avoid.

IF A VATA DIET IS WHAT YOU NEED, BUT YOUR DIGESTION IS SEN-
SITIVE TO THE ABUNDANCE OF RICH DAIRY AND OTHER HEAVY
FOODS TYPICALLY PRESCRIBED FOR VATA, THEN YOU CAN FOLLOW
THE LIGHT VATA DIET, PRESENTED AT THE END OF THE VATA
DIET RECOMMENDATIONS. THIS WILL SUPPLY YOU WITH ALL
THE NEEDED BALANCE FOR VATA WITHOUT AGGRAVATING YOUR
SYSTEM.

❧ FOODS TO FAVOR

In General:

• Favor foods that are warm, heavy, and oily, and with sweet, sour, and salty taste.
• Eat larger quantities of food, but not more than you can easily digest.
• Favor warm, creamy soups, hot cereals, bread, pasta (best with a rich sauce such as "alfredo" with butter and cream). Warm milk is always good. A substantial breakfast (warm, milky, and sweet, such as hot cereal, toast) will help balance Vata through the day.
• Although pungent (spicy) foods are generally not the best for Vata, foods such as Mexican and Indian are usually fine, as they are warming and are prepared with a good amount of oil.

Grains: Rice and wheat are best. Oats are all right, but only well cooked, as in oatmeal, not dry.
Dairy: All dairy products are good for Vata. Always boil milk before you drink it, and preferably drink it warm. Don't drink milk with a full meal.
Fruits: Favor sweet, sour, and heavy fruits, such as grapes, apricots, bananas, avocados, cherries, peaches, nectarines, melons, berries, coconut, sweet plums, sweet pineapple, sweet oranges, mangoes, fresh (not dried) figs, and papayas.
Vegetables: Vegetables should be well-cooked, not raw. The best are beets, cucumbers, carrots, green beans, radishes, asparagus, sweet potato, turnips.
The following vegetables are also acceptable in moderate quantities, especially if cooked in ghee or oil, and with Vata-reducing spices (see below): peas, green leafy vegetables, broccoli, cauliflower, celery, peppers, zucchini, potatoes, tomatoes, eggplant.
Nuts: All nuts are all right for Vata. Almonds are recommended.

Oils: All oils reduce Vata. Sesame oil is especially recommended.

Sweeteners: All sweeteners are good for pacifying Vata. Sugar-cane products and molasses are best.

Beans: Reduce all beans except tofu and mung beans (especially as *dal*, a soup made from split dried mung beans). Chick-peas and pink lentils are okay.

Meat and Fish: Chicken, turkey, and seafood are acceptable in small amounts.

Spices and Herbs: Most spices are good for Vata. Favor sweet and/or heating herbs and spices such as cinnamon, cardamom, cloves, ginger, cumin, black pepper (small amounts), salt, mustard seed. Also acceptable: allspice, anise, asafoetida, basil, bay leaf, caraway, cilantro, fennel, nutmeg, oregano, sage, tarragon, thyme.

❧ FOODS TO MINIMIZE OR AVOID

In General:

- Minimize foods that are cold, dry, and light. Avoid cold drinks.
- Minimize foods with spicy (pungent), bitter, and astringent tastes.
- Light diet and fasting are not recommended for Vata.

Grains: Minimize barley, buckwheat, corn, millet, rye; avoid dry oats.

Dairy: All dairy products are okay for Vata.

Fruits: Avoid dried or unripe fruits. Minimize apples, pears, pomegranates, cranberries. These are more acceptable if cooked.

Vegetables: Avoid cabbage and bean sprouts. See above for list of vegetables that become acceptable when cooked, especially with oils and/or spices.

Meat and Fish: Avoid red meat.

Spices and Herbs: Minimize bitter and astringent spices and herbs, such as coriander seed, fenugreek, parsley, saffron, turmeric.

❧ LIGHT VATA PACIFYING DIET

In General: Use this diet in case of low *agni* (low digestive fire) combined with Vata constitution (*prakriti*) or Vata imbalance (*vikriti*). Food should be fresh, well-cooked, tasty, liked, satisfying, and should be taken regularly and in a proper amount, in a suitable environment.

Grains: All grains should be one year old when used.

Make wheat preparations from finely ground whole wheat flour:
   a. crackers
   b. biscuits with low fat and sugar content
   c. light bread toasted
   d. unleavened bread such as light, fresh, and well-cooked chapati, Arabic bread, tortilla, etc.
   e. couscous
   f. semolina

Rice: Use basmati, red shali, or other wholesome rice with both husk and inner shell removed (polished).
   a. dry-fry the rice, then boil and prepare as soup
   b. dry-fry, then steam or boil
   c. steam or boil
   d. make light preparations from rice flour
   e. "puffed" rice

Oats should be cooked with water to light porridge.
Beans/Dhal: Best are yellow mung beans (with green husk removed).
   a. liquid dhal preparation (light soup)
   b. prepare with rice as thin soup (*peya*) or thicker soup (*vilepi*)

Dairy: Low-fat milk, goat's milk, buttermilk, lassi, ghee (clarified butter) in small amounts.
Fruit: All fruit should be ripe and in season. Grapes, raisins (soaked, chewed well, and in small amounts), pomegranate, papaya, pineapple, figs, apricots (fresh, not dried), oranges. Juices of Vata-pacifying fruits.
Vegetables: Should be well cooked in juicy or "soupy" preparation. Tender eggplant, white pumpkin, zucchini, cucumber, asparagus, artichoke, tomato (without skin), celery (not root), carrots (small amounts), spinach (small amounts), tender white radish (prepared with some fat), green papaya.
Sweeteners: All except honey, in small amounts.
Oils: All except coconut in small amounts.
Spices and herbs: Cumin, ginger, fenugreek, hing, mustard seeds, black pepper (small amounts), cinnamon, cardamom, anise, fennel, cloves, salt, lemon juice, tamarind. All others in small amounts only.

⸙ THE PITTA DIET

I gave the body-type questionnaire to a world-class triathlete I knew. Throughout his career he had fared extremely well when competing in cooler climates, but he had never done as well in long, hot races. When he found out that he was predominantly a Pitta body type and took a look at the foods that increased Pitta, he discovered all his favorite foods! His usual prerace meal was hot, spicy Mexican fare. When he realized that there were foods that actually had a cooling effect, he became very interested, especially in light of his pattern of having trouble competing in the heat. These effects, although subtle, have a cumulative effect on performance as well as health.

Many endurance athletes eat lots of bananas during competition to replenish the potassium needed to maintain a proper electrolyte and fluid balance. The logic appears to be sound from the standpoint of Western nutrition, since bananas do have lots of potassium. However, bananas increase Pitta, or heat, in the body. The resulting increased heat cancels out the effect of increasing the potassium intake. Pomegranate juice, on the other hand, is loaded with potassium and is one of the most cooling foods nature has to offer. This kind of understanding of how to work with the intelligence of nature can give you just enough of an edge to keep you in the Zone and put you in the winner's circle.

The Pitta diet consists primarily of sweet, bitter, and astringent foods. Their primary property is to be cooling, yet some of them are also somewhat heavy and dry. (Pitta, as you recall, is light, moist, and warm.)

If you have a Pitta constitution, the following will help you determine the best foods to eat and which foods to minimize or avoid.

✑ FOODS TO FAVOR

In General:

- Favor cool foods and drinks, especially in hot weather. Choose foods that are sweet, bitter, or astringent in taste.
- Salads are excellent, again especially in the summer.
- Pittas thrive on a vegetarian diet better than any other body type.

Grains: White rice, wheat, oats, and barley are best.
Dairy: Favor milk, butter, and ghee (clarified butter). Ice cream is acceptable, and egg whites are, too.
Fruits: Favor sweet fruits, such as grapes, avocados, cherries, melons, mangoes, pomegranates, coconut, as well as sweet, fully ripened plums, pineapples, and oranges.
Vegetables: Asparagus, cucumbers, potatoes, sweet potatoes, green leafy vegetables, broccoli, cauliflower, lettuce, celery, green beans, Brussels sprouts, cabbage, zucchini, sweet peppers, okra, peas, sprouts.

Nuts: Coconut, pumpkin seeds, sunflower seeds.

Oils: Coconut, olive, and sunflower are best. Soy is acceptable.

Sweeteners: All sweeteners are acceptable except honey and molasses, which are heating.

Beans: Chickpeas, mung beans, tofu and other soybean products are acceptable.

Meat and Fish: Chicken, turkey, shrimp, and pheasant are acceptable in small amounts.

Spices and Herbs: Most spices are too heating for Pitta, but the following are acceptable: coriander, cinnamon, cardamom, fennel, black pepper (in small quantities), cilantro, dill, mint, saffron, turmeric.

✢ FOODS TO MINIMIZE OR AVOID

In General:

- Minimize foods that are hot, spicy, salty, or sour.
- Most processed foods are full of salt and sour tastes, which aggravate Pitta.
- The sourness in alcoholic beverages, fermented foods, and coffee aggravates Pitta and should be avoided.

Grains: Minimize corn, millet, rye, brown rice.

Dairy: Stay away from yogurt, cheese, sour cream, cultured buttermilk, egg yolks.

Fruits: Reduce sour fruits, such as grapefruit, sour oranges, olives, papayas, and unripe pineapples and plums. Apricots, bananas, berries, cherries, cranberries, peaches should also be minimized.

Vegetables: Avoid beets, carrots, onions, garlic, eggplant, hot peppers, tomatoes, radishes, spinach.

Sweeteners: Avoid honey and molasses.

Beans: Avoid lentils.

Nuts: Minimize all nuts and seeds, especially cashews, peanuts, sesame seeds.

Oils: Reduce almond, corn, safflower, and sesame oils.

Meat and Fish: Avoid red meat and seafood.

Spices and Herbs: Minimize all pungent spices and herbs, such as salt, ginger, cumin, black pepper, fenugreek, clove, celery seed, mustard seed. Also cut down on barbecue sauce, sour salad dressings, vinegar, mustard, pickles, catsup. Completely avoid chili peppers and cayenne. Suggestion: Use some fresh lemon juice on salads instead of vinegar.

☿ THE KAPHA DIET

The Kapha diet is much like the modern-day health food diet, which is low in fat, has no sugars or sweets, and is high in carbohydrates. This is a very good diet for the Kapha type, particularly in spring, the Kapha season, to combat the tendency toward congestion and allergies. Raw-food diets, marcobiotic diets, and the Pritikin diet are also similar to the Kapha diet. All these are good for anyone on a short-term cleansing regimen. However, only Kapha types will find balance from these more austere diets over the long run.

Many of the so-called health food diets have value and work well for some people some of the time. But without knowing the constitutional needs of the individual, and the relevant season of the year, you could end up eating perfectly healthy foods that simply are not suited for your body type. The bottom line is: *There is no one diet that is suitable for everyone.*

The Kapha diet is made up of the pungent, bitter, and astringent tastes, which have the properties of being light, dry, and hot. It is a lighter diet, to help offset the Kapha tendency to become heavy and lethargic. If you have a Kapha constitution, the following will help you determine the best foods to eat and which foods to minimize or avoid.

☿ FOODS TO FAVOR

In General:

· Favor foods that are light, dry, and warm, and that have spicy, bitter, and astringent tastes. The bitter and astringent tastes will help curb the appetite.

· Favor spicy, stimulating foods cooked with a minimum of butter, oil, salt, or sugar. Indian and Mexican food are generally excellent for Kaphas.

· Always favor lightness in the diet, both in quality and quantity: smaller portions, lighter foods.

· Favor hot food over cold at every meal.

· Choose dry cooking methods (baking, broiling, sauteeing) over moist or oily methods such as steaming, boiling, frying.

· Raw fruits, vegetables, and salads are recommended.

Grains: Favor barley, corn, millet, buckwheat, rye. Wheat and rice are acceptable in smaller quantities.

Dairy: Low-fat or non-fat milk. Again, always boil milk before you drink it, and drink it warm. To reduce the Kapha qualities of milk, you can add one or two pinches of turmeric or ginger before boiling. A small amount of whole milk is acceptable.

Fruits: Take lighter fruits, such as apples and pears. Pomegranates, cranberries, and persimmons are also good. Dried fruits (apricots, figs, prunes, raisins) are okay.

Vegetables: Most vegetables are fine, including radishes, asparagus, eggplant, green leafy vegetables, beets, broccoli, Brussels sprouts, spinach, peas, potatoes, cabbage, carrots, cauliflower, pumpkin, lettuce, celery, sprouts.

Nuts: Reduce all nuts. Only sunflower or pumpkin seeds are okay.

Oils: Use only small amounts. Almond, corn, sunflower, and safflower are acceptable.

Sweeteners: Raw, unheated honey is the only sweetener that doesn't increase Kapha.

Beans: All legumes are acceptable, except kidney beans and tofu.

Meat and Fish: White meat of chicken and turkey is acceptable, as is shrimp, but only in small amounts.

Spices and Herbs: All spices are good for Kapha except salt. Ginger is recommended to stimulate digestion.

FOODS TO MINIMIZE OR AVOID

In General:

· Minimize foods that are heavy, oily, and cold. Reduce foods with sweet, sour, and salty tastes.
· Avoid overindulgence in dairy products.
· Avoid deep-fried foods of any kind.
· Main rule: cut down on sweet, rich foods.

Grains: Minimize large quantities of wheat and rice.

Dairy: Minimize dairy products, especially cheese, yogurt, butter, cream.

Fruits: Reduce sweet, heavy, or sour fruits, such as oranges, bananas, coconuts, pineapples, figs, dates, avocados, melons, pears, pomegranates, cranberries. These are more acceptable if cooked.

Vegetables: Reduce tomatoes, cucumbers, sweet potatoes, zucchini.

Meat and Fish: Avoid red meat, pork, seafood in general.

Spices and Herbs: Avoid salt.

CARBO LOADING BY BODY TYPE

Most of us know that foods rich in complex carbohydrates give us long-lasting energy. Athletes are famous for their carbo-loading feasts the night before competitions.

Recently, foods have been analyzed for their *glycemic index*—how quickly they provide sugar or energy to the blood and muscles. Certain foods break down quickly, others more slowly. The foods that are quickly absorbed into the bloodstream and quickly used by the muscles have a high glycemic index, while foods that break down slowly and provide long-lasting energy have a low index. (For more information on glycemic indexing of foods, see Edward Coyle's article, "Timing and Method of Increased Carbohydrate Intake to Cope with Heavy Training, Competition, and Recovery," in *Journal of Sports Sciences*, vol. 9, 1991.)

Pasta, probably the most common carbo-loading meal, is surprisingly found in the middle range. In other words, there are better foods than pasta to store up energy for a competition. Thanks to Bucky Black, an accomplished Ayurvedic chef, we have prepared three body-type-specific carbo-loading meals that have a low glycemic index and provide long-lasting energy.

For best results, carbo-loading meals should be eaten for lunch the day before competition.

CARBO-LOADING FOODS FOR VATA TYPES

- hot soups
- veggie burger
- yogurt shakes
- rice pudding, banana cream pie, or berry pie

CARBO-LOADING FOODS FOR PITTA TYPES

- salads with sweet lemon and olive oil
- pasta primavera (with veggies)
- mango shake
- sweet cherry or coconut cream pie

CARBO-LOADING FOODS FOR KAPHA TYPES

- apple juice
- salad with sprouts and low-fat buttermilk dressing
- black bean chili
- apple pie or gingersnap cookies

RECIPES

⚔ CARBO-LOADING MEAL FOR VATA

VEGGIE BURGER

½ cup split, peeled mung beans

3 cups water

1 tablespoon black mustard seeds

¼ teaspoon asafoetida*

1 tablespoon tamarind*

½ cup cracked or bulgar wheat

⅓ cup regular cream of wheat

⅓ cup toasted sunflower seeds

Salt and freshly ground pepper to taste

*These ingredients are commonly found in Worcestershire sauce.

Combine mung beans, water, mustard seeds, asafoetida, and tamarind in medium pot. Simmer until beans are tender but not broken, about 15 to 18 minutes (do not drain beans). Combine all remaining ingredients in same pot and mix into a thick paste. When mixture is cool (can be air cooled or refrigerated), form into patties about ⅓ lb each. This will make 6–8 patties. These may be covered air-tight and refrigerated until used. (This is a great advantage for athletes on the go, who can make several patties beforehand and cook them as needed.) Cook in oven under broiler or with butter in a skillet.

♠ CARBO-LOADING MEAL FOR PITTA

PASTA PRIMAVERA

Sauce

⅓ cup toasted chick-pea flour

½ cup cold milk

2 cups milk

12–15 threads saffron

1 teaspoon ground coriander

2 tablespoons fructose

⅛ teaspoon white pepper

Pasta

1 lb. pasta

1 cup broccoli (chopped)

1 cup cauliflower (chopped)

The sauce: Mix first 2 ingredients in bowl until smooth. Set aside. Mix all remaining sauce ingredients in a heavy skillet and stir constantly over high heat until just before boiling point, then lower heat. Stir in the cold milk-and-flour mixture until the sauce is thickened. Remove from heat. Transfer sauce to storage bowl. Continue stirring the sauce, to prevent the surface from forming a skin, till warm. Cover with plastic wrap for an airtight seal and refrigerate. The sauce can now be stored in the refrigerator as you would fresh milk. The pasta: Boil 4–5 quarts of water, and add pasta. Cook pasta as instructed on package. Add veggies to pasta 7–10 minutes before pasta finishes cooking. Drain off water and mix with sauce. Mix, heat, and serve. Will serve 4–6.

CARBO-LOADING MEAL FOR KAPHA

BLACK BEAN CHILI

This recipe uses a Kapha-balancing homemade chili powder that can be made ahead of time and used daily as a spice for Kapha types. It is particularly recommended for use during Kapha season. The degree of spicy heat will be determined by how many and what type of chili pod you use. A slow-cook pot is probably best for cooking the beans.

CHILI POWDER

4–8 large dried chili pods	½ teaspoon black peppercorns
1 tablespoon asafoetida	1 tablespoon oregano
2 tablespoons toasted cumin seeds	½ teaspoon thyme
2 tablespoons salt	¼ teaspoon rosemary
1 tablespoon ground coriander	¼ teaspoon sage
1 large spike of clove	2 tablespoons brown sugar
10–20 saffron threads (optional)	

All spice measurements are for dried spices.

To simplify, just use the first 4 ingredients. Cut the chili pods into 1-inch × 1-inch pieces and grind with the other spices to make a blend. Mix all ingredients for the chili powder.

BEANS

1 lb. dried black beans, washed, soaked at least 4 hours or overnight, and drained	4 tablespoons chili powder
	2 tablespoons olive oil
1 quart apple juice	
2 bay leaves	

Simmer the beans, apple juice, and bay leaves for 1½ hours, adding water to keep beans covered. When beans are done, sauté chili powder in oil, being careful not to let it smoke or burn. When oil is infused with spices (1–2 minutes), add a cup of cooked beans to the oil and spices. Turn to high heat, stirring for 1–2 minutes more, then mix back with main pot of beans.

To vary thickness: Mix *masa harina* (corn tortilla flour) with cold water to make paste, and add the chili to desired thickness. Makes 8 servings.

Remember, going the distance in making this chili powder can pay off in the long run, as you can use it as a condiment for almost all your meals in order to have a Kapha-balancing effect.

DIET—BY BODY TYPE AND SEASON

YOUR MIND-BODY TYPE	VATA SEASON (Winter)	PITTA SEASON (Summer)	KAPHA SEASON (Spring)
	V	V	V
	P	P	P
	K	K	K
	V	P	V
	V	P	P
	V	V	K
	V	K	K
	P	P	K
	K	P	K
	V	P	K

Find your body type on vertical axis, find the current season on horizontal axis and cross reference the appropriate diet.

PART THREE

8

SPORTS BY BODY TYPE

In chapter 3 I described the frustration and humiliation experienced by children who are forced to compete in sports, or to be tested in sports-related skills, that are not suited to their individual nature and body type. Asking a child who is endowed with the qualities of Kapha to climb ropes for speed, or asking a Vata child to throw a football for distance, is not going to build self-confidence and self-esteem or inculcate a love of exercise. On the other hand, the light-as-a-feather Vata child will fly up the ropes, and the big Kapha kid will throw the football a mile—and both will want to come back and do it again.

I once gave an interview to a very closed-minded, nonexercising radio host named Peggy Hart. She was quick to voice her point of view on why mainstream America doesn't exercise: "Basically we are all too busy for it. But if I had the time, I would surely do it, because as we all know, it's good for us."

I told her that if exercise were more fun, more of us would be doing it, "certainly more than the 15 percent or so who are involved in a regular exercise program. The basic theme of my program," I said, "is to bring the fun back into physical fitness by paying attention to the exercise needs of the body, according to one's body type."

Peggy rejected my logic. But later in the program I mentioned the statistic about 50 percent of American children experiencing their first failure in life as a sports failure, and I told some stories about kids who were humiliated because they were tested in sports for which they had no natural aptitude. This must have broken through Peggy's shell for a moment, because she immediately launched into a story from her childhood. For the next two minutes she related to me—and her radio audience—how she had been humiliated in gym class as a young girl.

It seems that when she was asked to bend forward and touch her toes, she couldn't do it. Her teacher would regularly call her up in front of the class and demand that she touch her toes. She repeatedly failed. She would go home and practice for hours, without success. Reluctantly, she would go to gym class each week, only to be humiliated again and again.

However, when I asked her, "Do you think the humiliating experience you had as a child could have anything to do with the lack of time you have for exercise now as an adult?" Peggy had no response.

Whether or not Peggy ever got it, it is clear to me that with the knowledge we have of body types, if children could be trained and tested in sports that are appropriate for them, sports in which they could easily and naturally excel or at least do well, most of us would still be exercising and enjoying it. But unfortunately, sports selection according to body type is virtually unknown.

There are new systems of body-typing emerging, such as somato-typing, which recognizes three main types called ectomorphs, endomorphs, and mesomorphs, and psychological typing, which divides people into introverts, extroverts, and other classifications. These varied systems of constitutional typing will always be limited because they don't connect man with nature.

Man is an extension of nature, possessing the same qualities as those found in foods, seasons, and times of day. Ayurveda understands man's individual nature as part of a larger, more intelligent system, which governs not only which foods or sports best suit us, but how we can live in harmony with nature's intelligence and enjoy a happier, more productive life, whether on or off the field.

This chapter provides detailed Level 1 and Level 2 descriptions and charts to help you select sports, exercise patterns, and a cross-training program best suited to your individual nature. With the information in this chapter, you will be able to quickly analyze your strengths and talents, combine them with your own likes and dislikes, and choose a sport or cross-training program to provide maximum health benefits, maximum results, and maximum enjoyment. With enjoyment will come longevity—that is, you are far more likely to stick with something that gives you success and satisfaction.

SPORT SELECTION BY BODY TYPE

Sport selection by body type is not a completely new concept. In 1984, CBS medical correspondent Dr. Robert Arnot and Charles Gaines wrote a pioneering book called *Sports Talent*. The book's theme is how to choose and participate in a sport or sports suited to who you are, so that you experience more pleasure and less frustration. The book provides scientific validation for the usefulness of this mind-body typing system.

Arnot and Gaines measured differences in body composition, frame size, muscle-to-fat ratio, and sizes of hearts and lungs, and analyzed muscle fiber to determine muscular potential for sprinting or endurance. They may have been the first modern researchers studying sports body-typing beyond the realm of simple somato-typing. Their research showed how differences in physical shape and size of various parts of the body combine to make unique individuals with specialized athletic aptitudes. Psychological profiles were touched on but did not play an important role in their recommendations.

Recent studies have shown substantial psychological differences in body types when under physical stress. Researchers at Florida State University studied two types of people during an exercise stress test, the now-classic Type A and Type B personalities. The Type A's, aggressive and highly motivated, were most likely Pitta-Vata in nature. The Type B individuals were less aggressive and more "laid back," probably possessing more Kapha qualities.

The study found that the Type A's needed no verbal support to push themselves to their full aerobic capacity, while the Type B's reached full capacity only when cheered on or otherwise supported. These results jibe perfectly with our understanding from Maharishi Ayur-Ved. Pitta types are naturally driven, while Kapha types need motivation and support.

GAINING THE COMPETITIVE EDGE

If knowledge of mind-body types were available from childhood on, performance results would be noticeably affected. This was proven in 1960, when the East German government began somato typing their athletes. At the time, East Germany was the size of New York in population. In 1968 they won only 9 gold medals, while the United States took home 45. In 1976, after a decade and a half of body typing, East Germany won 47 gold medals while the United States slipped to 37.

Body-typing was only one aspect of East Germany's massive, highly funded Olympic training program—but it was a crucial part. Only in the last few years has the United States begun investigating body-type sport selection.

Some of the most obvious results of the successful East German experiment have been in gymnastics. Have you ever noticed how the Eastern bloc nations always produce perfect, pint-size gymnasts? They all look about 8 years old and just "happen" to have the perfect body type for the perfect score. Fourteen-year-old Nadia Comaneci set the standard at the Montreal Olympics when she scored the first 10 in Olympic history. Nadia and Olga Korbut together carved into stone the body size prerequisite for success in world-class gymnastics.

Judges today make no bones about criticizing gymnasts who are of a larger body type. They feel that a smaller body just looks better, and they will most likely give a better score on that basis alone. Larger-framed gymnasts go into world-class competition well aware of this prejudice. The USA's Betty Okino was the victim of just such prejudice. Her skills were as good as any, but her size called attention to even the slightest flaw in her performance.

When you look at the American bench, you see a variety of different shapes and sizes rather than the uniformity of Eastern European teams. Some of these American girls are great young talents who often come up short in world-class contention simply because they reach puberty. Their hips and breasts mature and the girls are no longer the perfect pixy model required for supreme success in the world of gymnastics.

Another reason for body-typing appears a few years after childhood. In sports today, young athletes are placed under enormous pressure to excel. One of the consequences is that many of them, particularly (but not exclusively) women, develop eating disorders due to the fear of gaining weight. The most common disorder is bulimia, in which the young athlete fulfills his or her natural desire to chow down heartily and then induces vomiting, due to the fear of gaining weight and losing a competitive edge.

This behavior results in large part from forcing the body to perform outside its natural design. Not everyone is born to be a pixy. Nor is everyone designed to be a hulk—a fact that has led to the abuse of steroids by lighter body types. Although part of the problem facing athletes is the tremendous pressure to win, and part is the stressful "no pain, no gain" method of training, much of the problem begins with improper sports selection. Intelligent selection of sports by body type is the first step toward setting the situation right.

LIFELONG FITNESS

Critics of body-typing for sports selection with young children say that it will take away freedom of choice, that children will be pushed into sports rather than inspired by them. But the role of body-typing is not to force a child into a sport—it is to *expose* a child to activities in which he or she is likely to excel. Kids who are successful will be motivated and enthusiastic for the rest of their lives, because they are doing what comes naturally.

I once sat on a plane next to a wrestler coached by the famous Dan Gable of the University of Iowa. Coach Gable's philosophy belongs to the old school. Although Gable definitely squeezes the very best out of an imperfect system, this wrestler was totally exhausted from the experience.

I asked him, "What if you had to wrestle for the rest of your life?"

"No way," he said. "This is my last year, and I don't even want to think about wrestling again."

"How would you feel about wrestling for just one more year?"

"Even if I were eligible," he said, "I wouldn't do it. I'm just too tired all the time."

There are many reasons why this young man's attitude was so negative, all of which I address in this book. But one of the very first steps in making exercise a way of life is to select a sport that you like. This results in a level of enthusiasm that can arise only when a person is involved in an activity that suits his or her nature. It is natural for us to be attracted to something we do well—it is human nature.

Learning a child's constitutional type early in life, and giving the child the chance to choose activities that he or she can perform well, averts the danger of failure and humiliation that we have discussed. It can lead to lifelong physical fitness. Our surveys showed that when children are exposed to a variety of sports, they will naturally select the ones that are most appropriate for their body types.

Parents are often to blame for pushing children into sports to fulfill their own frustrated athletic ambitions, with little or no regard for the child's likes or dislikes. This kind of parental behavior may be the most injurious to the child's exercise perspective. Children forced into sports at young ages often spend a good deal of their adult lives trying to figure out why they haven't any desire to exercise.

The famous children's story "The Ugly Duckling" describes the humiliation of a misplaced baby swan trying to fit in with a family of ducks. The rejection and alienation experienced by the "ugly" duckling—who turns out to be a graceful and beautiful swan—is akin to the humiliation and alienation experienced by a Vata type being tested on a performance scale suited to Kapha types, and vice versa. When the activities chosen are in line with the natural talents of the person's body type, the risk of becoming the ugly duckling and experiencing failure in sports is dramatically reduced.

❧ THE SPORTS VATA TYPE

Pure Vata types have substantially higher Vata scores on the questionnaire in chapter 4, such as 31 Vata, 5 Pitta, and 5 Kapha. These individuals are like highstrung thoroughbred racehorses, always on the go, very restless and even jumpy at times. In baseball, they are the singles-hitting, base-stealing second-baseman types, where quickness and the short throw to first base make them the perfect choice. They are not endowed with power but are well endowed with speed and quickness.

They love fast, vigorous activity but can't handle too much of it if they are going to stay in balance. If anything, Vatas need to slow down, and nature often forces them to, since their endurance is not great and they tire quite easily. These people are quick to get involved in a fitness program, but due to their constantly changing interests, they are also quick to give it up.

When their Vata qualities are aggravated and out of balance, these individuals can become compulsive and get trapped in addictive behavior. When their addiction is to athletics, they can get caught up in what is known, in sports circles, as "addictive runner's syndrome." The same obsessiveness in business is sometimes called "workaholism." (This is a common Pitta trait as well.) These people become completely dependent on constant activity and can run their health, marriages, and jobs into the ground. Their compulsive Vata nature also makes them especially susceptible to overtraining and, consequently, to injury.

Because they are not well endowed with structural strength, pure Vata types will generally be inclined toward areas other than sports as a profession. However, there are certain sports-related professions that clearly require a Vata body type in order to excel, such as ballet and other forms of dance. These traditionally attract the lighter and more movement-oriented Vata individuals. But because of their lighter frames and lack of structural resiliency, Vatas may pay a price for their constant physical activity, ending up exhausted and injured.

More than any others, Vata body types need to know their limits—how much exercise is good and how much is harmful.

The same principle holds true for the elderly, who are in the Vata time of their lives. Their concerns are more for safety and longevity than simply avoidance of fatigue and injury, which makes sports selection and the coming sections of this book of paramount importance for them.

⚱ THE SPORTS PITTA TYPE

Pure Pitta types cash in at about 6 Vata, 27 Pitta, and 7 Kapha on the body-type questionnaire. Pitta translates as fire, both in personality and desire to win. The competitive nature and natural killer instinct of pure Pitta types make them high achievers and often big winners. They are hot-headed as a rule and must take care not to overheat mentally or physically. They are highly motivated and driven and are often not satisfied unless they win. For the purest Pitta types, it is *not* how you play the game but whether you win or lose that counts.

These are natural leaders and often will appoint themselves as team captain, whether nominated for the position or not. They are attracted to individual sports because of their strong ego and natural competence in most sports. Whatever it is, they can usually do it better than most, so they often end up doing it alone. Rock climbing, skiing, sky diving, racquet sports, and running are a few of the Pitta-dominated sports.

Pittas benefit from playing team sports because their competitive nature gains balance from passing the ball, working together, and sharing the accomplishment.

Pitta types make great athletes, but for longevity in any sport, it must be *fun*. The competitive Pitta mind can often drive the body into fatigue and exhaustion just to win or to be the best. This constant driving can take the enjoyment out of the game and ultimately strip the pleasure out of physical fitness and exercise. Pittas need to take it easy and enjoy the game itself, rather than live for the result.

Although Pittas make the best competitors in the world, celebrities such as John McEnroe and Stefi Graf have openly admitted that they rarely enjoy themselves during a match, when they are in the heat of the battle. Enjoyment begins only when they can relish a victory. Fortunately for these two, victory came often in their careers. Other Pitta types may not have been so fortunate!

The same Pitta temper that fired McEnroe to play at his best for many years now has to be controlled in order for him to keep his concentration. Earlier in his career, the hotter he got, the better he played; now, when he loses his temper, he finds it difficult to get himself back in the game.

Many Pitta types with less outstanding abilities find themselves losing interest in sport because they get too serious about their won-lost records. Some will tell you straightforwardly, "If I can't be the best, I'd rather not do it at all." This may be the psychology needed for the making of a champion—but it is hardly what's needed for fitness as a way of life.

Pittas have the speed of the Vata and the endurance of the Kapha, giving them fine potential for athletic excellence. Most pro athletes usually have at least some Pitta in their constitutions, along with some Vata and Kapha, depending on the specific needs for their sport.

⚕ THE SPORTS KAPHA TYPE

Kapha types are often late bloomers. Their development, mental, physical, or both, can be retarded until late in high school or even afterward. Coaches sometimes cut these kids from teams at a young age, only to watch them grow to become world-class athletes. Michael Jordan, probably a late-blooming Kapha type, was cut from his high school basketball team.

On the Body-Type Questionnaire, pure Kaphas might weigh in with something like 5s or 6s in both Vata and Pitta and a high 20-something in Kapha. They are more relaxed and easygoing, more naturally composed than other types. They love the camaraderie of team sports and are attracted to them. Most baseball players have this easygoing Kapha temperament and are not easily flustered. To stay calm and focused while thirty thousand opposing fans are chanting, "You're a bum!" requires a certain amount of composure.

As I mentioned earlier, Kaphas need to be motivated toward exercise; otherwise, later in life, they can all too easily multiply the pounds and become part of the sedentary population. For good health and mental and physical balance, Kaphas need regular exercise. Without it, they feel lethargic and complacent. Any aerobic exercise will benefit them—but to get them to do it, it has to have some charm. They are not often motivated to exert themselves.

For Kapha types who need vigorous exercise, a leisurely ride on a touring bike through the Napa Valley in California, stopping to do plenty of wine and cheese tasting along the way, will not satisfy their exercise needs. They will probably eat more calories than they burn. But this is just the kind of trip that would attract the easygoing (and food-loving!) Kapha. They are rarely in a hurry and are usually fairly content with life in general.

I once taught an aerialist on the U.S. freestyle team whose body type was Kapha. In comparing himself with his teammates, he said, "I really don't do it to win. If I hit each jump right, I'm happy. Each time I jump, I hope I find that place where you are totally aware of every part of your body moving through space, flipping through the air, and seeing the landing well in advance. It's being completely aware of the body from inside out. The other side of the experience is that when you jump, you find yourself thirty feet in the air, not knowing where you are in space, yet by some unknown phenomenon (probably called practice!) it all comes out okay and you land on your feet, hopefully."

The greatest reward for Kapha types usually has less to do with winning and more to do with playing. They are in it for the beauty rather than the glory.

COMBINATION BODY TYPES

In the next several sections I will review the traits of the remaining seven body types, which are combinations of qualities rather than the "pure" types I have discussed so far. One important point to remember is that when the qualities of each type are divided up, components such as mind, intellect, ego, emotions, behavior, likes, dislikes, talents, and strengths can land in either camp.

For example, a Vata-Kapha type can have a mind that is predominantly Vata (quick, lively, restless, poor memory, etc.) and a body that is predominantly Kapha (structurally stronger, heavier, slower). Or, a Vata-Kapha can have a Kapha mind (slow to learn, slow to forget, more relaxed and composed) along with a Vata body (lean, light, mobile). Or, yet again, some Vata and some Kapha qualities will go to the mind department, and others to the body.

Whichever way the chips fall, he or she is still a Vata-Kapha. This will create unique personalities within the type, each with the general theme of Vata-Kapha. In fact, the combinations are virtually infinite, leaving no two persons exactly alike.

BODY-TYPE FOCUS

ONCE YOU ARE FAMILIAR WITH THE GENERAL CHARACTERISTICS AND TENDENCIES OF THE TYPES, IT IS NOT TOO DIFFICULT TO FINE-TUNE YOUR UNDERSTANDING OF YOURSELF (AND OTHERS). A CLOSER INSPECTION OF THE PHYSICAL, MENTAL, BEHAVIORAL, AND ATHLETIC PROFILES, BASED ON THE SUBTOTALS OF THE BODY-TYPE QUESTIONNAIRE, WILL SHED LIGHT ON THE EXACT NATURE OF EACH INDIVIDUAL'S TYPE. WITH SOME BASIC PRINCIPLES UNDER YOUR BELT, THE DIFFERENCE BETWEEN A KAPHA, PITTA, AND VATA BODY OR MIND IS QUITE APPARENT EVEN TO A RELATIVELY UNTRAINED OBSERVER.

≝ ⚑ THE VATA-PITTA SPORTS TYPE

Questionnaire results here would be in the neighborhood of 21 Vata, 15 Pitta, 5 Kapha. Here, Vata is the major influence, with Pitta a close second. People of this type have the speed of the Vata along with the strength of the Pitta. Endurance will not be their strong suit; they will be quick and agile, excelling in sports that require short bursts of energy. The Vata predominance will make them susceptible to early fatigue and over-training.

The fire of Pitta will motivate them to excel in all that they do. But in exercise, the fiery mind can push the Vata body beyond its comfortable limits and increase the risk of injury. The combination of the air and fire from the Vata and Pitta can make for a very volatile, but also productive, personality. Being quick and getting things done quickly will be a part of this nature. But, as always when there is strong Pitta in the constitution, it is important for them to find the fun in exercise and to smell the roses along the way.

Vata-Pittas do well in gymnastics, ballet, dance, and other sports requiring primarily speed and secondarily strength. Since Vata controls the mind, they will be very pensive, and when engaged in sports they will quickly plan a cerebral strategy to accomplish the goal. Their mental propensity can often steer them away from athletics into more mental endeavors.

⚑ ≝ THE PITTA-VATA SPORTS TYPE

Here the scores will peak in the Pitta column, looking something like 15 Vata, 21 Pitta, and 6 Kapha. This type will have more of the strength of Pitta but will still be well endowed with speed from the Vata. The Pitta will give larger, quick-firing muscles. This muscle strength will combine well with the fast metabolism of the Vata to make good sprinters and middle-distance runners. Many marathoners on the world-class level are of this type, as marathons have increasingly become speed races. (Endurance events today are the ultramarathons, with runs up to 50 or 100 miles, and are dominated by the real endurance Kapha types—the elephants and camels of athletics!)

The smaller-framed Pitta-Vata types are usually very competitive, excelling in sports that require speed and strength, such as racquetball, gymnastics, aerobics, dance, and ballet. The Vata-Pitta type described above will also do well in these sports but will not possess the extremely competitive nature of the Pitta-Vata. Vata-Pittas will also lack some of the structural soundness of Pitta-Vatas. Both must take care not to overtrain, as they lack the structure and endurance of the Kapha.

Pitta-Vata types make the best shortstops, while their Vata-Pitta cousins are the best second basemen. On the basketball court, they excel in the guard position, dribbling, passing, and setting up plays. Their type combines the skills of a quick body and a quick mind.

The dominance of Pitta can manifest in business, in sports, and in life as a very fast-thinking, competitive nature. With all this Pitta up front, these people have a strong desire to win. This trait can often make the process frustrating. Physically, they break down quickly, while their mental stamina is second to none. They usually last longer in business than in sports. These are the types who will return to the athletic field in their thirties and forties with a more tempered attitude (after being burned out in their twenties), to stay fit rather than to smash world records.

🐾🦶 THE VATA-KAPHA SPORTS TYPE

A typical questionnaire result: 18 Vata, 5 Pitta, 16 Kapha. These people may be fairly slight in build and on the tall side. Or they may have a quick Vata mind along with a larger, more coordinated Kapha body.

Vata-Kaphas make great team players, and they enjoy what they do. They lack the killer instinct of the competitive Pitta type, but this doesn't mean they don't like to win. The world-famous underdog U.S. 1980 Olympic gold medal hockey team was selected intentionally to exclude any superstar, extroverted, Pitta-dominant players. Coach Herb Brooks's philosophy was that the whole is greater than the sum of the parts, and he chose Kapha-type men who would be team players.

These individuals have a good balance of speed and endurance. Possible physical limitations of the Vata are balanced by the strong Kapha. They do well in the heat because of the absence of Pitta. They excel in endurance sports that also require short bursts of speed. In basketball, they may play the forward position and provide great ability to balance their team. They often go unnoticed because of their selfless personalities.

Vata-Kaphas can be very tall and lean. With this combination, they are drawn to quick, graceful sports.

🦶🐾 THE KAPHA-VATA SPORTS TYPE

Questionnaire sample score: 16 Vata, 3 Pitta, 19 Kapha. Because of the predominance of Kapha, these men and women are more stable emotionally and physically than are Vata-Kapha types. They are bigger both in size and in weight, but they still tend to be on the lean side. Kapha-Vatas excel in endurance sports, while possessing a good measure of quickness thanks to their Vata qualities. Their Vata-Kapha close cousins will be quicker but have less endurance.

Both the Vata-Kapha and the Kapha-Vata need to avoid excessive exposure to cold weather. During the winter months, you will probably see both of these types wisely interested in indoor sports, rather than fighting the cold wintry elements.

Wide receiver is the perfect position for the Kapha-Vata type on the football field. They are big enough not to be massacred, but light and fast enough to outrun the defensive backs.

Kapha-Vatas can be very big and tall, with a certain amount of quickness and speed. If very oversized, they can easily overtrain and injure the less stable Vata structure. They are more naturally athletic than are Vata-Kaphas. The Kapha provides heightened mind-body coordination and a natural cool and composure during competition.

⚶ THE PITTA-KAPHA SPORTS TYPE

The questionnaire score for this type might be 3 Vata, 21 Pitta, and 17 Kapha. Pitta-Kapha types have the endurance of the Kapha along with the strength and drive of the Pitta. The strong-willed Pitta mind is just what the doctor ordered to keep the lethargic Kapha type physically fit. Kapha types need motivation, but when in shape these individuals are incredibly coordinated athletes.

They combine the competitive drive and will to win with the natural grace and composure of Kapha. This translates into a very powerful competitive package. The Kapha qualities ensure that the Pitta's zealous drive to win will be balanced with fun.

Because of the large amount of Pitta, people of this type can overheat easily and become angry if they get physically hot. But their predominance of Pitta gives good muscular definition. This, combined with the large body size and bulk produced by the Kapha influence, makes this type perfect for body building. These people gain weight fairly easily, but with Pitta at the helm, they rarely get fat. Their competitive nature makes them great winners, but with a tendency to be sore losers.

They make great power tennis players, great defensive backs in football, and will probably play third base, left or right field, or pitch in baseball.

Pitta-Kapha is a very resilient constitution. People of this type are rarely sick and do well in just about any physical activity. Their only red flags are the Pitta tendencies to overheat and to be so attached to winning that they cannot enjoy themselves. (See part III for a detailed discussion of this problem.)

♊♀ THE KAPHA-PITTA SPORTS TYPE

Questionnaire sample score: 5 Vata, 15 Pitta, 20 Kapha. The leading Kapha influence makes this type easygoing and easy to get along with, but there is still enough Pitta to get the job done. Their laid-back nature and need for external motivation attracts them to team sports such as hockey, football, basketball, and baseball. Their cool temperament makes team play extremely smooth; they can handle the pressure of being a winner as well as the agony of defeat.

Kapha-Pittas play because they love the sport, the team, and the fun of it all. They lack the killer instinct, yet they are highly motivated. They are gifted with the desire to achieve the goal, without the infatuation with attaining it at any cost. They are the team players in sports, business, and family life, always thinking how to help the cause rather than themselves.

Without proper training, Kapha-Pittas can easily get tired and suffer from a loss of concentration. Their very natural athleticism can remain dormant unless they are properly motivated. They do very well with a highly motivated coach who can spark their Pitta competitive fire. These types might find themselves labeled as teddy bears, good but not great. Yet, greatness is waiting to surface, if the inspiration is there.

In baseball, they make perfect catchers; in football, perfect linemen or fullbacks; in basketball, perfect centers.

These are the Babe Ruth types, with talent to spare. But as they grow older, if regular exercise hasn't become a way of life, their Ruthian talents can turn into major-league problems. A sedentary lifestyle, combined with too much or too heavy food, etc., can slowly wear them out.

In the strength and endurance department, Kapha-Pittas tower above all others. Their only lack is some speed, which, with training, they can make up for due to their exceptional athletic abilities. (Even Babe Ruth led the Yankees in stolen bases several times!) If I were to venture a guess on the most common body type in professional athletics, it would have to be Kapha-Pitta.

♊♀♊ THE SAMA SPORTS TYPE

The Sama type is an equal balance of Vata, Pitta, and Kapha. This may sound like an ideal, perfect type, but in fact, each constitutional type is unique and has its own areas of strength and weakness. The goal is not to be some particular type but to maximize your strengths and minimize your weaknesses by not exercising—and not living—against the grain of your nature.

This specific type, which is somewhat rare, has the speed of Vata, the strength of Pitta, and the endurance of Kapha. Their questionnaire totals might be something like 14 Vata, 16 Pitta, and 15 Kapha. The good news about this type is that they have the natural abilities to excel in just about any activity or sport. On the other hand, they have to be careful not to overtrain the Vata, overheat the Pitta, or undermotivate the Kapha. In this regard, they have to be more conscientious than most others to match their daily routine and sport selection to the season of the year.

Sama types, although rare, have world-class personalities. Their natural gifts are copious, and, with proper training and exposure to the right sports, they can be the best in the world.

It is true that if one constitution could be desired at birth, it would be this one. The Sama type is the balanced expression of Vata, Pitta, and Kapha, and, as a result, people of this type rarely get out of balance. But when they do, it can be difficult to get back in.

SPORT SELECTION INSTRUCTIONS

A person of any body type is capable of engaging in any sport or exercise. The following information is not intended to be restrictive. It is offered only to help enhance the experience of exercise, to make it a more appealing and therefore more important part of your daily life.

The remainder of this chapter has three main purposes. First, it is designed to help those who want to start an exercise program but don't know what sport or exercise would be best for them. Second, it is a useful guide for more serious athletes, who have already selected their sport but need to design a balanced cross-training program suitable for their body type. Third, it lists the sports in which the various body types are most likely to excel on a competitive level.

The chapter contains two sets of lists, Level 1 and Level 2. Level 1, called "General Fitness and Cross-Training," is to be used by anyone looking to design or start a fitness program, and as a cross-training or balancing guide for Vata, Pitta, and Kapha athletes—whether elite or of the weekend variety—who have selected their primary sports. Consulting this list will ensure putting "safety first" with respect to not overexciting Vata or overheating Pitta.

Use this list in the same way you used the diet listings in chapter 7. For example, the sports enumerated under "General Fitness and Cross-Training for Vata" are sports that will bring Vata back into balance, as would a Vata diet, and so on.

The Level 2 list, "Athletic Training," is for more serious athletes as well as individuals who are not comfortable with Level 1 selections. In this case, be sure to choose sports from Level 1 for cross-training.

Individuals are likely to excel in Level 2 sports because they are matched to the natural strengths of the body types. These sports increase the qualities of the three body types. (For example, the fast-paced Vata sports will increase the Vata tendency toward speediness.) Therefore, persons choosing these sports must take care not to aggravate their body types with overtraining, and should balance their programs by cross-training with a Level One sports selection.

If certain sports appear on both lists for a particular body type, then clearly these sports should be considered first for possible selection. They will have the most beneficial body-type-specific benefits.

CROSS-TRAINING BY BODY TYPE

Probably the greatest single contribution to mainstream athletics during the 1980s was the concept of cross-training. Cross-training allows athletes to train in other sports while still improving in their own area. One of the virtues of cross-training is that athletes are now able to train in a secondary sport and still benefit in their primary sport.

For years it was held that specificity of training was the only way to enhance performance. If you were a tennis player, tennis training was all you would do. Now, many athletes are finding that they can cross-train in another sport, while playing a little of their primary sport, and maintain the same fitness level and competitive edge.

This concept has proven invaluable after injury and during rehab. An athlete can let certain muscle groups rest after an injury, while training aerobically in secondary sports.

Our version of cross-training is slightly different. The purpose is not to allow individuals to push harder and farther toward their physical limits, but to balance *sport-specific* training with *body-type* training to ensure the highest unfoldment of physical potential without strain, overtraining, or injuries.

For example, if you put a classic Vata type on a racquetball court, where the ball is going 100 miles per hour during most of the match, he or she will be forced to follow the ball and move at a tremendous pace, thus driving the internal RPMs to the red line. Vata types are drawn to the quickness of this sport and excel in it because of the quick, agile nature of Vata. But if this person is pushing 100 mph at work, at home, and also on the racquetball court for any length of time, sooner or later both the mind and body will burn out.

The point is that even though Vatas do well at fast-paced sports, they do so at the risk of overtraining and psychophysiological imbalance if they participate in only that sport. The solution: cross-training in sports that help keep the body in balance. Instead of intense, high-speed activity on the Vata-aggravating racquetball court, Vatas should select more leisurely, low-intensity sports such as golf, swimming, or Yoga, which have a calming, relaxing effect on the high-strung Vata nature. These sports give them movement, which they love and need, but in the right amount.

SPORT SELECTION BY SEASON

To make the best use of this section, you must take into account not only your body type but the current season. Remember, fall and winter = Vata season, summer = Pitta, and spring = Kapha. Always select the sport or exercise that will balance your body type in conjunction with the season.

For example, if you are a Vata-Pitta type, you should choose Vata-balancing sports in winter and Pitta-balancing sports in summer. In spring, your selection is not crucial, just as we saw that diet decisions would not be crucial in spring for Vata-Pittas. If you're not sure, exercise to balance Vata, which is most predominant in your makeup.

If you are a pure Kapha type, the most important time to select the right sport is during spring, or Kapha season. During the remainder of the year, the Kapha type may choose any sport, but the Kapha-balancing sports will always be most appropriate.

If you are a Sama type, adjust your sport selection for each season: Vata-balancing sports in winter, Pitta-balancing in summer, and Kapha-balancing in spring.

At the end of this chapter, to expedite your selection process, is a chart to help you determine the seasonally best balancing sports for each body type.

Please remember that when choosing your sport and exercise program, enjoyment is the highest priority. Any sport can be performed by any individual, as long as it is comfortable. The following section will ensure that you have maximum safety and longevity in a sport, by applying the knowledge of body types, sports qualities, and seasons.

❦ LEVEL 1: GENERAL FITNESS AND CROSS-TRAINING FOR VATA

Vata-balancing sports or exercises require slow, calming activities that facilitate rejuvenation rather than exhaustion. Some examples:

aerobics (low-impact
  or dance)
archery-kyudo
badminton
ballet
baseball
bicycle touring
bowling
canoeing and
  easy rowing

cricket
dance
doubles tennis
golf
hiking
horseback riding
martial arts
  (nonviolent Aikido
  and Tai Chi)

Ping Pong
sailing
stairstepping
  (moderate)
stretching
swimming
walking
weight training
Yoga

⚑ LEVEL 1: GENERAL FITNESS AND CROSS-TRAINING FOR PITTA

Cross-training and general fitness sports for Pitta types must balance the excessive heat and competitive spirit with sports that provide enjoyment rather than a focus on competition and winning. Some examples:

basketball and
  other team
  sports
cycling
diving
golf
hockey
ice skating

kayaking/rowing
martial arts
mountain biking
noncompetitive
  racquet sports
sailing
skiing (downhill)

skiing (recreational
  cross-country)
surfing
touch football
water skiing
wind surfing
Yoga

● LEVEL 1: GENERAL FITNESS AND CROSS-TRAINING FOR KAPHA

These sports must be stimulating and vigorous to maintain balance in the slow-to-get-started Kapha types. Some examples:

aerobics
basketball

body building
calisthenics

cross-country running
cross-country skiing

cycling	martial arts	sculling
fencing	par course running	shot put
gymnastics	racquetball	soccer
handball	rock climbing	stairstepping
javelin	roller blading	swimming
lacrosse	rowing	tennis
		volleyball

There may be many other sports that fit the three body types; the above is only a selection of some of the most common sports. If one sport appears in more than one section, that indicates the more universal nature of that sport.

If you find a balancing sport in the Level 1 General Fitness and Cross-Training list that is your primary sport, you need look no further. That sport is ideal to keep you in a balanced state of health and fitness. If you don't find one there that appeals to you, then choose a sport you enjoy from the Level 2 Athletic Training lists below, choose at least one other sport from the cross-training list for balance, and be sure to use the Three Phase Workout and the breathing techniques described in later chapters.

LEVEL 2: ATHLETIC TRAINING

Competition sports are the ones a person will be drawn toward and in which he or she will most easily excel. These lists are primarily for the more serious athlete, but anyone looking to excel in sports, rather than just to improve general fitness, can select from it.

Sports on the Level 2 lists support performance gains, but cross-training measures must be taken from Level 1 to ensure balance. In the same way as too much hot food will overheat a Pitta type, too much of the Level 2 sports will overstimulate a particular body type and risk overtraining, injury, and even addictive behavior. To balance this tendency while keeping up fitness levels, cross-train from the appropriate Level 1 list.

Remember, performance gains at the expense of the integration of mind and body will provide enjoyment only in the short term. For lifelong health and fitness, we must respect and train both the mind and the body.

❦ LEVEL 2: VATA ATHLETIC TRAINING

Vata types excel in fast-moving sports requiring speed, agility, and short bursts of energy. These include:

aerobics	handball	skating
ballet	martial arts	sprinting
dance	Ping Pong	squash
fencing	race walking	swimming
gymnastics	racquetball	tennis

⚲ LEVEL 2: PITTA ATHLETIC TRAINING

Pitta types are drawn to individual sports that exhibit their great strength, speed, and stamina. Some of these are:

archery-kyudo	gymnastics	sky diving
baseball	horseback riding	soccer
basketball	ice skating	surfing
body building	kayaking	swimming
canoeing	martial arts	tennis
cross-country skiing	rock climbing	track and field
cycling	roller blading	weight lifting
diving	skiing	

⚲ LEVEL 2: KAPHA ATHLETIC TRAINING

Kapha types excel in endurance and mind-body–coordinated skills, particularly when under pressure, due to their calm, easygoing, stable nature. Their prime competitive sports include:

archery-kyudo	football	mountain biking
baseball	golf	sailing
basketball	hiking	skiing
body building	hockey	surfing
bowling	horseback riding	tennis
cricket	martial arts	volleyball
cycling		

There may be many other sports that fit these categories. The above is only a selection of some of the more common sports.

SPORT SPECIFICS

In this section we will approach the situation from the reverse angle. Up to now, we've been looking at the different body types to see which sports are good for them under different circumstances—as a primary sport, for cross-training, and in what season. Now we will briefly focus on a number of major sports to see what body types are most suitable to engage in them. This list will help you to cross-reference your original selection in terms of the individual nature of each sport.

Body-type icons next to each sport appear in sequence according to the benefits and enjoyment each sport will provide for that individual. For further details, see Level 1 and Level 2 lists. Remember: All sports can be enjoyed by all body types when used in conjunction with the Three Phase workout in chapters 11 through 15.

AEROBICS

Aerobic exercise provides a good cardiovascular workout, which makes it beneficial for Kapha types and somewhat good for Pitta types, as long as they don't get overheated. Although Vatas will be attracted to the fast pace of aerobics, they will be at high risk for overtraining and burnout. Vatas must practice aerobics with some restraint in order not to overtrain.

ARCHERY

Archery is very balancing for the unsettled Vata type and is probably best mastered by the more sedate Kapha. In Zen archery, or kyudo, hitting the target is not the major concern. The entire focus is on the form and process. This may be difficult for goal-oriented Pitta types but is quite valuable for them.

BADMINTON

This sport demands speed and agility, which are abundant in both the Vata and Pitta types.

BALLET

This is a profession more suitable and enjoyable for the Vata and Pitta types, who love to move and have the lighter frames necessary to fly through the air. Although the vigorous, aerobic nature of ballet would be good for Kaphas, they are usually not particularly successful at it, for obvious reasons.

BASEBALL

As a sport of individual exhibition, baseball will attract Pitta types. It also demands great composure, found mostly in Kaphas. Although there are Vata types in the sport who are often at home playing second base and hitting singles, baseball demands the combination of coordination and strength most abundant in the Kapha-Pitta type.

BASKETBALL

Basketball is best suited to the giant Kapha and Kapha-Pitta types. Again, they need great mental composure, but even more, those who excel here possess exceptional coordination and grace, inherent in the Kapha and Pitta natures. This is a sport where size is a dominant factor; it is definitely not suited for the small-framed pure Vata type. Kapha-Vata types, however, can excel in this sport. They are often very tall and thin, Vata providing the thin and Kapha the tall.

BODY BUILDING

This sport attracts Pitta types, who love to look at and admire themselves. But this can be a wonderful sport for all types, especially if they can build bodies, not just muscles, from the inside out. Don't get caught up in the result; focus on the process. Vatas can use the extra bulk; strong, structurally large Kaphas naturally excel at it; Pittas can self-motivate themselves to any achievement.

BOWLING

There is not a great deal of strength involved in bowling, but some endurance is definitely required. The biggest demand comes from mental pressure, especially in competitive, championship play. This can be handled best by Kaphas and a little less successfully by Pittas. This is why the best bowlers are usually the full-framed Kaphas or Kapha-Pittas.

CALISTHENICS

Much like aerobics.

CRICKET

Much the same as baseball.

CROSS-COUNTRY SKIING

This sport is said to develop the most complete fitness of any sport. It is good for all types, but because of the sport's demanding nature, Vatas have to be careful not to overtrain. Indoor skiing machines can easily be regulated to different levels of exertion, which makes them useful for all types. There is no vertical impact on the body, so it is one of the few aerobic activities Vatas can do long-term. Pitta and Kapha types excel in this sport.

CYCLING

In general, cycling is good for all types, because of its lack of structural impact. There are three main types of cycling: sprinting, touring, and road racing. Touring is best for Vata. While Kaphas are attracted to it, it may not provide enough exercise for them. Pittas excel in sprinting, and Kaphas benefit most from road racing. Also see mountain biking.

DANCE

Much like ballet.

DOWNHILL SKIING

This is a great sport for Pitta types because it is for the most part pure, cool, noncompetitive enjoyment. Vatas usually shy away from the cold, while Kaphas relish the scenic beauty. Ski racing is usually dominated by the midsized but competitive Pitta or Pitta-Kapha types.

FENCING

A sport of quick bursts of energy, fencing is more suitable for Pittas and Vatas than for the more heavy and methodical Kaphas.

FOOTBALL

Nowadays it is rare to see a pro football player who is not gifted with some of the Kapha qualities, whether he be Pitta-Kapha, pure Kapha, or Kapha-Vata. The sheer size of Kapha is a prerequisite to play in the NFL—and at just about any other level of football, from sandlot to college. Although Pittas may have the drive, they probably won't have the bulk to keep from getting hurt. Recreational touch football is fine for the lighter-built Vatas—otherwise, this is not their department.

> REMEMBER: ANY SPORT CAN BE MASTERED BY ANY MIND-BODY TYPE. THIS CHAPTER GIVES GUIDELINES THAT REPRESENT THE MAJORITY OF PARTICIPANTS. THERE ARE ALWAYS EXCEPTIONS TO EVERY RULE.

GOLF

Golf, if played in a calming and relaxing manner, is great for Vata types. It is not vigorous enough to give Kaphas a good workout, although they will excel in it because it so perfectly matches their methodical, slow-paced nature. Pitta types have to stay cool, both physically and mentally, in order to do well; they often get frustrated.

GYMNASTICS

Vata-Pitta type is the winning combination here. Kapha types can do well in certain aspects of gymnastics and find it enjoyable and stimulating, but they are simply not in their element. This is a good cross-training sport for Kaphas.

HANDBALL, RACQUETBALL, SQUASH

These sports require quick bursts of energy as well as agility and a great deal of endurance when played on a competitive level. Pitta types usually excel because they have Vata speed, Kapha endurance, and their own usual will to win. Handball, because of bilateral involvement, offers another dimension of mind-body integration to indoor court sports.

HIKING/WALKING

Great for Vatas, probably boring for Pittas, and not vigorous enough for Kaphas—unless you're going up the Rockies toting a 40-pound pack.

HOCKEY

This team sport is dominated by Pitta and Kapha combination types. Hockey players need to be aggressive, fast, big, and strong—although not too big, as they need quite a bit of agility, too. Kapha-Pitta types make great team competitors and are the usual call in hockey.

HORSEBACK RIDING

This sport does not provide enough exercise for Kaphas. Although they are attracted to it, they will need to cross-train for more aerobic conditioning. Vatas are perfectly suited for it, both in size and temperament. Pittas also do well, but the Vata-Pitta types win the gold.

MARTIAL ARTS

The martial arts are really for the development of mind-body coordination and the unfoldment of maximum potential. They are good for all constitutional types, as long as the teaching has an integrated, spiritual base rather than one being focused on fighting.

MOUNTAIN BIKING

A sport that will challenge all types. Vata types can gear down and enjoy the beauty. The Pitta types will have the unlimited terrain to challenge them. (Pittas must be sure that getting to the top is not more important than the process itself.) Kapha types will be dually challenged and motivated to keep coming back for more.

ROCK CLIMBING

This sport requires both the agility and the drive of a Pitta. Most rock climbers are either Pitta-Vata or Pitta-Kapha. This drive to conquer can be a double-edged sword, which must be realized if Pitta rock climbers are to maintain the much-needed balance in this sport.

ROLLER BLADING

This is a very good endurance sport that develops cardiovascular fitness. Although it is dominated by Pitta types, Vatas and Kaphas can do well and enjoy it, too. Vata types enjoy the quick, short bursts of speed and practicing trick maneuvers, while Kaphas relish the long, gliding, speed-skating workouts.

ROWING

Balance, coordination, endurance, and strength are required for excellence in this sport. This makes it especially suitable for Kapha and Pitta types. However, if done in moderation it is a very balancing sport for Vatas. The calming influence found near or on the water is additionally soothing for the Vata and appealing to the Kapha.

RUNNING

Because of the pounding incurred by the body, excessive running should be avoided by Vatas. The lean Vata body type lacks the shock absorption needed for vigorous running. In moderation, on soft surfaces, it is okay. Kaphas and Pittas are well suited for this sport, but it is the Pitta-Vatas who excel. The ultraendurance runners are usually the bigger, slower, more endurance-paced Kapha types.

SKATING

Skating requires the talents of all three types. Although Pittas often excel at it, Vatas and Kaphas also do well. The types correlate to various skating styles: quick, aggressive, and graceful. Speed skaters usually have more Kapha qualities, while figure skaters have more Vata and Pitta.

SURFING

This sport demands balance, patience, and coordination, all qualities found in abundance in the Kapha type.

SWIMMING

Swimming is excellent for all body types. Vatas and Pittas excel in the short-distance events, while Kapha types excel in the longer, more endurance-oriented events. Basically, swimming is recommended for everyone who enjoys it.

TENNIS

Tennis requires the assets of all three major body types, although a Pitta-Kapha combination or Sama is probably best suited for success at the game. The exertion of singles can often be too much for an unconditioned Vata type. Doubles provides the needed exercise without the risk of over-doing it. Kapha types tend to play power tennis, and Pitta and Vata combinations play touch tennis. Sama types have all-around skills.

TRACK AND FIELD

Sprint/pole vault. The best sprinters have the best of all three types—Vata speed, Pitta strength, and Kapha endurance—needed to handle all the intense training.

High jump. This requires a lighter-framed Vata-Pitta body type, or the taller Vata-Kapha.

Shot put. Kapha-Pitta size and strength are required to excel.

Discus and javelin. The balanced Sama types excel, but the Kapha-Pitta nature also does well.

VOLLEYBALL

In this game, height, quick reactions, jumping ability, and power all come in handy. The Kapha qualities must be strongly present and are usually complemented by the Pitta type's drive to win. The Pitta-Kapha or Kapha-Pitta types excel, although the very tall Kapha-Vatas can also play a dominant role.

SPORTS SELECTION BY BODY TYPE—BASED ON BODY TYPE AND SEASON

YOUR MIND-BODY TYPE	VATA SEASON (Winter)	PITTA SEASON (Summer)	KAPHA SEASON (Spring)
	V	V	V
	P	P	P
	K	K	K
	V	P	V
	V	P	P
	V	V	K
	V	K	K
	P	P	K
	K	P	K
	V	P	K

Find your body type on vertical axis, find the current season on horizontal axis, and cross-reference the appropriate sports selection.

9

CHECKING THE BRAKES

I remember racing to the airport one cold, wet Boston morning only to find that my plane was delayed. The reason: one of the tires was low on air. I figured that at most it would be a five- to ten-minute delay.

Two hours later we were still on the ground, the tire was still low, and the "special pump" was still on its way. Even though I was late, I was happy to know there were strict safety standards and that the airline wouldn't cut corners. There are a series of preflight inspections that must check out, or they don't even start the engines.

It's the same when you get on a bicycle. If the brakes don't work, you don't go bike riding. If you get in your car and the headlights are out, you don't drive at night.

It seems only logical that we would treat our bodies with similar respect. When we're preparing for exercise, it seems worthwhile to run a few safety checks to make sure our bodies are ready, willing, and able to keep up with our enthusiastic minds.

WHEN TO REST

How do we know when the body is ready? And perhaps more important, how do we know when it is not—when, in fact, it needs to take the day off and rest?

The problem with knowing when to rest is that the mind almost always thinks that the body can do more than it actually can. The mind simply doesn't get as tired as the body while exercising, and if it is too busy to listen or has its own agenda (like the late Jim Fixx's rule that he run 10 miles every day, rain or shine), we can easily neglect the body's need for rest.

In endurance sports, athletes relish the days known as the "TV taper." These occur when an athlete, after training at high intensity for many months in order to be in peak form for a certain race, begins to taper down two or three days before the event, to get some much-needed rest. It's called a TV taper because almost everyone sits around watching TV during the time normally spent training.

Something fascinating happens to many athletes in this situation. In short, they get sick. A sore throat, a cold, a stomach flu, or some other ailment pops up. On race-day morning, the main topic of conversation is often how lousy the athletes feel. Many chalk it up to race-day jitters or use it as an excuse for poor performance. But I believe it is more than that.

When we push ourselves daily into exhaustion, whether in a health club or at home, or pounding the pavement, we are building a debt of fatigue and strain in the body that we will eventually have to settle. It's like borrowing money from the bank. Eventually you have to pay it back, and with interest.

When we keep pushing ourselves beyond our natural limits, the body must compensate to achieve the goals we have set. Over time, the fatigue of overtraining builds up. When the individual begins to taper down the training regimen, the stored-up fatigue and strain find their way out, often in the form of illness.

This happens because rest for the body means an opportunity to repair and rejuvenate itself. If the body has been overdriven, then the energy available from the increased rest begins to clean house. So, if some version of the TV-taper blues happens to you when you cut back on your exercise program, you can be pretty sure you've pushed yourself too hard.

THE DAILY STRESS CHECK

There is a very simple way to check how your body is doing, without any invasive blood tests. You can objectively assess whether you are overtraining, whether you should work out hard or easy, or if it might be better to take the day off and rest.

STEP 1
Take your resting pulse every morning for a few weeks to establish an average pulse rate. This is best done first thing in the morning, before getting out of bed. Keep a pulse-rate log next to your bed. (If you are not

familiar with how to take a pulse rate, refer to chapter 13, where I explain how to do it.)

Step 2

If the average pulse rate increases or decreases from one day to the next by more than 10 beats per minute (BPM), you should rest. If the heart changes its rhythm by 10 BPM, the body may be gearing up the immune system to fight an invading bacteria or virus, or it may just be under some extreme stress. The last thing the body needs to do on this day is a 20-mile run or a hard-driving aerobics class. It needs rest, to conserve energy. The body needs to properly restore its internal balance and return to its normal metabolic rate. If you didn't rest and went to work out, I can assure you it would be one of those days when you feel you "just don't have it"—you feel weak during workouts, and, as much as you push yourself, you just aren't performing properly, and you know it.

Keeping a daily morning-pulse log will give you an early clue to what kind of day you can expect. Whenever possible, when your heart rate is off, make it an easier day. Of course, you can't schedule your life around your morning heart rate. But within reason, and as much as possible, respect the needs of your body. When your gas gauge is on E, you give your car gas. When your body asks for rest, give it rest. The more we can exercise in accord with the body's needs, the greater degree of mind-body coordination we can access down the road.

Example: Suppose your average heart rate in the morning is 60 beats per minute. Maybe it fluctuated between 58 and 63, but generally it was about 60 every morning for a month. Then, one morning, you woke up and it was 70 BPM, for no apparent reason. This is an indication that you should take it easy that day. Don't schedule your hardest workout or log any overtime at work if you can help it. Try to stay relatively sedentary until your heart rate returns to normal.

As you learn more about your body and your pulse rate, you will be able to see how an elevation corresponds to how you feel. Many times we are so conditioned not to listen to our bodies that we can't hear them even when they are shouting at us.

THE LUNAR CYCLE

In earlier chapters I have spoken of the seasonal and daily cycles, but I have not yet mentioned the monthly cycle of the moon. The tides are regulated by it, moods are often affected by it, and some plants' growing cycles are entrained (linked up) with it.

Without a doubt the most recognized lunar cycle in the human realm is the menstrual cycle. The menstrual cycle is a monthly cleansing cycle in which women have a great opportunity to eliminate built-up waste from their bodies. This is considered a great boon in Ayurveda, and a distinct advantage over men, who recognize no apparent connection with the cycles of the moon.

I remember that when Maharishi Ayur-Ved doctors first came to the United States some years ago, they made many comments about the inordinate number of menstrual problems in this country. They were also surprised to find women who were symptom-free routinely taking estrogen to prevent postmenopausal bone loss or osteoporosis. In India, women rarely get osteoporosis later in life, and the use of estrogen is relatively unknown.

Also, hysterectomies—shockingly, the most frequently performed surgery for women in the United States—are performed only in very extreme situations in India. This was something they couldn't fathom. After many months of touring the United States and consulting with thousands of patients, they drew some conclusions as to why menstrual difficulties and other problems with the female reproductive system were so prevalent.

The doctors concluded that women in the West are not reaping the benefits of the lunar cycle. They seem to regard this time as no different from any other time of the month, and as a result they experience only the problems, and not the benefits, of menstruation.

For some women, it has become a sign of weakness to admit to feeling anything but normal during this part of the monthly cycle. As a result, many women (including most women athletes) don't break stride at all; they move right through the menstrual period as if it weren't there. But it is there.

Just as seasonal changes trigger a cascade of transitions in nature that we need to respond to in order to maintain balance—in terms of our dress, diet, and behavior—the monthly menstrual cycle also demands a behavioral response to the obvious physical changes taking place.

The initial three days of menstruation are considered to be *resting days.* In ancient times, and to some extent in India today, women have been encouraged to take it easy during those days. The responsibilities of a menstruating woman are taken up by members of her extended family, leaving the woman free to engage only in light activity, if any.

The rationale behind this minivacation is that during this time the body is sloughing off the unfertilized lining of the uterus, as well as trying to move impurities down and out of the system through the reproductive organs. If large amounts of physical—or mental—activity are performed during this time, the energy (known as "prana" in Sanskrit) is redirected toward that activity rather than toward organizing a complete and efficient process of purification. If the policy of being active during menstruation is continued for many years, some symptoms will ultimately result.

> DOCTORS BLAME THE EXCESSIVE HORMONE DEPENDENCY, THE HIGH RATE OF HYSTERECTOMIES, AND THE MAJORITY OF MENSTRUAL COMPLAINTS ON OUR SOCIETY'S FAILURE TO UNDERSTAND THE BENEFITS OF REST DURING THE MENSTRUAL PERIOD.

This part of the monthly cycle can be an opportunity for a woman to completely rejuvenate and revitalize herself. Some even postulate that it is thanks to this regular cycle of menstrual cleansing that women live longer than men. Of course, we do not yet have proof of this, but men clearly lack this cleansing ability.

It is not realistic to ask Western women to conform to guidelines set down by an ancient and very different culture. Most women cannot simply shut down and do nothing during their menstrual flow. But they *can* moderate their schedule at that time of the month.

In business, for example, don't work long days during your period, and don't push yourself as you might during the rest of the month. If you are an athlete or if you exercise a lot, don't plan heavy workouts or races around that time. Grete Waitz, the world-class Norwegian runner, after many years of training finally realized that she didn't race as well during her period, and now she alters her training around that time.

Taking the time to nourish yourself during these few days will ensure a more productive and balanced mind and body during the rest of the month. It is an important part of respecting human nature, and it is a powerful means to ensure graceful menopausal changes later in life.

AMENORRHEA AND EXERCISE

We have been hearing experts say, "Listen to your body," for years. But how and what do we listen to? And is anybody really doing it?

Let me give you an example. A controversial phenomenon occurring among women athletes today is the large number of instances of amenorrhea, or cessation of menstruation. Researchers haven't pinpointed the exact cause, but a consensus is building that points to the combination of vigorous exercise and low body fat.

One report indicated that irregular menstrual cycles occur five times more often in women runners than in the general population. Women who chalk up many running miles and also have low body fat run an even higher risk of irregularity. In one study, 50 percent of women runners with both low body fat and high mileage had amenorrhea.

In some athletic circles, amenorrhea is actually regarded positively, as a physiological sign that training has reached new heights. But some research is telling quite a different story.

In a *Nova* documentary on the subject, Dr. Barbara Drinkwater compared the X rays of a 76-year-old woman suffering from severe osteoporosis with the X rays of a 22-year-old aerobics teacher who was suffering bone loss much like that seen in women after menopause. The aerobics teacher was overtrained physically, which resulted in extreme loss of body fat. Reduction of body fat is believed to disturb the hormonal balance, so that a normal amount of estrogen is not available. This triggers a menopausal response, and the monthly cycle stops.

When a woman repeatedly goes without a menstrual period, bone loss begins. In fact, the X rays of the 22-year-old aerobics teacher showed a virtually identical bone density to the 76-year-old woman with severe osteoporosis. This is dangerous for a physically active young woman. Fortunately, with proper diet and a reduced exercise load, the aerobics teacher saw her bones return to normal, and her menstrual cycle came back as well.

Certainly this is an extreme case, but personally I cannot imagine the body screaming more loudly for attention than in this example. Although many people believe that amenorrhea is a "normal" process for women athletes, I think it is one of the clearest examples of an overzealous mind driving the body into physiological imbalance. Is it necessary to put yourself through these changes in order to reach your fitness and competitive goals? If there was a way to reach your goals—and beyond—and still maintain a normal menstrual cycle, would that not be more desirable?

This issue takes us back to the central theme of this book. The reason why people do not exercise, and most people never experience the runner's high, is the same reason why women override their body's needs and thereby disturb the balanced functioning of their menstrual cycle. When you ignore the body's signals and push yourself to or beyond your limits, with no knowledge of how much exercise is good for you and how much more can be harmful, the results won't go unnoticed.

Many women who compete professionally maintain perfectly normal menstrual cycles. There are two ways to train: by listening, or not listening, to the needs of the body. The menstrual cycle is not a deterrent to athletic success. As a matter of fact, if respected rather than overruled, it can provide monthly rejuvenation along the way to maximum fitness.

GOING AGAINST THE GRAIN OF
MODERN SCIENCE

These recommendations may sometimes go against the trends of modern allopathic medicine. A customary medical remedy for PMS and menstrual discomfort is increased exercise, and many women do find that exercise helps them deal with a painful or uncomfortable period. However, this clearly departs from the viewpoint presented above. Exercise is fine during the pre- and postmenstrual phases of a woman's cycle. But during the menstrual period itself, vigorous exercise is contraindicated.

The rationale behind this recommendation can be understood only with some further knowledge. As noted above, if the prana, or vital energy, needed to maintain normal menstrual functioning is siphoned off to support the energy needs of exercise or work, ultimately it will lead to imbalance and the body's inability to menstruate efficiently. The reproductive organs, weakened by overtraining during the menstrual period, will drain the body's energy reserve, creating the classic PMS symptoms. It's like running or swimming right after a big meal. Everyone knows that this takes energy away from the digestive process, weakening the digestion.

So why do some women feel better if they exercise while menstruating? During the period, exercise can force the body to adapt and compensate, to take much-needed energy from the reproductive organs in order to produce a temporary sense of well-being. This can only leave the body in a more depleted condition, susceptible to future menstrual difficulties.

Many healthy women can get away with not taking extra rest during their menstrual flow. In the short run, they will be symptom-free. But from a preventive point of view, for later in life during and after menopause, give your body the chance to take rest if it needs it. If you never ask it, you'll never hear it. And if it's screaming, you'd better listen.

10

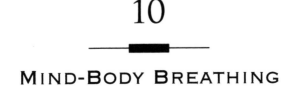

MIND-BODY BREATHING

When my three children were infants, I noticed that they could only breathe through their noses. For them, things were simple: the mouth was for eating, the nose for breathing.

At about two or three months old, my youngest one caught a cold and became so congested that he could barely breathe. At one point he was trying so hard to get air through his nostrils that I was afraid he might suffocate. The more congested he got, the harder it was for him to sleep, as he attempted to fill his lungs through his nose.

I wished I could tell him about breathing through his mouth. But his breathing strategy was genetically in place and, for the time being, not about to change. He simply did not know how to breathe through his mouth. As far as he was concerned, air was not a substitute for breast milk.

Humans come into this world as nose breathers. We are "obligate nose breathers," to be scientific, which means that we do not possess the voluntary ability to breath through our mouths. Mouth breathing is a learned response triggered by emergency stress.

If an infant's nose becomes completely obstructed, he or she will fight for nasal air until he begins to suffocate and starts to cry. The crying forces air through the mouth and into the lungs. Mouth breathing is a means of getting large quantities of air into the lungs quickly in order to deal with the emergency. Once the emergency is over, the child will go back to breathing through his or her nose until the next threat to survival.

The survival response triggers certain emergency fight-or-flight receptors in the sympathetic nervous system, which help the infant deal with the extreme stress. This shift from nose breathing to mouth breathing seems to be triggered only by stress. When infants are relaxed and calm, all their breathing is through the nose. Their first encounters with mouth breathing are survival-based and stress-ridden. When babies have to breathe through the mouth, they cannot nurse; thus, the loss of their primary source of nourishment and security is associated with the need to breathe through the mouth.

Thus it is that from an early age we are conditioned so that under the first sign of stress, including exercise stress later in life, we shift into our emergency mode of breathing—through the mouth. You can see this if you watch people running and exercising. Although the method of exercise breathing currently in favor is to inhale through the nose and exhale through the mouth, I don't see very many people doing it. If you visit a health club or a 10 K race, you will see that the vast majority of people have their mouths wide open.

NATURE'S WAY

In this section I will reintroduce you to a style of deep nasal breathing that you once knew: It comes as standard equipment in every newborn.

During exercise, there are two basic forms of breathing:

- chest and clavicular
- diaphragmatic

Utilizing *both* of these in sequence, along with the proper nasal breathing technique, will provide the simplest and most efficient means of respiration during exercise.

DIAPHRAGMATIC BREATHING

Diaphragmatic breathing is the most efficient means of respiration. Infants and young children are restricted to this kind of breathing because the physical structure needed for proper chest breathing is not yet sufficiently developed. There is a remarkable parallel in the calming and relaxing influence of deep, nasal, diaphragmatic breathing on a nursing infant, and on an athlete experiencing the runner's high during exercise. Reproducing this state of composure and calm is the key to making the experience of the Zone available to everyone.

The diaphragm is a flat, parachute-shaped muscle at the base of the lungs. As we inhale, this muscle contracts, drawing air into the lungs. This diaphragmatic action is particularly important, as it pulls air into the lower lobes of the lungs first. The blood supply to the lower lobes is gravity dependent, so that while we are upright there is far more blood available for oxygen exchange in the lower parts of the lungs. It is for this reason that diaphragmatic breathing, which draws air into those lower regions, is such an essential component of optimal exercise breathing.

During inhalation, as the diaphragm contracts and flattens out, the lower rib cage expands and the abdomen feels protruded. During exhalation, the contracted diaphragm relaxes into its dome-shaped parachute position. Exhalation, for both types of breathing, results primarily from the natural elastic recoil of the lungs. A tension on the inner surface of the lungs will retract the lungs, create the dome shape of the relaxed diaphragm, and expel the CO_2 and other gases. To completely expel the CO_2 from the lower lobes, the abdominal muscles have to engage, to squeeze out the residual air.

You can try this right now. As you exhale normally, you'll see that in order to squeeze the last bit of air out of your lungs, your abdomen has to contract slightly.

CHEST AND CLAVICULAR BREATHING

Most people in our society breathe mainly in the chest. This breath is performed largely by the expanding and lifting of the rib cage via the intercostal muscles. In extreme states of air hunger, the collar bones (clavicles) can also be lifted to lengthen the chest cavity and aid inhalation. This action is more difficult than diaphragmatic breathing and requires more work and a higher heart rate to perform.

Chest breathing fills the middle and upper portions of the lungs but doesn't efficiently engage the blood-rich lower lobes. Although it is easier to get large quantities of air in and out of the upper and middle lobes, the ample blood supply needed for a quality exchange, especially during oxygen-demanding exercise, is in the lower lobes. For chest breathing to supply enough oxygen, both breathing and heart rate must be faster.

THE BEAUTY OF THE BEAST

It is my belief that man, like most mammals, is designed to breathe through the nose and eat through the mouth, except in extraordinary circumstances when access to nasal air is insufficient. If nose breathing is performed correctly, the proper balance of diaphragmatic and chest breathing is naturally coordinated, without thought and without effort. We should not have to think about how we breathe; it should come naturally.

But we have forgotten how. We have been conditioned away from using the nose as our primary breathing instrument during exercise.

I have consulted with many comparative anatomists, and they all agree that animals in their natural state breathe through the nose when running. Some of the best runners in nature, such as horses, breathe only through the nose. Like infants, horses are obligate nose breathers. The unique shape of their palate makes it almost impossible for them to breathe through the mouth. When they run, their nostrils expand considerably to accommodate the large quantity of air needed for respiration.

Kangaroos clip along at about 35 miles per hour, comfortably breathing through the nose; elk, deer, zebra, and moose are other examples of nature's nose-breathing runners. Experts agree that most animals breathe only through the nose unless under stress, at which time they will mouth breathe. For them, as for us, the nose is for breathing and the mouth for eating.

Animals that do not sweat through their skin, such as the carnivorous dog, cat, lion, and wolf, must cool the blood supply to their brains by panting. However, even these animals are essentially nose breathers and breathe through the mouth only when they become overheated. Horses, camels, cows, deer, and the majority of the vegetarian mammals have porous skin like humans', which sweats for temperature regulation; nose breathing is their mode of respiration.

THE NOSE KNOWS

The nose, with its intricate design, is man's best choice for optimal respiration during both rest and exercise. To better understand the rationale behind the recommendation of nose breathing over mouth breathing, let's compare the two. Most modern physicians adhere to the belief that there is no significant difference. "The air all goes to the same place," they say. I disagree. The destination may be the same, but how it gets there, and in what form, can make all the difference in the world.

Consider the phenomenon of hyperventilation. Hyperventilation occurs due to deep or rapid mouth breathing, which takes in so much oxygen that it cannot be exchanged for CO_2 fast enough; oxygen builds up, creating a state of hyperoxygenation, or too much oxygen in the blood—potentially resulting in dizziness or fainting.

It is easy to hyperventilate while breathing through the mouth and next to impossible while breathing through the nose. You simply cannot get enough oxygen into the lungs fast enough through the nose. When air enters the body through the nose, it does so in a more refined, rarefied stream, compared with the huge quantity of air capable of being gulped through the mouth. This makes the two breathing instruments very different.

Hyperventilation is typically associated with anxiety and fear. Could this stress-triggered mouth breathing be a carryover from the infant's mouth-breathing survival response to the threat of suffocation? Many studies support this view. Some researchers have suggested that chronic mouth and chest breathing can actually stimulate a sustained fight-or-flight form of arousal, common in states of anxiety and fear. This contrasts sharply with other studies that have shown the usefulness of nose breathing techniques to *relax* body and mind—exactly the opposite response.

During exercise, it is common for unnecessarily high levels of oxygen to be exhaled along with carbon dioxide. You can see this if you watch a pack of cross-country runners coming across the finish line. They are usually hyperventilating, huffing and puffing with their mouths wide open. Their purpose is to blow off more carbon dioxide in order to absorb more of the desperately needed oxygen.

One of the problems with push-to-the-limit training is that with increased exercise and increased blood flow to the lungs, the time the blood stays in the lungs for oxygen exchange is shortened due to the faster heart rate, which pushes the blood through more rapidly. So, even though the mouth/chest breathing is providing an abundance of oxygen to the mid and upper lung, the accelerated heart rate is decreasing the time for the lungs to exchange it. This respiratory *inefficiency* shows the crucial need for nasal, diaphragmatic breathing, which accesses the blood-rich lower lobes and takes the stress off the heart.

Remember the formula for the exercise high: dynamic activity coexisting with composure, comfort, and silence. Watching the breath will be our first step toward success.

In one of our case studies on breath rate during a bicycle stress test, we found that as the exercise load increased, the breath rate went up, peaking for the subject (see Graph D) at 47 breaths per minute using conventional mouth breathing. At the maximum breath rate, all of our subjects were anaerobic, gasping for air and pushing right to the edge of their capacity.

The same subject was tested two days later on the same stress test, except that he used nasal breathing and the techniques of Invincible Athletics. This time the breathing was comfortable the entire time, even at the highest level of stress, and the average breath rate was 14 breaths per minute. This result is even more impressive when you consider that the average breath rate for people *at rest* is around 18 breaths per minute.

All of our subjects had been using the Invincible Athletics techniques for at least 12 weeks prior to the testing. This particular case study was a

Graph D

Breath Rate
Invincible Athlete vs. Conventional Athlete

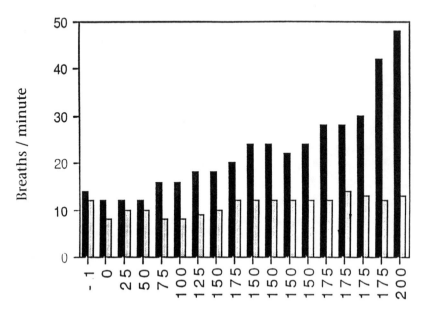

WATTS
(resistance increasing over time during bicycle ergometer submaximal stress test)

■ Conventional Athlete
□ Invincible Athlete

demonstration of a state of maximum respiratory efficiency developed from using this program. If, with training and patience, you can perform the same exercise workload with only 14 breaths per minute instead of 47 using conventional techniques, what reason could there be not to do it? "I will never breathe through my mouth again" was the sentiment of all the subjects after completing both tests. Why burn 8 miles to the gallon when you can get 30?

PERCEIVED EXERTION

I think it's safe to say that we all feel exercise requires physical strain in order to be effective. When the strain is taken away, many people feel, at first, "I'm not doing enough." When our subjects completed this comparison, they were amazed at how different the two tests felt. During and after the mouth-breathing sessions, they were physically strained. During and upon completion of the nose-breathing workouts, they felt surprisingly invigorated.

This was measured using the Borg Scale of Perceived Exertion (see graph C on page 17). This test measures how the individual feels, in terms of comfort and exertion, on a scale of 1 to 10, with 10 being maximum effort and strain. As you can see, the individual using conventional mouth-breathing techniques took himself to the maximal level of exertion at the maximal load. Two days later the same individual performed the same work using our principles, and the perceived level of exertion was about half.

I'm sure you will agree that exercise is more enjoyable when it is performed with more efficiency and you experience less strain.

PREMATURE NOSE FAILURES

It is said that breathing through the nose is 150 times more difficult than breathing through the mouth. This is probably the reason why the exercise community has dismissed the nose as an efficient breathing device. When people begin training with nose breathing, they frequently feel they are working with an insufficient source of oxygen. But with practice, they realize they are replacing quantity with quality.

If you tested an average individual—untrained in nose breathing during exercise—one day with mouth breathing and the next with nose breathing, you would surely find that the mouth easily outperforms the nose. I remember that when I first started running using nose breathing, I couldn't come close to the pace I was accustomed to. But, after 3 months, I noticed a remarkable improvement. After 6 months, my nose decidedly outperformed my mouth.

The one drawback—if you consider it a drawback—is that it takes some time to recondition the body to breathe correctly, particularly during high-intensity exercise. We usually want instant results from a fitness program, and results that are measured in quantities: how much weight you can lift, how fast you can run, and so on. With this program, the measurement of your success will not be limited to how much you can do, but, more important, with how little effort you can it do. You will also find that your exercise experience will take an enormous leap in enjoyment.

When you see yourself running faster every day, with your breath rate stable at 15 or 20 breaths per minute, you will begin to feel the true meaning of the word *fitness*.

It doesn't take a lot of skill to go out and push yourself to exhaustion with daily exercise. Sure, it takes discipline and commitment, but if you pour that same intensity into this program, before long you will be runing as fast as your legs can carry you, effortlessly, as you continue to breathe comfortably through your nose at a resting breath rate. The amount of time it takes to adjust your system to this new style of breathing, to the point where you feel comfortable exercising, averages between 3 and 10 weeks. This is a broad time span, but the difference is simply because we are all unique.

I recently received a phone call from a cross-country coach in a private midwestern high school. He said, "John, you've got to come and videotape our girls coming across the finish line using your principles."

The typical scene at the end of a high school girls' cross-country meet can only be described as insane. If you're not familiar with it, I suggest you watch a meet at your local high school. The girls are pushed, cheered, and coaxed to drive themselves across the line with every last gasping breath in their souls! You will see them screaming, crying, cursing, celebrating, and throwing up. This whole gamut is usually represented, but the common denominator is total exhaustion.

Coach Schutt continued, "This is our second year doing the program, and our girls are now crossing the finish line with the winners, medaling, and feeling totally composed, breathing comfortably through the nose. The contrast is unbelievable. Our girls are finishing with ease, while the other teams cross the line hyperventilating and screaming with exhaustion.

"Our best girl, Rohini Grace, is only a sophomore. She sprints the last half-mile and still maintains an easy breath rate through her nose. She places in nearly every meet. We've tested her, and her average heart rate after an all-out finish is 140 BPM. [This remarkably low heart rate corresponds to the low breath rate. I will talk more about it in chapter 12.] She qualified for the state championships, not bad for a sophomore.

"The other coaches used to think I was crazy for not pushing my kids, and would constantly criticize the program—but this year the tables have turned. Now the coaches are always asking about the program, and commenting on the talent that we have. One coach said to me, after he saw Rohini cruise across the finish line, 'Why aren't you pushing that girl?' But before I could say anything, another coach stepped in and said, 'Don't worry about her, she's in good hands.' "

I commonly get reports from serious participants in the Invincible Athletics program, telling me that they never have to breathe through the mouth, even during an anaerobic sprint workout. Runners like Warren Wechsler, the athlete I described in chapter 1, can nasal breathe through high-intensity sprint workouts without strain. When the body becomes adjusted to nasal breathing, the nose provides the same sufficient flow of oxygen to the human lungs as does the nose of a Thoroughbred racehorse to the lungs of the horse.

When you first apply the breathing techniques in this chapter, be prepared to cut your performance in half. If you're willing to backpedal for a few weeks, you will soon see yourself doing the same workouts as before, only now you will be breathing with full respiratory efficiency, comfortably through the nose. After that—the sky's the limit.

INSIDE THE NOSE

An analysis of the anatomy of the nose leaves no question that it is the primary breathing apparatus for humans. Inside, it is made up of turbinates, or ridges, which act as turbines to swirl the air into a refined stream most suitable for oxygen exchange. The entire passageway is lined with a protective mucus-producing membrane, to keep it moist and ward off infection. (With mouth breathing, the mucous membranes in the throat dry out, increasing the risk of irritation and infection.) The mucous membranes work together with small hairlike cilia to clean, filter, and prepare the air for maximum oxygenation. The air is warmed, cooled, or moistened, depending on the conditions, by the highly sophisticated design of the nasal passage.

The mouth, on the other hand, is the more direct emergency route. It bypasses all the preliminary phases, and the cold, dry, unfiltered air is allowed to enter directly into the lungs. This is risky business and is therefore reserved only for emergencies, as with the overcongested infant.

The shunting of air directly from the mouth to the lungs appears to trigger a survival response, and as a result activates the fight-or-flight response from the sympathetic nervous system. This aspect of the autonomic (involuntary) nervous system is designed to deal with stress-related emergencies. It is the same response you would have if you were frightened by a bear in the woods: a mouth-open, loud, fearful gasp for air. Your heart rate would increase and adrenaline would shoot into your blood as a means of gearing up for a potentially needed burst of energy.

This natural response is wonderfully effective in life-or-death emergencies. But when you are breathing with large, gasping mouth breaths while running around the block, your nervous system is getting the same survival message. There's no bear, and no reason to fear for your life, yet your body is gearing up its emergency response pattern.

LEVEL 1 BREATHING

Before I explain more of the differences between mouth and nose breathing, I'd like you to experience them both for yourself.

Sit comfortably, up straight, and take a big breath, inhaling and exhaling through your mouth. Take a full, maximum breath in, and let it all out, breathing only through the mouth. Repeat this 3 times.

Then take 3 deep breaths through your nose. Maximum breath in and maximum breath out. Breathe only through the nose.

Repeat this cycle a couple of times, and try to notice the differences.

I have performed this little experiment with literally thousands of people and have polled their experiences. Maybe you had a similar response. The most common observations were:

"It takes longer to breathe through the nose." This is due to the smaller stream of air allowed by the nasal passages. Also, because the breath is naturally deeper, it takes more time to fill the lungs with the narrower stream of nasal air.

"I get dizzy when I breathe through the mouth." This is due to the hyperventilation response discussed above. The mouth can inhale more oxygen than the lungs can exchange, creating a potential state of hyper-oxygenation and a feeling of lightheadedness.

"Through the mouth it seems more shallow." A natural and spontaneous mouth breath will usually fill the upper chest or upper lobes of the lungs first, giving the experience of a more shallow breath.

"It feels deeper through the nose." The nasal breath is a more relaxed breath, which spontaneously allows both the upper and lower parts of the chest cavity to expand. The slower nasal breath also allows time for the diaphragm to engage in pulling the air into the lower lobes, making the breath feel deeper.

"Through the mouth it feels like it is from the upper chest only." Because the mouth breath is a faster breath, with a larger quantity of air being transported, the upper rib cage expands first to accommodate the rush of oxygen. It takes longer to penetrate the lower lobes, which are often not fully inflated by an upper chest breath.

"I feel calmer when breathing through the nose." Because it takes longer to draw the air in through the nose, the diaphragm has time to suck the oxygen into the lower chest. This lower diaphragmatic activation is said to stimulate the parasympathetic nervous system, which, by contrast to the sympathetic fight-or-flight response, actually calms and relaxes the body. This is why nose-breathing techniques have been recommended for thousands of years for dealing with anxiety and nervous system disorders. (See chapter 16.)

"It is uncomfortable to breathe through the mouth." As we have seen, breathing through the mouth is associated with a survival response. A deep mouth breath excites and stimulates the body to guard against stress, and may impart an uncomfortable experience of nervousness.

"Through the nose the breath comes from the diaphragm. It feels better to breathe through the nose." It usually feels better to breathe through the nose for the exact opposite reasons why the mouth breath feels uncomfortable. With the nose the breath takes longer, bringing a more relaxed feeling. Its deeper penetration triggers the parasympathetic nervous system, which calms and relaxes both the mind and the body.

In Level 1, simple nasal breathing will provide maximum respiratory efficiency. Let the comfortable rhythm of the breath through the nose set the pace during exercise.

Level 2 breathing can be employed even from day one, as long as it is comfortable.

LEVEL 2 BREATHING

Although nose breathing is more efficient than breathing through the mouth, it too can be improved upon. There are specific breathing techniques that can dramatically enhance the effectiveness of nose breathing during exercise.

In her book *Never Be Nervous Again*, Dorothy Sarnoff tells a story about the late Yul Brynner doing what seemed to her an odd exercise to calm himself before going on stage. She saw him pushing against a wall, making some strange grunting sounds. When she asked why he was doing it, he responded that it helped him control his nervousness. She concluded that for some reason, when Brynner contracted his abdomen, it somehow calmed him down. Sarnoff then modified his method for use by apprehensive public speakers, to help them control their nervousness before going out to speak.

A breathing exercise known as *ujjayi pranayama* has been recorded throughout the ages to have an effect on calming the mind and body. For exercise we use a similar technique that I like to call Darth Vader breathing because of the sound it makes.

STEP 1 Inhale normally through the nose. At first, do not take a large breath. It will be easy to master this technique with shallow breaths in the beginning.

STEP 2 During the exhale, breathe out only through the nose. As you exhale, constrict the throat slightly, as if you were lightly snoring. The sound should be a little like Darth Vader. You will notice that in normal nose breathing you can feel the air coming out through the nostrils, similar to the feeling you get when you blow your nose. In this technique you will feel a sensation in your upper throat; it doesn't feel as if the air is moving through your nostrils at all. Of course this is just an illusion; your mouth is closed, and there is simply no other way out!

STEP 3 Try making this sound during the nasal exhale, without contracting your abdominal muscles. Go ahead and do it now. If you are doing the Darth Vader breathing correctly, you will find it impossible to make that sound without slightly contracting your stomach muscles.

STEP 4 If you're not sure you've got it right, try it this way: Instead of focusing on exhaling through your nose and constricting your throat, think about squeezing the air out from your tummy by tightening your stomach muscles. You will find that the tighter you make your stomach during the exhale, the more pronounced the Darth Vader resonant sound will be.

STEP 5 If you're still not sure, take out a pair of sunglasses and blow on them, with your mouth open, as if to fog them up for cleaning. You will make a HAAA sound that comes from inside your throat rather than your mouth. Now, close your mouth and make the same glass-fogging sound, but through your nose. It is the exact same breath, only done with the nose rather than the mouth. The only slight difference is that, instead of just a short glass-fogging burst, I want you to carry that HAAA sound throughout the exhale. The same breath that cleans your glasses with the mouth open will mimic Darth Vader with the mouth closed.

STEP 6 Now that you have mastered making this sound with a shallow breath, begin to increase the size of the breath, ensuring a quality, resonant, Darth Vader sound! Keep increasing the depth of the breath until you are taking in every last bit of air and squeezing out every last bit. Practice this as much as possible while sitting or walking, because the better you make this sound now with a deep maximal breath, the easier it will be to apply it to your exercise program.

THE LEVEL 2 BENEFIT PLAN

As discussed in steps 3 and 4, the abdominal muscles have to contract to perform this breathing properly. We forget that the abdominal muscles are one of the primary muscles of exhalation. Without them, we wouldn't be able to move all the air (primarily carbon dioxide) out of the lower lobes of the lungs. Like most people, you probably don't feel your stomach contracting during ordinary breathing. Most of us breathe like rabbits, little tiny shallow breaths from the upper chest, known as *costal* breaths. To say the least, this kind of breathing is extremely inefficient.

The problem is that after so many years of this shallow, rabbit breathing, the rib cage becomes frozen. It moves up and down a little but loses most of its ability to move dynamically—that is, to expand and contract. A complete expansion and contraction of the rib cage for each breath are essential for good health. The ribs should be like ribboned levers that expand and contract with each breath, internally massaging the thoracic organs, abdominal organs, and spine. If the ribs are supple like ribbons and moving fully with proper breathing, the massage they provide helps maintain a flexible, young, supple body and mind.

The average adult breathes 26,000 times per day. If done correctly, each and every breath can be rejuvenating and invigorating. If not done correctly, the rib cage becomes truly a cage, locking up and restricting the normal functioning of the respiratory system.

All twelve of our ribs attach to the spine. With proper respiration each breath ensures flexibility and resiliency in the spine and the central nervous system, which is housed within it. If caged in by improper breathing, before long the spine becomes rigid and stiff. This is one main reason why people later in life are often in the chiropractic office, trying to relieve stiffness and pain. Just breathing correctly for one day would provide 26,000 opportunities for the body to become normal and flexible once again.

The effect on the spine of proper breathing is greater than you might think. Joseph Bollin was a 55-year-old runner who took my course. He loved to run but had recurring bouts of mid-back pain and headaches, which forced him to limit how much exercise he could do. He applied what he learned in the course to his running and soon began to realize that he could run without pain.

In the beginning he was running much more slowly than his normal pace, but within a few weeks he saw himself improving. Despite a little impatience, he decided to stick with the program. I spoke to him six months later. He was headache-free and only vaguely remembered the mid-back pain that used to plague him when he ran.

There are many reasons why people feel better structurally when exercising in this way, but the breathing alone can provide a subtle but powerful massage from the ribs to the joints of the spine and ultimately throughout the entire body.

If you are a swimmer, by now you have no doubt asked the question, "How do I swim and breathe through my nose?" First of all, before you can breathe correctly in the water, you must learn to breathe on land. After you've developed a certain level of nose-breathing skill during aerobic activity on land, you can apply the same skill while mouth breathing. Breathing correctly with the mouth is not imposssible, but if the habit of taking short, big, upper-chest gulps of air becomes the norm, the ability to take air into the lower lobes of the lungs efficiently is lost. With practice, you can learn to take a deep mouth breath while swimming, filling both the lower and upper lobes of the lungs. The exhale during swimming would still be through the nose, using the Darth Vader technique. This will allow the exhale to be longer and the number of strokes per breath to be greater. As you contract your abdomen during the exhale, your buttocks are naturally pushed out of the water, creating a planing effect. With practice, this breathing can give you more ease, comfort, and efficiency as you pull yourself through the water.

LEVEL 2—DARTH VADER MAGIC

The use of the diaphragm, particularly during Darth Vader breathing, ensures the filling of the lower lobes of the lungs, where the majority of the oxygen exchange takes place. Some experts project that as much as two-thirds of the population never accesses these more efficient lower lobes. Making full use of every square inch of the lungs' capacity for oxygen exchange is the necessary first step in high-performance respiration.

In Darth Vader breathing, contraction of the abdomen is a natural and consistent component of the breathing process. As you've seen, it is impossible to make the Darth Vader sound without contracting the abdomen. This makes proper breathing simple: *Just make that sound, and the rest will happen automatically.* The abdominal contraction pushes the abdomen up against the diaphragm and the lungs' lower lobes, squeezing out the CO_2 from the bottom up. Once the CO_2 is effectively removed from the lungs, the freshly inhaled oxygen can access the more capillary-rich lower lobes for potential oxygen exchange.

I have spoken to hundreds of people who have taken expensive Yoga classes and courses in breathing. Despite all their classes, they often ask me, "Does the stomach go in or out when you inhale?" I tell them—politely—that they would be better off not knowing. When you breathe correctly making the Darth Vader sound, the stomach naturally does exactly what it's supposed to do for optimal breathing. Before long, the Darth Vader sound becomes second nature, and the thinking process can be removed from the complications of breathing.

The contracting of the abdominal muscles is also said to put a slight pressure on the heart. Yoga experts say that this has a positive effect on the mechanics of the heart's pumping action, improving its efficiency. The diaphragmatic contraction is also said to have a "pulling" effect on blood flow to and from the heart, further increasing cardiovascular efficiency. These effects, although not yet confirmed by research, would occur only when breathing is complete, deep, and normal.

A more established benefit of abdominal contraction is its effect on the parasympathetic nervous system. The vagus nerve (tenth cranial nerve) regulates much of the parasympathetic activity in the body. The vagus nerve attaches to the heart and is stimulated by the pressure initiated by the abdominal muscles pushing on the diaphragm and the heart during exhalation. This stimulation activates the parasympathetic nervous system to lower the heart rate, producing a calming effect.

In practical terms, this means that the fast heart rates, sweaty palms, and prerace jitters associated with sympathetic dominance are controllable with the parasympathetic influence of deep nasal diaphragmatic breathing.

In our research, we found that the calming parasympathetic activity actually increased during exercise using our techniques, while sympathetic survival activity decreased. (Autonomic nervous system activity was measured from heart rate variability during a submaximal bicycle stress test.) As far as we can tell, activation of the parasympathetic nervous system during exercise is an unprecedented finding. Normally, as you might expect, this calming system is suppressed during exercise, while the sympathetic system becomes dominant.

The sympathetic system increases the heart rate and stimulates the adrenal glands to produce stress-fighting hormones, which are useful in preparing for and dealing with exercise stress. However, this natural production of adrenal steroids ultimately has a catabolic effect on the body—that is, it breaks the body down. (In the same way, taking anabolic steroids allows for the creation of larger muscles, but accelerates the degeneration of other body tissues.) In our exercise program, the catabolic, degenerative effect is markedly reduced, thus giving rise to fewer injuries and less physical wear and tear.

BREATHE AWAY BUTTERFLIES

A TECHNIQUE TO QUICKLY DISSOLVE TENSION
BEFORE COMPETITION

It's all right to have butterflies in your stomach. Just get them to fly in formation.

Ancient nasal breathing techniques like the one I have nicknamed Darth Vader breathing have been known for centuries to have a calming effect on the nervous system. One I recommend is called *ujjayi pranayama*. It is very effective in times of stress and has been reported to be helpful in states of anxiety, fear, worry, and insomnia.

The technique gives an athlete a wonderful way to maintain composure while waiting to compete. The pressure of race-day stress for an athlete is unparalleled; the intensity of waiting for the start of the event can be overwhelming. This simple breathing technique, performed while sitting down waiting for your event, can be of great help in fighting stress and warding off unproductive thoughts.

Traditionally in *ujjayi pranayama*, you make the snoring sound on both the inhalation and the exhalation. You will find that to make that sound while inhaling, you will constrict your throat in the same way as when you exhale, but you will have to breathe with considerably less force. This is particularly true in the beginning, when you are first finding out where in the throat it is most comfortable to make the sound. *Ujjayi pranayama* is usually done while comfortably seated, for about 5 to 10 minutes per sitting.

Laura Rarig is an avid runner and marathoner in Los Angeles who took my course shortly after she had endured her first marathon. Laura had battled with knee and ankle pain throughout her training; only physical therapy and chiropractic care had allowed her to keep on. On the day of her first marathon, the pain returned soon after she started running. Determined, she endured the pain and finished in 4 hours 20 minutes.

Shortly afterward, Laura scheduled another marathon for six months down the road. She also took my seminar and started training using the principles in this book. She started out slowly, as she needed to build respiratory efficiency, and gradually picked up speed. She had discontinued treatments for her knees and ankles, figuring that she would deal with the problems when they came. To her surprise, the aches and pains never reappeared. She trained right on schedule, and, using the Invincible Athletics methods, finished the race—pain-free and 25 minutes faster than her previous time.

THE SCIENCE OF PRANA

There is yet another factor that makes breathing supremely important. In many cultures, the breath has long been associated with the force of life itself. The Greek word for breath, *pneuma* (from which we get words like *pneumatic* and *pneumonia*), also means "soul" or "spirit." In China this life energy is called *chi*, in Japan *ki*, and in India it is known as *prana*. In the martial arts, Zen archery, and Yoga, the knowledge and control of one's prana is considered the key to mental and physical success. Although the existence of prana hasn't yet been verified or measured by objective scientific methods, its existence and effects are well known.

I would venture to say that most coaches recognize the need to develop both the mind and the body to succeed in today's competitive world. Prana is that which connects the mind and the body. The body's life force, or prana, is carried into the body by oxygen, water, and food. This is why copious amounts of pure water and fresh, well-cooked food, along with breathing exercises, are fundamental components of all the ancient sciences.

When you breathe in through the nose, prana, which is carried by oxygen, enters the nasal cavity. The air while in the nose is prepared for exchange in the lungs, but the prana is said to travel into the brain along the olfactory nerve, which transports a smell or scent from the nasal passage to the appropriate centers in the brain. The first stop for the prana is therefore in the brain, which when enlivened can coordinate with any or all parts of the body engaged in physical activity.

When we breathe through the mouth, the air and prana move directly, unprepared, into the lungs. The air, along with its prana, travels in and out of the body, never entering the brain via the nasal passage.

If exercise is for the purpose of enhancing mind-body coordination, doesn't it make sense to access the brain first and then the rest of the body? With proper nasal diaphragmatic breathing, the role of prana is heightened, as it is capable of nourishing the control centers in the brain as well as penetrating the deepest levels of the lungs and bloodstream.

In *Science Studies Yoga*, Dr. James Funderburks describes a 106-pound Indian Yogi who exhibited remarkable strength for his 67-year-old body. He strapped a ³⁄₈-inch metal chain around his waist and to his feet. The chain was previously tested to withstand 650 pounds of pressure without so much as bending. The small Yogi began with a minute of preparatory breathing exercises, then as he exhaled he pushed his feet against the chain. The chain shattered!

DARTH VADER BOARD BREAKING

Popular images of the martial arts in the media have made us all familiar with the breaking of boards and bricks with a version of the famous karate chop, usually accompanied by a shout. When studying karate, the beginning student learns the value of that shout, known as the *kya*, a loud, short, forceful yell that engages the solar plexus with the breath. (The solar plexus is the junction between the rib cage and the abdominal muscles.)

During a board break, the student will yell "Kya!" while contracting this area. If one held the breath during a board break, the body would become rigid, the coordination of mind and body would break down, and the attempt would most likely fail. The kya is a method of focused breathing in order to enhance mind-body coordination during physical activity. Tennis star Monica Seles is famous for her center-court kyas.

The focused energy of the kya is very useful. During a golf swing, for example, if the breath is held tight, the body becomes rigid and loses its rhythm. If breathing is too relaxed and without control, the brick-breaking focus of the kya is lacking. A loud, bellowing kya accompanying each swing probably won't get you many new golf invitations. Fortunately, however, the same effect can be had without all the ruckus. During Darth Vader breathing, the abdomen is contracted and the focal point of contraction is the solar plexus, as it is during the kya.

With a properly coordinated nasal breath, a golfer can have both the focus provided by a held breath and the power and fluidity of a kya. Do it this way: Inhale during the backswing, and as you initiate the swing, begin the exhale, making the Darth Vader sound. This sound, although slightly audible, is much less noticeable than the board-bashing kya.

The primary role of prana, however, is not in hitting tennis balls or breaking bricks with your hands. Its function is to establish the highest coordination of mind and body. Remember according to history, exercise is for rejuvenation and to perfect the coordination of mind and body, in order to access more of our unlimited human potential; for our forebears, this was the highest purpose life had to offer.

When prana is flowing most efficiently in the body, it produces a state of natural euphoria. Charlie Morenus wrote me this letter, relating his first runner's high experience:

"I normally run about three or four miles a day. I would start out running at about a 7½-minute/mile pace and keep it there. My usual experience was that after about a quarter of a mile, I'd wonder how I was going to finish the workout. I now know I was in oxygen debt right away. As you can imagine, this was sort of drudgery, but being from the old school, I sucked it up and ran through it.

"When I started to run using your principles, all that changed. And my last workout was incredible. I warmed up properly and got into a comfortable breathing pattern, in and out through my nose. After about a mile, I had a feeling of euphoria that I never had in activity before. I was so settled in that pace, and so comfortable with it, that I was running for periods with my eyes closed! (Fortunately, I was in a park with lots of open space.) This experience continued for two miles or so. When I finished running, it was the first time in my memory that I didn't feel the least bit tired."

Charlie wasn't out to break any records, but he was still able to experience the runner's high. More important, he felt rejuvenated after running. This experience of joy and increased vitality is essential to the success of an exercise program. If the "old school" provides only drudgery during each workout, is it surprising that the exercise routine falls apart and a sedentary lifestyle sets in?

TRAINING TIP NO. 10
THE PERFECT SWING

Hold the golf club in your left hand (for a right-handed swing). Swing the club back and forth, breathing in during the backswing and using a Darth Vader exhalation as you would strike the ball. Repeat until you can do 30 in a row without strain. In the beginning it seems cumbersome only because the breathing is not customary. It will soon become second nature and thought will not interfere. This same breathing and swinging technique can be applied to almost all racquet sports with great success.

Euphoria is definitely a motivator to a continued fitness program, but so is improving the performance and fitness curve. For a fitness program to work on a permanent basis, it must provide all the essential ingredients. It must be enjoyable, so people will want to continue. It must regularly provide the euphoric experience of the exercise high. And it must provide the incentive to be "the best." Not the best in the world, perhaps, but a personal best. Human potential is unlimited, and people often use exercise as a tool to taste a sliver of that potential.

DARTH VADER FOR KIDS

One ingredient missing from most exercise programs is its application to children. As I discussed earlier, our habitual likes and dislikes regarding physical fitness as adults are often shaped during childhood. If you grow up hating exercise, chances are you won't seek it out as an adult. Thus, keeping the kids excited about exercise is the only real solution to establishing a fit America.

Kids, because they are so pliable, respond very quickly to these breathing techniques. When a child sees that this breathing method works and doesn't have to hurt—in fact it makes you feel better—a growing interest in exercise and athletics is cultivated. Betty Pollack wrote me a note about the success of her 15-year-old daughter:

"I taught my daughter the Darth Vader breathing technique over the summer. Last year, at the end of the track season, she had run the mile in 10 minutes plus, with side aches and dizziness. (This was not fast enough to pass the class, according to the standards of the President's Council on Physical Fitness and Sports.) She tried out for field hockey in September, having had little vigorous exercise all summer. Using this breathing, she ran the tryout mile in 8 minutes and 36 seconds with no side pains or dizziness until the last few seconds, when she switched to mouth breathing to sprint to the end."

THE NASAL HIGHWAY

In the beginning stages of retraining with Darth Vader breathing, it is common and sometimes necessary to breathe through the mouth at the end of a race, when the body has its response to competitive stress. As long as you do this only part of the time, the cumulative results of exercise will be lasting and enjoyable.

The very best way to gauge your state of respiratory efficiency is to compare your current workout level, before starting this program, with the same exercise performed only with nose breathing. If you cannot perform at the same level using your nose, then there is room for improved breathing. In just a few weeks you will begin to see nose breathing supporting more and more vigorous exercise. It is a matter of reconditioning, and while it can be slow going in the beginning, it is well worth it in the end.

For those who have nasal congestion, believe it or not, nasal breathing is the best cure. It is more difficult in the beginning, but, in time, exercise levels will improve and the once-congested nose will be open and pumping prana into the mind and body. One of the worst things you can do if the passageway is blocked, even structurally, is not to use it. If you don't use it, it will surely never work properly.

If you suffer from such breathing difficulties, it will be extra slow going at the outset, and you will probably have to switch to mouth breathing more often, but with time, your nasal passages will open and accommodate optimal respiration.

In short, there is no excuse for not breathing through your nose! Set new goals. See how much work you can do with the least amount of breaths. Less is definitely more when it comes to breathing and the amount of effort needed to become physically fit.

HELPFUL HINT

For excessive congestion in cold weather, or other difficulties with nasal breathing, try this:

Sniff a little sesame oil first thing in the morning, before bed, and before each workout. Soak a Q-tip with cold-pressed uncooked sesame oil and lubricate the inside of your nose a couple of times, sniffing after each application to draw the oil upward. Sesame oil is good for most any body type, but the pure Pitta types may prefer to use ghee (clarified butter) or coconut oil for an enhanced cooling effect.

11

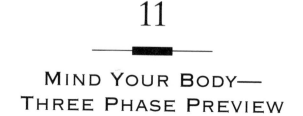

Mind Your Body—
Three Phase Preview

When putting all the information together into a workout and fitness plan, there are a few basic ingredients to factor in. First is knowledge of your body type (chapter 4), which will act as a blueprint. All aspects of your workout can be structured according to the needs of your individual constitution. The appropriate time of day for your workout (chapter 6) can be selected according to your body type. If you haven't yet decided on a sport, you can choose from a large variety, according to body type and season (chapter 8). And, since fitness is not just a matter of exercise but of total health, body-type–specific nutritional and dietary recommendations are given in chapter 7.

Once you have accomplished this, you're ready to start the Three Phase Workout. If the Darth Vader breathing (chapter 10) is uncomfortable for any reason, then begin by using deep, nasal, diaphragmatic breathing during the workout. Once you are accustomed to the nasal breathing, add the Darth Vader technique. Darth Vader breathing will become second nature and will be the breathing technique during the entire workout. In time, you'll never leave home without it.

The Warm-Up—Preparing the Mind

Before starting the workout, we must, as in any fitness program, warm up the body. Because this is a mind-body fitness program, we must start by integrating the mind with the body. Many techniques are available today, such as visualization, biofeedback, and subliminal programming, but only one predates them all by more than five thousand years. Defined as the union of mind and body, it is called Yoga.

In this workout, we will use Yoga to establish maximum coordination of mind and body at the very beginning. Then we will gracefully build a workout based on the needs of the mind and body together, rather than just the desires of the mind. The Yoga mind-body coordination established up front is maintained throughout the workout to ensure regular experience of the exercise high.

In chapter 1, this integration was demonstrated by the production of alpha waves in the brain during an exercise stress test. These results proved dramatically different from the typical beta brain activity seen during conventional exercise, indicating a mind and body under stress. Here we begin the workout by exercising the mind, creating silence and alpha brain waves, or what I like to call the eye of the hurricane. From here we will slowly build the activity or exercise around this silence until we have successfully created a mature hurricane, totally silent while incredibly dynamic.

Since the athletes who find the Zone always report that it is effortless and automatic, let's not start our workouts with any other experience. Let's allow the experience of comfort to set the pace for the workout in terms of how much weight to lift or how fast to run. With the experience of comfort in place from the outset, the Zone can be established at the first step of every workout and maintained to the last.

To help you achieve deep mind-body coordination, we will use the Vedic exercise known as *Surya Namaskar*, or Sun Salute. The is the only classical series of Yoga postures linked with the breath. Since the breath moves prana, and the movement of prana coordinates the mind and body, this is the perfect exercise to initiate a workout and capture the experience of the Zone from the word go.

THE RESTING PHASE—EXERCISING THE LUNGS

Once you've coordinated mind and body using the Sun Salute, you are ready to start the workout. In the Resting Phase, you will begin the run, the tennis warm-ups, the exercise bike, etc., but only for 5 to 10 minutes. You will keep the exertion level unusually low and the breathing unusually deep.

In this phase we are primarily exercising the lungs. By *this* intentional maximized breathing, all the lobes of the lungs and the hard-to-reach corners of each lung are totally perfused. This is happening without any of the physical demands of exercise. Here, by exercising the lungs first, we are preparing the body to achieve an effortless level of performance and fun.

Instead of a random or insufficient warm-up, we want to be sure to prepare the body physically so that we don't incur any exercise stress. This is a time to build up an oxygen reserve so as to avoid a premature oxygen debt in the first few minutes of the workout. It is a window in which the circulatory system can prepare and adjust to the increased demands of exercise.

The coordination of deep-breathing techniques with very low levels of exercise helps to pump prana into every cell of the body in preparation for maximal exertion later. It also ensures the early removal of any systemic waste products that could subsequently impair cellular respiration during exercise. We want to maximize the body's ability to function efficiently during aerobic exercise, without the build-up of waste or lactic acid. In addition, this is a sort of nasal hyperventilation where the lungs are being completely perfused and therefore prepared for maximal efficiency when the exercise load begins to increase. It is necessary to take these forced deep nasal breaths to drive the oxygen into the very small and usually dormant alveoli in the lungs. It is only by using every square inch of the lungs that we will be able to accommodate these dramatically lower breath rates and the experience of comfort during vigorous exercise. (See Graph C in chapter 1 and Graph D in chapter 10.)

During this phase, we begin to exercise the body, but the mind is already established in silence. The calm and composure of the mind is a prerequisite to carry the experience of effortlessness or the Zone into higher levels of exertion. The exercise load is gradually increased to about 50 percent of one's maximum capacity. The precise location of this 50 percent will be determined through the monitoring of heart and breath rates, form, comfort, and awareness, which I will discuss in depth in chapters 13 and 14.

At 50 percent of one's capacity, there is a point (I call it the breaking point) where the body shifts from an experience of comfort and balance to one of fatigue and exhaustion. As exercise increases above that 50 percent threshold, there will be an associated feeling of discomfort as the body shifts out of the comfort zone.

Unfortunately, many of us are conditioned, probably from childhood, to power right past the 50 percent mark, and we usually exercise at somewhere around 70 or 80 percent. This takes the body to a point where the lactic acid build-up is so great that muscle function is compromised, resulting in a tangible experience of discomfort. This discomfort is a signal that you are at the end of your aerobic rope. If pushed further into an overdrive performance mode, the body will shift into an anaerobic state of metabolism, which is highly inefficient, waste-producing, and short-lived.

Actress Catherine Oxenberg came to our health center a few years back, very interested in my athletic program. She is a runner and at the time was logging about 4 miles 3 to 5 times a week. I taught her the breathing techniques and the Sun Salute (of which she already knew the basics). With heart monitors on, we started the workout. We went through the Sun Salute and spent about 10 minutes in the Resting Phase maintaining a brisk walk.

As soon as we decided to go into the Listening Phase and started to run, within 10 steps her heart rate went from 100 to 160 beats per minute. This was far over her 50 percent limit, and I immediately slowed her down to a walk. We tried it again, this time running more slowly. Again her heart rate jumped from 100 to 160 in about 10 steps.

After three or four more attempts at it, I said to her, "Catherine, you are absolutely conditioned to exercise at a heart rate of 160 BPM. It doesn't matter what you do; your heart jumps automatically to 160. What your body is telling you is that it needs rest, not speed, and a brisk walk would probably be enough.

"In time, you'll be able to run 7-minute miles naturally and without strain, but right now your body wants rest. You may be keeping your muscles firm, but pushing yourself this much isn't necessarily healthy. You're working too hard for insufficient results. Eventually, you'll be able to increase the pace without the high heart rate, and I would expect your enjoyment level to increase as well."

Catherine is a Vata type, with a very fast mind and a strong desire to get things done quickly. Knowing that, I didn't really expect her to follow my advice and slow down to the extent she needed. But the concept of doing less and accomplishing more made sense to her, and she could see that she was straining physically even during a normal workout.

Three months later she came back to the center and asked me if I would run with her. We cruised through the Sun Salute and the Resting Phase, and, to my surprise, when we began running in the Listening Phase, her heart rate was stable. We built up the speed to about an 8-minute-mile pace, and her heart rate remained stable at 130 beats per minute.

I was amazed that she had improved so quickly. She said she had followed the workout and gradually was able to run faster and faster while maintaining the lower heart rates. It is just a matter of conditioning, I told her. Like most of us, Catherine was conditioned to exercise at unnecessarily high levels of strain and exertion. We are accustomed to taking the body to 160 BPM or more, because that's where the real discomfort starts, and we think we need to feel the strain for the workout to have any value.

THE LISTENING PHASE—
THE AEROBIC LIMIT

The role of the Listening Phase is to condition the individual to recognize that point at which the body shifts out of the comfort zone into a state of discomfort. When we fail to listen to the signal of strain and push ourselves out of our comfort zone, we leave the experience of the runner's high. Without both the comfort and the exercise high being carried into higher levels of performance, efficiency and enjoyment are dramatically reduced.

I've taken hundreds of runners out to introduce them to these principles. The experience is always the same, and always very surprising to them. I strap a heart monitor around their chest, programmed to beep at 50 percent of their maximum heart rate. We then begin the workout. Without fail, they charge right by the 50 percent mark, not realizing that they are exercising too hard. Then, after a couple of attempts at exercising up to the breaking point but going past it, they suddenly notice that a couple of seconds before the beeper went off, they did feel some discomfort. It wasn't much, and surely wasn't enough to slow them down according to conventional wisdom, but nonetheless it was there.

The more they slowed down to listen, the better they grasped that there was definitely a point where the ease and comfort of exercise shifted into the initial experience of discomfort, strain, and potential exhaustion. This subjective awareness of strain at the breaking point can be in the form of labored breathing, a pounding heart, or the breaking down of form.

Physiologically, this experience occurs just before the body kicks into anaerobic activity, when it reaches what is known as the "blood lactate threshold." This is the point at which the accumulation of blood lactate begins to impair the ability to manufacture energy and transport oxygen to the muscles, and the muscles begin to notice the slight decrease in the oxygen supply. Usually, we wait until the lactate build-up is inhibitive to the functioning of the muscles, and then we either go anaerobic or stay aerobic, building up more and more exercise-waste metabolites.

What I am recommending is that instead of pushing to this limit, train yourself to recognize the point at which your body first shows signs of fatigue and accumulating metabolic waste. In this way, you can maintain maximum efficiency during exercise.

I truly believe the human body is unlimited in potential, but if you break it down by constantly pushing it to exhaustion, this potential will never be realized. The Listening Phase is a time to recognize the point of maximum exercise efficiency, and respect it.

During this phase, we exercise up to the point of discomfort, then back off for a period of time in order to prepare the body for an even higher level of fitness. We repeatedly ask the body to go faster, push harder, and run farther, but we never push it beyond its internally set limitations of comfort.

Ask for more, and if the body responds to the increased workload with strain, then back off and reestablish the experience of comfort with a slower pace. A couple of minutes later, ask the body again to go faster. If it responds with strain again, then respect it and back off. In time, the body will accommodate the request for higher performance. If you keep forcing it beyond its limitations of efficiency and comfort, then the enjoyment will be stripped away as well as the opportunity to discover your personal best.

Yes, it might take a little longer to reach a specific goal. But with this program you are more assured of getting there and of enjoying the process along the way. The experience of the Zone with each workout will soon become the norm, and the cumulative perfecting of mind-body coordination will carry you to higher levels of achievement.

The Listening Phase is also the time to assess whether you are overtrained, whether you need rest, and whether you need a hard or an easy workout. It is difficult to decide weeks in advance what the body will want to do in a training run *today*. How can the mind know what the body will be able to do, weeks in advance? And will it know today, if we never ask?

The 1991 short-course world champion triathlete, Colleen Cannon, said this about the Listening Phase: "I think that's just what a lot of athletes don't do, they don't listen, they just go out and hammer. They run right out the door and don't listen to what their body's telling them, and as a result, they get injured.

"For me, this program helps me listen. You ask your body if it wants to run today, then go through the warm-up and Listening Phase, and if it's not responding and you don't feel good, then you go home because it's really not ready. When you listen to your body it responds so much better, because it's getting paid attention to. It doesn't have to knock you around and sprain an ankle or pull a hamstring to get your attention."

During the Listening Phase, your body is talking. If you pay attention, your performance will improve naturally. You will have fun again, too, because every step of the way you are receiving feedback from your body and either increasing or decreasing your workload, based on its request. By respecting the needs of the body and the desires of the mind as one integrated whole, you virtually eliminate the risks of injury, boredom, and overtraining.

THE PERFORMANCE PHASE—EXERCISING THE MIND AND BODY

As you develop greater respiratory and cardiovascular efficiency you will begin to access the perks of the Performance Phase. In this stage of your workout, the exercise high you cultured in the earlier phases is fully mature, and peak experience is within reach. This is not "for elite athletes only." The beauty of this program is that the things that work for Olympic athletes work for toddlers and teenagers and everyone in between. Reaching the Zone is the result of a properly structured workout, and the experience is available at every level of fitness for every individual.

If you've been warming up for a competition, this is the point at which you will start the match or the race. Now that the body has successfully completed the Listening Phase, it is properly warmed up and ready for a safe and comfortable stab at competition. If you're out for a walk, the experience will be colored with the same thrill as if you were achieving a personal best. Regardless of the activity or its intensity, the Performance Phase carries the coordination of mind and body that you have established, the composure of an alpha state, gracefully with you into a more vigorous or competitive level of exercise.

Now, instead of being distracted by the opposition, you will find it easy to stay within yourself and play your own game, not worrying about the competition or the final score. This doesn't mean you don't care about winning. If winning is the goal, then so you shall win—but not at the expense of your mind or body. Winning will become the natural side benefit of a performance from the inside out.

During the Listening Phase, the strategy was to keep asking your body to go faster, but not pushing if you felt some strain or resistance. The Performance Phase is the natural extension of the Listening Phase. The comfort and balance you carefully established is taken with you as your performance naturally goes higher and higher. You'll find your legs going as fast as they can, but the experience inside is still relaxed, composed, and comfortable.

One of my graduates, a 40-year-old housewife who is a noncompetitive runner, said, "Once you set up the proper parameters, what you experience is this state of euphoria, a complete, total feeling of happiness. And there's no feeling of the body moving. I remember running quite rapidly at one time. It was almost comical to see how fast my legs were moving, yet there was no heavy breath, and no feeling of running. I had no feeling of effort or motion whatsoever."

This is the time when you ask your body for more, and it says an enthusiastic *Yes!* There is no strain, and the exercise high remains a part of you, whether you're shooting baskets or throwing horseshoes.

You can experience the Zone, the exercise high, at every level of fitness during every workout. Remember that we've defined the Zone as that place where the body and mind are perfectly coordinated at an exercise level comfortably suited for the individual. If you lose the experience of comfort, then adjust your pace to reestablish it. For each person there is a certain pace that provides maximum integration of mind and body. The low end of that pace will be established during the Listening Phase, while the high end will be found in the Performance Phase.

If you roll an automobile tire down the street, the speed at which you roll it will determine the balance of the roll. If pushed too slowly, it won't have enough momentum and will start to wobble. If pushed too fast, it will start to bounce. Neither of these extremes offers the right conditions for a straight, balanced roll. If it is pushed just right, at the proper speed, it will roll in perfect balance without a wobble or a bounce.

If you took two high-speed side-view photos of this tire, one in perfect balanced motion and one standing at rest, they would look identical. The tire in motion would possess the same balance, and look as still, as the tire at rest.

The perfectly balanced, smoothly rolling tire exhibits the two essential yet opposite qualities of the Zone. Appearing to be still while in motion, it possesses the silent composure of rest and the dynamic action of motion, simultaneously coexisting.

These are the qualities fundamental to all aspects of nature, best illustrated by our earlier example of the hurricane. For the powerful gale winds of the hurricane to exist, there must be the silent eye, which coordinates the hurricane's dynamic forces.

The sequential Three-Phase Workout will first create the eye of the hurricane (silence) up front during Yoga (union of mind and body) established in the Sun Salute. This state is measured by the production of alpha or composure in the brain. In the Resting and Listening phases we begin to move the winds around the eye of the hurricane as we slowly increase the exercise load. Here we are always monitoring the experience of comfort as measured by the production of alpha. By the time we enter the Performance Phase we have established a fully mature hurricane where the exercise is maximal and the brain, heart, and breath are composed and calm. Reproducing this experience is an absolute requirement for exercise to be truly fun and your potential to be unlimited.

The Three Phase Workout helps you to make the choice for more efficient, effortless functioning. Brent Mayne of the Kansas City Royals said of the program, "It enables me to reach my peak performance without a maximum effort. I can now get that peak performance that was previously sporadic. Sometimes you're really hot, sometimes really cold. But with this program, you can *bottle* that feeling, and get it every time you play."

THE COOL-DOWN

The cool-down also serves as an early warm-up for the next exercise session. By properly cooling the body, we ensure the removal of accumulated waste products deposited from the exercise session. This, along with the tendency to manufacture less waste, will prevent the muscle soreness that is experienced all too often after starting a fitness program.

Soreness indicates that you've pushed beyond your body's limits of comfort. Although some soreness here and there may occur, it doesn't have to. I've received many reports from people who begin exercise programs, and although they anticipate the usual next-day stiffness, it never comes.

Carmen Owen is a 38-year-old businessman and ardent windsurfer. Carmen lives in the Midwest and for several years has taken an annual midwinter sailboarding extravaganza in Hawaii. He rarely did any other exercise back home, and was basically out of shape when he arrived in Hawaii. Each year, after the first day of sailboarding, he would wake up feeling about as stiff as his board. This spoiled two days of his hard-earned vacation, and he lost sailing time thawing out.

Then he tried the principles of Invincible Athletics. He did Sun Salutes on the beach and the Resting and Listening phases during a walk-run before he got on his board, ready for performance action. He then sailed for the next several hours, feeling quite good.

Carmen had always told himself to take it easy the first day, but he was repeatedly overwhelmed with excitement, and ended up going all-out, knowing full well that he would pay with sore muscles the next day. This time was no different—he went for it totally. To his amazement, he woke up the next day without any stiffness. Each day he went through the Three Phase Workout, and found he had completely avoided the soreness he had learned to accept as a small price to pay for his pleasure.

During the cool-down, you wind down the same way you wound up. Spend 5 to 10 minutes in the Resting Phase, where you combine deep Darth Vader breathing with low levels of exercise. This will act as a pump to remove any built-up blood lactate and other waste products. Then do about 5 to 10 minutes of Sun Salutes. These postworkout stretching and breathing exercises will further facilitate the removal of waste from the muscles, as well as make great strides toward increased flexibility.

12

HERE COMES THE SUN

If the mind and body are not working harmoniously together before you begin to exercise, chances are you will not enjoy your workout. Without the fun factor, the likelihood of continuing a fitness program for any length of time is slim. This is proved by the fact that, despite good intentions and even good beginnings by many people, only about 10 to 15 percent of Americans exercise regularly. Therefore, if our goal is to make fitness as much a part of our way of life as eating and sleeping, we'd better bring back the fun and get the mind and body coordinated.

Since Yoga is defined as the union of body and mind, by definition it will be the most effective means of integrating mind, body, and sport.

THE SUN SALUTE (SURYA NAMASKAR)

The Sun Salute is the only series of Yoga postures that coordinates breathing with movement. Traditionally, Yoga postures are performed with an emphasis on being still and quiet, without specific breathing instructions. The Sun Salute is a series of 12 flexion and extension postures, linked together as one fluid movement, with a rhythm established by the natural and comfortable pattern of the breath.

THE BREATH RATE

During exercise, the Darth Vader breathing technique is recommended during the exhalation only. During the Sun Salute, however, you have the option of adding the Darth Vader technique during the inhalation, although it is a bit more difficult. (If you need a reminder of the technique, please review chapter 10. Nasal breathing with the Darth Vader technique is one of the key ingredients for success in this mind-body fitness program.)

The reason why I recommend using Darth Vader only on exhalation during exercise is this: During the exhalation, you can force the air out very quickly, which is important during vigorous exercise. Using the technique on inhalation would not allow the lungs to get the needed oxygen quickly enough to support an exercise work load.

SOLAR BENEFITS

The Sun Salute, in addition to setting the mind and body in a coordinated motion, has some very profound physiological benefits that have been written about in the Ayurvedic texts for thousands of years. First, as the body is flexed and extended during these 12 postures, the internal organs of the pelvis, abdomen, and chest are deeply massaged. In addition, the sequence takes the spine through almost every possible range of motion, including flexion, extension, lateral bending, lengthening, compression, and rotation, thereby breaking up any tensions or muscle spasms that could possibly restrict its full range of motion.

The coordination of the breath with the flexion and extension postures considerably enhances the effects of the Sun Salute. When the body is moving into extension during a back bend, for example, the rib cage, spine, and muscles are all stretched or lengthened. With an inhalation coordinated with back-bending extensions, the diaphragm is moving in the opposite direction. During this inhalation the diaphragm must contract downward in order to pull oxygen into the lungs.

During the contraction of the diaphragm (inhale) the Sun Salute posture is always one of extension. During this exercise, as the body extends upward, the diaphragm (located at the base of the lungs and attached to the rib cage) is contracted downward. This provides a deep internal massage, particularly for the diaphragm and the muscles of the rib cage.

The rib cage is often restricted in its ability to expand and contract, due to years of improper breathing. The Sun Salute introduces a scissorlike motion, which can effectively break the hard-to-get-to muscle spasms in the rib cage that make breathing into the lower lobes of the lungs more difficult.

With continued practice of the Sun Salute, the rib cage will reestablish its normal range of motion and flexibility, making deep diaphragmatic nasal breathing—the preferred breathing technique both during exercise and at rest—easier to perform.

PNF AUTO PILOT

The abbreviation PNF stands for peripheral neuromuscular facilitation. This technique is commonly used by trainers to increase the flexibility of certain muscle groups. Trainers will spend an hour or so with an athlete doing this technique before the start of a competition.

PNF is based on the principle that if you want to make a muscle more flexible, you must contract it first, before you stretch it. PNF provides the alternation of contraction and relaxation by flexing and extending the designated muscle—the exact same formula inherent in the 12 flexion and extension postures of the Sun Salute.

The Sun Salute reproduces all the benefits of the PNF technique naturally. It can be very effective for all the major muscle groups and can be completed in 5 to 10 minutes, without the time and costly attention of a personal trainer.

Kyle Cleveland, the 1991 Iowa State high school tennis champion, said, "Normally you do stretching before any physical activity, but when you do the Sun Salute you don't have to think, 'Well, I'm going to stretch my calves, and now I'm going to stretch my hamstring.' " Or as a professional body builder said, "It just seems to stretch every major muscle group. It's such a simple exercise, but for me to mimic that by doing a series of other stretches would take me three times as long."

THE FRUITS OF THE SUN

The Sun Salute is, by itself, a complete exercise. It has been practiced for thousands of years, and today you can still find men lined up along the Ganges at sunrise performing dozens, even hundreds, of repetitions. For many, it is their only exercise.

Here is a summary of the benefits of this excellent warm-up and cool-down exercise:

• Deeply massages the internal organs

• Takes the spine through the entire range of motion, thereby ensuring maximum flexibility

• Breaks adhesions and spasms in the rib cage that inhibit deep nasal diaphragmatic breathing

• Coordinates movement and breath and thereby pumps prana into every cell of the body, making it the perfect preparation for any physical activity

• Increases strength, flexibility, and endurance of every major muscle group in the body

• Naturally reproduces the PNF technique, thereby dramatically increasing flexibility, whether you use it before and after exercise, or as an exercise by itself

• Improves circulation, energy, and vitality

A graduate of my Invincible Athletics seminar says that when she does Sun Salutes as a cool-down at the end of her exercise class, "you feel a liquid gold flowing through your body."

MIND/BODY RAYS

Surya Namaskar consists of 12 postures, which take about 5 seconds each to perform, adding up to a total of about 1 minute for a complete cycle. For a good warm-up, I recommend anywhere from 5 to 10 cycles (or minutes); or, if you like mathematical formulas, do all 12 postures 12 times each, which will take you about 12 minutes.

Actually, you may perform this exercise as many times a day as feels comfortable, but be sure it starts and ends your fitness routine.

While doing the Sun Salute, be sure to breathe in and out maximally. The slow, deep, comfortable rhythm of the breath will set the pace for both the Sun Salute and your subsequent exercise. As mentioned earlier, Darth Vader breathing can be performed during both the inhalation and the exhalation, if it is comfortable, but always do it on the exhalation.

Take each posture to a comfortable stretch. If you feel some pain or tension developing, stop short of that point and exercise that muscle group *within the experience of comfort.* Soon the comfort will overflow into the stiffness, and within a week you'll find yourself stretching far beyond what limited you before. The flexibility gain is natural and comes as a result of not straining or pushing the muscle. With some practice, always erring on the conservative side, you will become familiar with the amount of stretch that provides maximum results along with comfort.

Remember, when athletes experience the Zone, they always feel that their performances are effortless. They feel no strain, yet they may find themselves smashing world records. If we are to reproduce this experience, let's capture it from the first step of the workout and never let it go. The Sun Salute is the way to provide the initial integration of mind and body needed for that effortless flow, and to set ourselves up for a consistent experience of the Zone.

FROM THE INSIDE OUT

There are two ways you can perform the Sun Salute: with attention, or without it. If your mind is off thinking about where you'd like to be, or what you're going to do after these postures, you will reap only minimal benefits and relatively no integration of mind and body. To realize maximum benefits from this exercise, the awareness has to be from the inside out. When you do it just right, the mind is totally settled, not distracted.

To heighten this experience, do the postures more slowly. This will also slow your breathing to a more efficient rhythm, which will carry over into the rest of your exercise.

As you flex into a posture, there will be a place where you begin to feel a slight stretch. If you are going slowly enough, and your mind is settled enough, your attention will naturally flow to the point of the stretch, whether it's in your calf, your back, or your hamstrings. This naturally focused attention will bring the mind and body together in that area and help to dissolve whatever is causing the restricted range of motion. If there is effort or strain to make it happen, the natural coordination between mind and body will break down.

Our habit is to force and push. When you want more flexibility in an area, the tendency is to push and pull on that group of muscles. To touch your toes, standard operating procedure is to stretch and bounce until you make it. In the long run, this forcing only ties the muscles into knots and spasms, which ultimately make the body less flexible than when you started.

Respect the experience of comfort. Your body is smarter than you think! Rather than always telling it what you want it to do, give it a chance to prove itself. It will come through in the end. But it only speaks the language of comfort. As soon as you push and force it, the body will adapt and compensate, and lose its ability to stay on track toward its full potential and an ultimate personal best.

MIND-BODY SUN SALUTE TIPS

- Go slowly
- Breathe as deeply as possible
- Think from the inside out
- Let your awareness flow to the area of the stretch
- Take every posture slowly, to the very limit of a comfortable stretch
- Breathe through the nose using the Darth Vader technique
- If you're having trouble settling into it and find yourself distracted, try going through the postures with your eyes closed

Remember: Be sure to consult your physician before beginning any fitness program. During pregnancy this exercise is not recommended.

THE POSTURES

1. **The Sunrise Pose** (Nasal exhale)
   Begin by standing tall with the feet together in a parallel position. Stand evenly on both feet and lengthen the spine upward. Place palms together in front of the chest as you look straight ahead.

2. **Raised Arm Position** (Nasal inhale)
   On the inhalation, slowly extend the arms over the head. Reach up and slightly back as you continue lengthening the spine, while allowing the head to look upward. Keep breathing evenly as you continue right into the next pose.

3. **Hand to Foot Position** (Nasal exhale)
   As you exhale, bend the body forward and down, lengthening the spine, arms, and neck. Let the knees soften or bend freely, bringing the hands to the floor. Keep the elbows and shoulders relaxed, and don't lock the knees.

4. **Equestrian Position** (Nasal inhale)
   On your next inhalation, extend the right leg back and drop the back knee to the ground. The front knee is bent and the supporting foot remains flat on the floor. Simultaneously extend or lift the

spine and open the chest. Allow the head and
neck to lengthen vertically.

5. **Mountain Position** (Nasal exhale)
   On the exhalation, bring the left leg back to meet
   the right leg—feet at hip width apart, hands at
   shoulder distance. As you raise the buttocks and
   hips, press down with the hands. Stretch the heels
   down toward the floor and lengthen through the
   backs of the legs. Relax and gently flex the head
   and neck. The body forms an even inverted V
   from the hands to the feet.

6. **Eight Limbs Position** (Hold briefly)
   Gently drop both knees to the ground and slowly
   slide the body down at an angle as you bring the
   chest and chin to the ground. All eight "limbs"—
   feet, knees, hands, chest, and chin—touch the
   floor. Hold this very briefly and then continue to
   move into the next pose.

7. **Cobra Position** (Nasal inhale)
   On the inhalation, pull the chest up using the
   muscles of the spine. Keep the elbows close to the
   body and continue to extend the spine upward.
   Let the upper back widen and lengthen. Do not
   initiate this movement with the head or lift the
   body with the neck.

8. **Mountain Position** (Nasal exhale)
   Repeat position 5. On the exhalation, raise the
   buttocks and hips, press down with the hands,
   and allow the spine to release upward and back.
   Stretch the heels down toward the floor and
   lengthen through the backs of the legs. Relax and
   gently flex the head and neck.

9. **Equestrian Position** (Nasal inhale)
   Repeat position 4. Inhale and swing the right leg
   forward between the hands. The left leg stays
   extended back, knee to the ground. The front
   knee should be bent, with the foot flat on the

floor. Extend the spine, lifting the chest forward
and up. Allow the head and neck to lengthen
upward.

10. **Hand to Foot Position** (Nasal exhale)
    Repeat position 3. As you exhale, step forward
    with the left leg and continue to bend the body
    forward and down, lengthening the entire spine.
    The arms and head follow in line with the spine.
    Both hands remain on the floor. Let the knees
    soften or bend freely. Keep the elbows and
    shoulders relaxed.

11. **Raised Arm Position** (Nasal inhale)
    Repeat position 2. On the inhalation, lift the
    arms from the upper back. Extend the arms over
    the head, reaching slightly back. Keep the
    breathing smooth, deep, and continuous.

12. **Sunset Position** (Nasal exhale)
    Repeat position 1. Exhale as you lower the arms
    and bring the palms together in front of the
    chest. Stand tall with the feet in a parallel po-
    sition at hip distance. Lift the chest and expand
    the ribs as you look straight ahead. Vertically
    lengthen the spine and neck.

IMPORTANT POINTS TO REMEMBER IN THE SUN SALUTE

1. Let the knees be supple or slightly bent in postures 3 and 10.

2. During the first time through the postures, bring the *right* leg back in
posture 4 and forward in posture 9. On the second time through, bring the
left leg back in posture 4 and forward in posture 9.

3. In posture 7, do not push into the cobra position with your arm
strength. Use your back muscles to pull yourself off the ground.

4. Posture 6 is a shorter pose, as the breath is suspended until the inhale
in posture 7.

5. Take each posture slowly to the maximum comfortable stretch.

6. Inhale and exhale maximally, finishing each breath as you finish each posture.

7. Employ Darth Vader breathing.

8. Continue as a warm-up or cool-down for 5 to 10 minutes.

9. Don't rush. Let the deep, comfortable rhythm of the breath set the pace from one position to the next.

13

THREE PHASE WORKOUT: LEVEL 1—GENERAL FITNESS PROGRAM

The workout in this chapter is designed for people who are not exercise fanatics or fitness enthusiasts, but who simply want to start a fitness program, stay healthy, or make their walks around the block more fruitful and enjoyable.

Because this system works for novices and elite athletes alike, *all should familiarize themselves with the instructions for Level 1.* The Level 1 program could stand alone for even the most competitive athletes and should not be disdained as being "too elementary." The principles outlined here will serve as a basis and prerequisite for the understanding and practice of the Level 2 Athletic Training Program described in chapter 14.

Please recall the case study discussed in chapter 1, in which athletes trained in the principles of Invincible Athletics look two bicycle ergometer exercise stress tests. The first time they took the test, the athletes used conventional exercise techniques, like the ones taught in your local health club. Two days later, they went through the same test, using the Invincible Athletics principles and procedures you are learning in this book.

Using these techniques, the subjects produced a heightened state of alpha in the brain, representing a degree of mind-body integration that conventional techniques do not produce. (See graphs A and B, chapter 1.) Their breath rates were relatively stable at around 14 breaths per minute (BPM), compared to 47 using conventional methods. (See graph D, chapter 10.) While the breath rates were stable, the brain maintained a state of integration. When the breath rates began to increase (during conventional exercise), the integration was lost.

Subjectively, the experience of the Zone was sustained as long as the breath rate remained slow and constant. When the breath rate sped up, the experience was lost. This tells us something very important: In order to reproduce the experience that goes along with the alpha brain wave pattern, we must maintain the comfortable rhythm of the breath set during Yoga (union of mind and body) throughout the entire workout.

What does this mean in practical terms?

AS SOON AS YOU FIND YOUR BREATH RATE INCREASING, SLOW DOWN YOUR EXERCISE PACE TO RECAPTURE THE ALPHA BREATH RATE. THE COMFORTABLE RHYTHM OF THE BREATH ACTS LIKE A METRONOME FOR A MUSICIAN; IT SETS THE EXERCISE PACE. THIS EXERCISE BREATH RATE IS ESTABLISHED DURING THE SUN SALUTE AND CARRIED THROUGH THE WORKOUT.

WHEN USING THE THREE-PHASE WORKOUT ONE CAN EXERCISE EVERY DAY IF DESIRED. THE PREMISE OF THIS PROGRAM IS BASED ON THE REDUCTION OF STRESS DURING EXERCISE, SO ONE CANNOT OVERTRAIN. ON THE OTHER HAND, TO ACHIEVE A CARDIOVASCULAR BENEFIT, 30 MINUTES OF EXERCISE MUST BE PERFORMED AT LEAST THREE TIMES A WEEK.

WARM-UP: SUN SALUTE SETS THE BREATH AND CREATES ALPHA

Throughout the phases of Level 1, the breath rate should not change. The deep, comfortable breathing rhythm generated during the Sun Salute sets the rate for the entire workout, so be sure to establish a good rhythm at the outset. Remember as you go through the postures to take maximal breaths, going to the next posture only when you have taken each inhalation and exhalation to its limit. (See graph E.)

It is recommended by convention that before stretching one should engage in light aerobic activity like walking for 5 to 10 minutes to warm the muscles prior to stretching them. The Sun Salute, when combined with deep nasal breathing, can be performed slowly and without maximal stretching during each posture to accommodate this requirement. These postures can produce this light aerobic effect when performed gently, slowly, and fluidly for the first 5 minutes. The second 5 minutes can be a time to focus on deeper breaths and more completed postures. If you are very inflexible then a short stretch may be the appropriate way to start your workout. Let comfort be your guide.

THE RESTING PHASE—EXERCISING
THE LUNGS

The Resting Phase is the time to start your run, walk, bike ride, swim, or whatever your selected exercise is—but start slowly. For 5 to 10 minutes (the duration of the Resting Phase), go at an unusually slow pace, while maintaining the same deep breath rate established during the Sun Salute. Remember, this is the breath rate that got the mind and body integrated, and we want to hold on to it during the whole workout. Don't lose it by exerting yourself too much here.

If you are scheduled to go for a run, take a brisk walk during the Resting Phase. If you're on an exercise bike, freewheeling with little or no resistance would be sufficient. If you are going for a walk, walk slowly for these 5 to 10 minutes. Be sure to maintain the slow, even, deep Darth Vader nasal breath.

Breathing deeply during light exercise will feel very different from what you are used to. Usually, we breathe deeply only when we have to—when we are short of breath and need more oxygen. In this case, we make a concerted effort to keep up the same depth and rate of breathing established during the Sun Salute (see graph F), even though our exertion is minimal.

If you are playing tennis, racquetball, basketball, soccer, or any other sport that demands unpredictable full-out bursts of energy that could distract your from your breathing, there are two options for the Resting Phase:

Graph E

Level 1
Breath Rate During Three Phase Workout

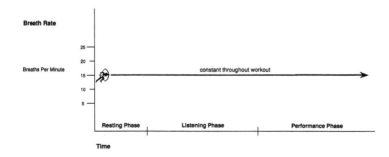

The breath rate is constant throughout the entire Level 1 workout.
The breath rate is set during the 5–10 minutes of the Sun Salute Warm-up.
The average breath rate is 10–20 BPM.

Graph F
Level 1
Exercise Intensity During Three Phase Workout

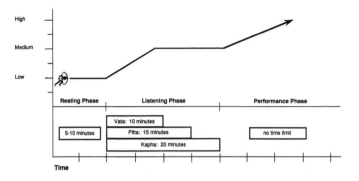

Resting Phase
The exercise level is very low, while breathing is slow and very deep.
The breath rate is set during the Sun Salute Warm-up.

Listening Phase
Gradually increase exercise level.
If the breath rate increases beyond the rate set during the Sun Salute, slow down the pace of exercise and maintain the original breath rate.

Performance Phase
As the fitness level and skill increase, the intensity level of exercise can increase while the original breath rate stays the same (see graph D in chapter 10).

· Warm up with a walk or light jog before entering the court or the field to play. I recommend that you complete both the Resting and Listening phases before starting the game.

· Go through the Resting and Listening phases on the court or field during warm-ups. In tennis, for example, tell your opponent, "I'm not going to chase warm-up balls for a while, just hit them right to me for a few minutes." In this way, you can focus on your shot and your breathing without being forced to lose your breath rate while chasing balls. Your opponent will probably gain more by hitting the ball right at you than by hitting away with no real sense of control. Tennis players often find themselves completely out of breath within the first 5 minutes on the court, due to chasing wild warm-up shots.

If you can't arrange to take the time on the court, arrive early and jog or walk nearby.

In the beginning stages of this program, it is easier to use a steady-state exercise such as running, walking, cycling, or cross-country skiing. With these activities, the level of exertion can be closely monitored. This is necessary to properly condition the mind to listen to the needs of the body.

THE LISTENING PHASE—BEGINNING TO EXERCISE THE BODY

During the Listening Phase the breath rate again remains the same as during the Sun Salute. (See graph F.) In this phase the exercise pace is gradually increased as you monitor your body's response.

If the exercise level goes too high, you will be forced to increase your breath rate. The oxygen intake from the Sun Salute breath rate will not be sufficient to maintain your body's new level of exertion, and your breathing rate will naturally pick up. Just at this point, where the breathing begins to become labored or increases beyond the Sun Salute rate, there will be an associated feeling of discomfort. At that point, respect the feeling and slow the pace until you can reestablish the original breath rate.

The purpose of the Listening Phase is to become aware of what happens when the exercise level forces the breath rate upward. This breaking point will be correlated to the heart rate, and to the form and awareness monitors discussed in the Level 2 Athletic Training Program.

By maintaining the Sun Salute breath rate throughout the workout, the exercise level will be perfect for those who do not want to overdo it and who are concerned about exercise safety. This will also ensure the maximum integration of mind and body, which translates into more enjoyment during the entire workout.

LISTENING PHASE—EXAMPLE

If you are a runner, during the Listening Phase you will keep asking your body to run faster, and you will pay attention to how it responds. If you pick up your pace a little and the Sun Salute breath rate remains even and steady, you know you can go that fast without any problem. You can then try speeding up still more.

You can continue going faster until your breathing increases beyond the original rate. Then slow the pace to reestablish the comfortable rate. After a minute or two of a stable breath rate, you have the option of again asking the body for more. If the body says no and the breath rate increases, then slow down again and reestablish the Sun Salute breath rate.

Soon you will become sensitized to exactly how much exercise is beneficial and when you start to strain. The experience of comfort and ease, reported by all the greats when at their best, will become a natural guide to keep you exercising along the high-performance curve.

Actually, this is one of the most important unanswered questions of modern exercise science: What is the correct (i.e., most beneficial) amount of exercise for each individual? For anyone who wants to gain maximum benefits from an exercise program, in terms of both health and performance, knowing the right amount is paramount.

As you develop the ability to tune in to your body, you will find it shouting out the answer. In Level 1, the point of maximum return continues right up until the breath rate established in the Sun Salute begins to increase, and your comfort begins to be lost due to overaggressive demands on yourself.

The benefits are greatest when exercise and breath rate are matched, and the body is exercising at the maximum comfort level. There is just enough stimulation in the system to remove waste, improve circulation, and help the body repair itself. When the metabolic rate is raised to this stage and not beyond, the body experiences itself functioning with a high degree of efficiency.

On the other hand, when the breath rate becomes labored beyond the Sun Salute rate, it is because the body is being forced to adapt and compensate to meet the demands of increased exertion. Then the benefits start to diminish and stress starts to accumulate.

It's like a test drive. You can't tell what might be wrong with the car until you drive it. When you employ the Listening Phase during exercise, if there are any weaknesses in the system, the body can address them before the increasing demands of exercise shift the system into a higher gear.

The marvelous thing about our bodies is that we have a built-in mechanic who will fix problems on the spot, as long as the system is not overstrained. As soon as the body shifts into its fight-or-flight stress response, all repairs are put on hold until the workout is over. At that time, recovery is the priority and the metabolic rate drops too low to troubleshoot the system properly.

Exercise was originally designed as a stress-reducing, rejuvenative activity. The principle behind this concept is that only when all the stress is cleared out of the system can the body and mind fully integrate and fully express their potential. That is why it is especially important not to incur *new* stress at a time when the system could be becoming increasingly stress-free. The Listening Phase of the Three Phase Workout will help you know exactly how much exercise will support this growth to higher potential, and how much will oppose it.

It is simply a matter of repeatedly asking the body for more without crossing over the line into discomfort and strain. This procedure is based on the belief that the body's capabilities are essentially unlimited, and that the best way to access its potential is to give it a chance to accommodate to your performance desires naturally, in its own time, without forcing it. The result is a graceful upward performance curve that produces a permanent level of fitness.

This is altogether different from the rubber-band effect well known to conventional exercisers. Many people have been shocked to discover, after months of getting into shape by driving themselves, that they were back almost where they started after just a week or two of not exercising. When the body is forced, it will snap back to its original condition as soon as the stressor is gone. On the other hand, if exercise is gracefully expanded, the body will have a chance to assimilate the fitness gains gradually and develop a fitness level that becomes a way of life rather than a burned-in temporary experience.

THE DURATION OF THE LISTENING PHASE DEPENDS ON ONE'S BODY TYPE:

• FOR THE VATA TYPE, THE MINIMUM TIME NEEDED IS 10 MINUTES.
• FOR THE PITTA TYPE, THE MINIMUM TIME NEEDED IS 15 MINUTES.
• FOR THE KAPHA, THE MINIMUM TIME NEEDED IS 20 MINUTES.

(SEE CHART AT END OF CHAPTER 14 FOR DETAILS ON ADJUSTING LISTENING PHASE TIMES.)

As your body becomes more fit and stress is removed, it will respond more and more positively to your requests. When you ask your body for more, it will say yes, and your performance will soar while your breath rate remains stable. When this happens naturally, you can flow smoothly into the Performance Phase.

THE PERFORMANCE PHASE—MAXIMIZING MIND AND BODY

There is no time limit or requirement in the Performance Phase. This is when you would start the actual race, tennis match, or other competition. Now the body begins to perform at its highest levels, while the breath rate and feeling of comfort and balance continue with you into the competition.

If you look back at the graphs in chapter 10, you will notice that the breath rate during the Three Phase Workout decreases slightly at the maximum workload. While the "conventional" breath rate is going through the roof, the Invincible Athletics breath rate is actually coming down.

When we exercise at a competitive level, we begin to require more oxygen. In order to get this oxygen into the lungs, the body can either breathe faster, as it tends to do with conventional exercise, or breathe more efficiently. The subject in Graph D (see chapter 10) was breathing more efficiently. I can tell you from experience that there is nothing more enjoyable than to watch your breathing become slower and more efficient while your legs carry you faster and faster

We are accustomed to correlate high-level exercise with more strain, yet, when Roger Bannister broke the 4-minute mile, he trained only 45 minutes a day. Of his historic run, Bannister said, "I felt no pain or strain; I felt I was going slow." Effortlessness is a new experience for most people, but it is the common testimony of those who have found themselves performing in the Zone.

It is the experience of opposites: The faster you go, the more composed physically and mentally you become. We can condition ourselves to have that experience on a regular basis.

Warren Wechsler, the 38-year-old runner whose rise from sedentary businessman to marathoner was described in chapter 1, told me that he would marvel at how he would pass people in the last miles of a 10 K race, watching them huffing and puffing in pain while he would be pushing almost to sprint speed. Even toward the end of a race, he would still be breathing quietly through his nose, feeling absolutely comfortable and composed.

Warren said that even during his sprint workouts on the track he never had to breathe through his mouth. "You reach a point where your lungs are not the limiting factor to how fast you can go," he said. Such a statement, from a runner committed to nasal breathing, is possible only because of the high degree of respiratory efficiency that comes quite naturally when you let the body and the breath, not your desires, dictate the performance curve.

In the beginning weeks of your Invincible Athletics workouts, if you listen carefully to your body, you may find yourself never going beyond the Listening Phase. If this happens, it is because your body is protecting you from yourself. It won't let you hurt yourself if you listen to it.

In the Listening Phase you are repeatedly asking the body for more and monitoring its responses. In the Performance Phase you are on cruise control at an exercise level you established as your maximum comfort zone in the Listening Phase, just before your exertion level reaches the breaking point. That subjective experience is then carried into the Performance Phase. The level of performance may differ from one person to the next, but the exercise high will be experienced throughout.

If you are exercising on your own, you can stay in the Performance Phase as long as the experience of comfort remains. If you are involved in a competition where your exertion level is dictated by the game, then you must go with that. As long as you successfully completed the warm-up and the Resting and Listening phases, the body is ready for competition and short bursts beyond the comfort zone will be fine.

Ultimately, when you become truly fit, the experience of comfort will be with you every step of the way, even into the most intensely competitive situations. (Sprint training and competition are discussed in detail in chapter 14, the Level 2 program.)

THE COOL-DOWN

Just as jockeys walk their horses extensively after a race to ensure a proper cool-down, you need to spend some time cooling down, too. Basically, you cool down the same way you warmed up.

STEP 1. Begin with 5 to 10 minutes in the Resting Phase, where you combine deep nasal breathing with low-level exercise. (Review the instructions given earlier in this chapter.) This will ensure the removal of any accumulated blood lactate or other postexercise circulatory waste products.

The cool-down not only discourages next-day muscle stiffness, it acts as a preparation for your next workout. If waste products are completely removed from the muscles after each workout, the body can spend more time on rejuvenation, repair, and increasing performance levels during subsequent workouts.

STEP 2. After 5 to 10 minutes of the Resting Phase, immediately move on to 5 to 10 minutes of Sun Salute. The best flexibility gains can be made when the muscles are warm, immediately after a workout. The Sun Salute, because of its counterposing flexion and extension postures, is one of the most effective means of gaining flexibility.

Johnny Ray had been training for flexibility for years in a gym, to improve his karate form and kicking ability. He was a Pitta-Kapha type whose muscles were fairly bulky and not overly flexible. He would train for at least an hour every day using different stretching exercises. He improved quite a lot, but he could never perform splits or sit in the lotus posture (the cross-legged Yoga position in which the ankles sit on opposite thighs), which he wanted very much to do.

I taught Johnny the Sun Salute sequence, and after doing two 15-

minute sessions per day for just two weeks, he sat in the lotus posture for the first time in his life.

The Sun Salute is not just a generic Yoga exercise stuck in the front and back of the workout. It provides strength, flexibility, and endurance to each of the major muscle groups, completely naturally, while increasing the flow of prana throughout the body. It also provides a greatly heightened state of neuromuscular integration. Ending a workout with 5 to 10 minutes of Sun Salute is the best way to train your body to take the alpha state into your daily life.

14

THREE PHASE WORKOUT:
LEVEL 2—ATHLETIC TRAINING
PROGRAM

In this chapter, we will take a comprehensive look at the Three Phase Workout with the goals of competition in mind. I use the word *competition* to include all those who are serious about their exercise and want to take a more active approach to their workouts.

Level 1 provides a slightly more conservative workout, to ensure safety and maximum mind-body integration for those who may exercise at random rather than with strict regularity, and who may not want to study the process deeply. Level 2 is a more aggressive program, from which an individual can make faster performance gains while still staying on the exercise high performance curve (the exact amount of exercise for your body type, to keep you in the Zone).

This chapter instructs athletes in how to integrate conventional training with the Three Phase Workout when competitive goals demand immediate results. The application of speed work and intervals, and specific-sport applications, are also covered.

LEVEL 2 WARM-UP—CREATING ALPHA

STEP 1. The Level 2 warm-up is basically the same as Level 1. If you're feeling nervous preparing for competition, try using the *ujjayi* breathing exercise (see chapter 10). If you're playing a tennis tournament, for example, and have an hour wait during which you find yourself getting anxious, use this technique intermittently, for a few minutes at a time, to maintain your composure.

STEP 2. Begin the Sun Salute, exactly as it is performed in Level 1. The breathing is deep, and you can use Darth Vader breathing during both the inhalation and exhalation postures. The comfortable rhythm of the breath will set the pace of the workout, but the rhythm will not necessarily be set by the Sun Salute as in Level 1.

In Level 1, the breath rate established during the Sun Salute is extended throughout the workout and is the sole monitor for success. That is, you pay attention to your breath throughout the workout, and when you find the breath coming faster than the Sun Salute rhythm, you cut back and regain that comfortable rhythm. In Level 2, we will not adhere so strictly to that exact breath rate. We will use other monitors, such as heart rate, form, awareness, and comfort, as well as breath rate, to focus on an even more aggressive but still balanced performance curve.

Perform the Sun Salute as a warm-up for about 5 to 10 minutes. (See chapters 12 and 13 for Sun Salute benefits and instructions.)

OPTIMUM TRAINING HEART RATE

The classical Ayurvedic text, *Sushruta Samhita*, states that exercise will be most beneficial when kept at 50 percent of one's capacity. The training zones currently recommended by the American College of Sports Medicine now range from 60 percent to 80 percent of maximum heart rate. Sixty percent is usually for general fitness and 80 percent for performance enhancement. We will use 50 percent for both fitness and performance gains.

To put this into perspective, we must remember that it wasn't very long ago that training-zone ranges were as high as 70 to 90 percent. But with the focus of science on the true limits of exercise safety, and with people like Jim Fixx and Pete Maravich dropping dead right after vigorous exercise, the experts were compelled to reassess the maximums.

It is interesting to watch the training-zone percentages slowly but surely come down toward 50 percent as the scientific community keeps changing its mind. This points to one of the strong suits of this training program: It hasn't changed in some five thousand years and isn't likely to change in the near future!

Critics brought up in the stress-and-recover school of training will argue that 50 percent of maximum heart rate is too low to produce any significant cardiovascular benefits. This is simply not correct. Dr. Steven Blair of the Cooper Institute for Aerobics Research conducted a study while he was at the University of North Carolina. He showed "highly significant improvement in aerobic fitness" for young healthy male subjects who exercised at 50 percent of their maximal performance levels (based on predicted maximum heart rates). The men trained for 30 to 40 minutes, 5 days a week, for 10 weeks.

The University of Arizona studied a group of 14 men and women with mild hypertension. Their exercise regimen consisted of walking, 3 days a week for 1 year, at 50 percent of maximum heart rate. They lowered their blood pressure an average of 9 points.

The fitness benefits when exercising at just 50 percent are well documented. So why aren't we all exercising at 50 percent? It would certainly be a lot easier!

I believe there are several reasons. The first is that performance gains, though apparent at 50 percent, are not as quickly acquired as when exercising at 80 percent. I think that when conventional techniques are used, 50 percent will never be as appealing as 75 or 80 percent in terms of instant results. But when a 50 percent training program is combined with maximum respiratory efficiency, developed through proper breathing techniques and a body-type–specific, sequential Three Phase Workout that keeps you locked in to the exercise high and comfort zone, 50 percent can provide both immediate and long-term achievements to satisfy any competitive athlete.

The second reason, as sad as it is true, is that we are simply conditioned to the experience of strain during exercise. Without it, many people feel unsatisfied, as if they haven't pushed themselves hard enough.

My goal is to change that bias and to give you satisfaction far beyond what you will reap from exercising according to the "no pain, no gain" mindset. You can also have a shot at peak performance, without the strain conventionally required. We aim to reproduce nothing less than the experience and results of those outstanding athletes whose testimony defined the term *the Zone.*

The formula we use to establish the optimum training heart rate (OTR) is the Karvonen formula for 50 percent of a maximum heart rate of 220.

TAKING THE HEART RATE

For about $100 you can purchase a fairly good heart rate monitor that will give you a continuously adjusting readout of your current heart rate on a device that looks like a wristwatch. The best ones have a remote chest-strap sensor that signals the wrist device. For less money, you can get a version that connects the chest-strap sensor to the watch via a wire. This can be slightly inconvenient at times, but it too is an accurate means of heart monitoring.

The least expensive way to monitor your heart rate, of course, is to take your pulse manually, at either the wrist or the carotid artery on the neck. On the wrist, the strongest pulse is on the thumb side, just below the wrist joint toward your elbow on the radial artery. The carotid pulse, on the neck, can be difficult to find when you are at rest, but it pounds during exercise, making it much easier to find. It is located about one inch on either side of the front of the neck's midline, about one inch up from the Adam's apple, just below the jaw.

You can calculate your beats per minute by taking your pulse for 6 seconds and then adding a zero to the score to get BPM. For example, if you felt your pulse for 6 seconds and counted 9 beats, you would have 90 BPM; if you felt 13 beats, it would be 130 BPM. This is the quickest and simplest method and will give a fairly accurate ballpark figure. However, you can get a more accurate figure by taking a slightly longer reading. Taking the pulse for 10 seconds and multiplying by 6, or 15 seconds and multiplying by 4, will give a more precise count.

The problem is that taking the pulse during exercise will probably require you to stop for a few seconds. You can get used to this, but it sometimes breaks up the exercise rhythm.

HOW TO DETERMINE YOUR OPTIMUM TRAINING HEART RATE (OTR)

OTR = 220 − Age + Resting Heart Rate ÷ 2.

Example: a 40-year-old with a heart rate of 60 beats per minute.

OTR = 220 − 40 + 60 ÷ 2 = 120 beats per minute (BPM)

Step by step:

$$220 - 40 = 180$$
$$180 + 60 = 240$$
$$240 \div 2 = 120$$

OTR = 120 (see below for body-type adjustment)

If the resting heart rate is 60 beats per minute or below, then adjust the formula as follows, according to your body type:

　 types add 5 BPM to OTR
　 types add 10 BPM to OTR
　 types add 15 BPM to OTR

THE RESTING PHASE—EXERCISING THE LUNGS FIRST

The Resting Phase in Level 2 is much the same as in Level 1, but the primary monitor is heart rate rather than the breath rate. You will most likely find that the two are intimately linked, and that when one increases, the other follows. The formula for the Resting Phase heart rate is:

$$RPHR = OTR - 30 \text{ BPM}$$

If the OTR, or optimum training rate, was calculated to be 130, then the Resting Phase heart rate is 100 BPM. During this part of the workout, you will exercise up to that heart rate, and not above it, for 5 to 10 minutes. This very low heart rate will be combined with very deep maximal Darth Vader breaths and a very low exercise level. The philosophy behind the Resting Phase, and the benefits of carrying out this phase thoroughly and well, are described in chapters 11 and 13.

The amount of exercise needed to push the heart rate above 100 BPM (or whatever the Resting Phase heart rate is) is minimal, so be careful. Try not to be anxious about going at a faster pace during this time. Instead, focus on taking bigger and deeper breaths. Because the exercise level is unusually easy and will not force you to breath more deeply, you will need repeatedly to remind yourself to continue the maximal breathing during this phase. It takes a little effort at the outset to prepare the body to enjoy maximum exercise along with the regular experience of the Zone.

THE LISTENING PHASE—EXERCISING THE BODY/MIND

After 5 to 10 minutes in the Resting Phase, begin to increase your exercise pace. If you are running, gradually run faster. If you're playing tennis, begin to chase more balls and play more aggressively.

During the Level 2 Listening Phase we will listen to several monitors such as heart and breath rate, form, and awareness to help determine how much exercise is most beneficial. The breathing rate monitor explained in Level 1 is only one of them.

While Level 1 is fairly automatic, the athlete in Level 2 is more involved mentally and physically. Level 2 provides a more accurate assessment of mind-body needs and therefore will have more appeal—and benefit—for the more experienced athlete.

The best way to get acquainted with this program is with a sport that provides a steady level of intensity that can be gradually increased or decreased, such as walking, running, rowing, or cross-country skiing. New technologies have made exercise equipment available at reasonable prices, so that this training method can be mastered in your living room. Stair-stepping machines, cross-country-ski machines, rowing ergometers, and stationary bicycles make this exercise reconditioning very easy. As you become skilled with the program, you can apply it to sports requiring varied intensity, such as basketball, tennis, skiing, and cycling.

MONITOR 1—HEART RATE

The exercise level in the Listening Phase is increased up to the optimum training rate (OTR) described above, adjusted for body type if the Resting Phase heart rate (RPHR) is 60 beats per minute or less.

THE DURATION OF THE LISTENING PHASE DEPENDS ON BODY TYPE:
• THE MINIMUM TIME FOR VATA TYPES IS 10 MINUTES.
• THE MINIMUM TIME FOR PITTA TYPES IS 15 MINUTES.
• THE MINIMUM TIME FOR KAPHA TYPES IS 20 MINUTES.
THESE ARE THE MINIMUM TIMES NEEDED FOR PEOPLE OF THESE CONSTITUTIONS TO GAIN MAXIMUM AEROBIC BENEFITS.

During the Listening Phase, gradually increase the exercise intensity up to the OTR, also called the "breaking point." Your monitoring of heart rate, breath rate, form, and awareness will all cross-reference the experience of the breaking point.

The breaking point is that point at around 50 percent of maximum heart rate at which the integration of mind and body established in the warm-up phases begins to break down. At this stage, the athlete feels a certain subjective feeling of discomfort or strain. The "objective" monitors reflect this initial subjective experience of disintegration. I will discuss each monitor in detail later in this chapter, but for now let's focus only on the heart rate monitor.

Again, the purpose of the Listening Phase is to learn to recognize the subjective experience at the breaking point. As you gradually bring up your exercise workload, begin to "listen" for any signs of strain as your exercise approaches the OTR (130 BPM in our example). A good learning method would be to exercise up to 130 BPM and continue to 135 BPM. At 135 BPM, begin to bleed the exercise level back to about 125 BPM. Stay at 125 for 1 to 2 minutes, then begin to increase the load once again, carefully watching and listening to how your body feels.

The exact number is not what is important. What matters is *how you feel*. You are learning to gauge your mind-body breaking point. So, if you noticed no subjective experience of strain at 130, move up again from 125 to 135 to find it. At 135, slowly back off the pace and stabilize at 125 once again. This "rinsing" effect gives you a comparative look at comfort becoming discomfort as you subjectively measure the difference from 125 to 135.

Somewhere in this range, you will perceive a point of initial strain. Our habit has been to exercise right through this point without even noticing it. With focused attention around the 50 percent mark, the breaking point becomes as clear as the severe strain that occurs at the aerobic threshold, around 70 to 90 percent of maximum heart rate. (Details on the aerobic threshold are in chapters 11 and 13.)

In the beginning weeks of this program, you will notice that it doesn't take much exercise to reach your OTR, and with any significant exercise your heart rate will spike to 150 to 170 BPM automatically. When Warren Wechsler from chapter 1 began his training, he could barely pedal his stationary bike without seeing his heart rate jump to 180. He was like most of us, totally conditioned to an exercise heart rate of 150, 160, or 170 BPM.

When I saw Barry Norton six months after he started this program, he told me of his experience: "When I began the program, I became very frustrated. Every time I would start to run, my heart monitor would start beeping, as it was set to my 125 OTR. Your ears must have been ringing, because I was cursing you out daily for the first couple of weeks. I wanted to quit, but my friends encouraged me to stick with the program, and to my surprise, within three or four weeks, I was running as well as before, only with a lower heart rate, and breathing through my nose the entire time.

"Within eight weeks, I was able to finish my run, which normally took me 25 minutes, in 18 minutes. I must say, in the beginning I never thought this was going to work, but within a couple of weeks, it was clear that things were changing. I think the most rewarding part of the program was how I felt after my run, compared to my usual feeling of exhaustion."

The shift of the heart rate to a slower rhythm is one of the last indicators of invincible fitness to appear. Lowered breath rates and lower perceived exertion rates come first, and more easily, than the sometimes stubborn heart rate. The reason for this is that the heart rate is intimately connected to the sympathetic nervous system. If there is any unnecessary fight-or-flight exercise stress, the heart will respond accordingly. As you become properly trained to maintain composure at higher and higher competitive levels, the sympathetic nervous system will not be called upon as much, and the parasympathetic nervous system can come forward to balance it.

In our preliminary study, both systems, the emergency sympathetic and the relaxing parasympathetic, were balanced, keeping the mind and body highly coordinated. If one becomes dominant, then the balance of rest (parasympathetic) and activity (sympathetic) cannot be maintained. These two opposite systems were balanced in our study to set up neurologically the exercise high. This is probably the reason why more of the coherent alpha brain waves were seen in all of our subjects when using the Three Phase Workout.

If we are to create a hurricane in the body and mind of an athlete, then every step of the way we must establish the opposites. The winds must revolve around the eye and its silence. Its enormous strength comes from the silence. As exercise increases, the Listening Phase monitors will display this level of silence. If the silence is lost, then it must be reestablished before going on. Holding on to this experience is the formula for lasting success.

This experience is real and reproducible, as long as you have the desire and patience to respect the needs of your body. It is just a matter of conditioning the body to function more efficiently. Why push your heart rate to 170 or 180 when with a little retraining and patience you can accomplish as much or more with a heart rate of 130 or 140?

Soon the motivation for exercise goals will be turned inside out. Your performance goals will become secondary to the perceived exertion economy—how much work you can accomplish with how little effort. By learning to achieve more but expend less effort, you are developing the coexistence of opposites that is our formula for the Zone and the road map to an unlimited and enjoyable competitive performance curve.

MONITOR 2—BREATH RATE

The way to monitor the breath rate was described in detail in the Level 1 program. The success of Level 1 is dependent solely on the breath rate. Please review the Level 1 breathing instructions now, as they are the basis for Level 2 training.

As in Level 1, the breath rate is established in the Sun Salute, but there is a slight difference. While the Level 2 breath rate is maintained at a comfortable rhythm, it is not exclusively the Sun Salute breath rate.

Because you are using other monitors to listen to your body's responses, you can allow your breath rate to increase beyond the Sun Salute rhythm and still remain on the performance curve. Although the breath may be slightly faster, it is still comfortable and deep. A 2- to 3-second count on the inhale and 2- to 3-second count on the exhale would be a minimum comfortable rhythm, with a maximum around 5 or 6 seconds. In the beginning, the need for mouth breathing in order to be comfortable is common, and is the first indicator that you are pushing too hard. You will reach your breathing limits early in the beginning, but respecting them is the key to the long-term success of your fitness program.

MONITOR 3—FORM

When Mark Spitz won an Olympic-record seven gold medals, breaking world records in all seven events, his form was perfect. One analyst noted that during the 100-meter freestyle, for example, he took 45 strokes per length of the pool, compared to his nearest competitor's 60 strokes.

Swimming requires mastery of the subtleties of perfect form in order to achieve the perfect stroke. On swim teams, children from ages 8 to 18 sometimes log 15,000 to 20,000 yards of swimming per day. It is only after such intensive practice that one can find the form to be a world champion. The better the form, the better the performance—and the more effortless it becomes.

As the saying goes, "Form follows function." When form looks strained, it is only reflecting a body overloaded with mental, physical, or emotional stress. If form could be used as a monitor, it would give insight into the inner functioning of the body, an aspect that we sometimes overlook or unconsciously overrule.

With a group of friends, I was watching the Ironman Triathlon in Hawaii on *Wide World of Sports* a few years back. At the start of the race, a cascade of about fifteen hundred bobbing orange caps churned the Kona surf. Then, starting about a quarter of the way into the swim, a helicopter camera began singling out one lone swimmer.

He seemed in last place, because he looked like he was going very slowly, and there wasn't another swimmer in sight. Despite his position, he seemed in no hurry. His strokes were slow, relaxed, and quite rhythmic. We figured he had gone off course. Why else would national television spend so much time on a last-place swimmer unless he was swimming out to sea and might be in danger?

But as the helicopter panned away from this swimmer, it turned out that he was alone all right—100 yards ahead of the pack, in first place. It was amazing to all of us that this guy, whose strokes were so slow, could be dominating the race. His form: perfect. His performance: perfect. When you're doing it right, it always looks easy.

In the Three Phase Workout, establish perfect form from the outset and never let it go. When a boxer's arms begin to drop, his broken-down form sends up a flare of defeat. When a weight lifter recruits muscles not intended for a certain lift, his form must break down. This defeats the purpose of the lift. The body is forced to endure an unproductive and unnecessary level of stress. This curtails the mind-muscle coordination needed to reap maximum results from the workout.

Pay attention to form during the entire workout, but with particular care during the Listening Phase. As the exercise intensity approaches the breaking point, the heart rate begins to spike and the breath rate becomes labored. At this point, proper form is likely to break down as well. If so, slow down the pace until proper form is reestablished. Keep trying to run faster or bike harder, but when your form slips, listen to it, respect it, and adjust your pace until you get it back.

Many of us are unaware of the value or even the experience of proper form. The best way to get acquainted with it is to listen to the body during the sequential Three Phase Workout. This will allow a close look at the form during every stage of the workout. Soon, form will be a lively monitor in your exercise-stress gauge.

As the form becomes perfect, the function gets easier, to the point where the whole thing just flows. The San Diego Padres' Tony Gwynn, one of baseball's all-time great hitters, described his experiences in the Zone: "I see the ball leave the pitcher's hand and then leave the bat, with no recollection of physically moving my hands, wrists, or hips." Gwynn, a perennial .300-plus hitter, finds the place where form and function blend together as one. There's no resistance, no thoughts, just a body and mind in motion.

Tim Flannery, the Padres' shortstop, found that same place: "When I'm locked in, I feel like a giant eye. I don't feel my hands or my stride, I just see the ball and the rest just happens." When form is perfect, physiological resistance, strain, and fatigue are eliminated and the elusive Zone becomes a reality.

MONITOR 4—AWARENESS

I have been discussing the final monitor throughout the book, although I haven't called it by name. It is our own consciousness, or awareness, as we tune it to perceive what is going on with our body.

Two basic experiences shape our reality: comfort and discomfort. We have been conditioned to expect and accept the discomfort of exercise, yet we are constantly searching for the place of supreme comfort called the Zone. Through this program, you learn to set up that comfort from the start.

At the breaking point, the feeling of comfort created during the Sun Salute and the Resting Phase will begin to shade into the feeling of discomfort. If you remain alert, you will recognize that initial experience of strain, the point where mind and body begin to disintegrate, as the point where the heart rate crosses the 50 percent mark, the breath becomes labored, and the form begins to break down.

The perceived level of exertion will ultimately become your primary exercise monitor. Recent studies have shown that perceived level of exertion can be as accurate as a heart monitor in predicting the current heart rate. This reconditioning may take a couple of months to establish, but once it is in place, you will know the exact amount of exercise you need for maximum performance, health, and fitness, and you will know it from the inside out.

AWARENESS THERAPY

If exercise is for the removal of stress, then we should not be surprised if that actually happens. Yet many conventional sports practices increase stress rather than dissolve it.

For example, it is not uncommon for an athlete, during a run or any other sports activity, to suddenly acquire a knee or hip pain that lasts anywhere from a few hours to a few days. There are two ways to deal with this type of exercise pain—or, for that matter, any kind of pain.

The first is summed up in the common advice "run through the pain." But pushing the body into overdrive, in order to meet the demands of the exercise, forces the body to compensate for the structural weakness that is causing the pain. Usually the pain does go away after a while, but three or four days later it appears somewhere else. It is not uncommon for an athlete to be able to track a pain, which began in the knee, down to the foot, then into the lower back, until it finally settles into the neck as chronic neck and shoulder tension. It no longer interferes with running, but it is a constant nag that simply won't go away.

I call this "dealing with the pain on the level of discomfort," because we simply shift the discomfort from one level to another, never really getting free of it. Many of us handle pain this way. The pain is not eliminated from the body but is driven in deeper, often taking up permanent residence. This method defeats the purpose of exercise, expressed many centuries ago as the elimination of stress and imbalance from the body.

Another way to deal with pain is "on the level of comfort." This seems a contradiction, since it is obvious that when pain comes, comfort must go. But if exercise is a technique for stress reduction and removal, then it makes sense that when stress pops up in the form of pain, we have an opportunity to get rid of it. Training through the pain only buries it, but respecting it can eliminate it.

When the pain comes and the comfort goes, slow down your pace until the pain dissipates and the comfort returns. Keep on bleeding back the intensity by going slower and slower until the feeling of comfort gradually replaces the feeling of discomfort.

If the pain persists, slow down to a walk. If this is what the body wants, then, in the name of longevity, listen to it. If needed, take that day off and try again tomorrow. Exercise up to the point of pain and discomfort and back off until you can stabilize comfort. When the comfort overflows into the pain, you can go back to raising the intensity level once again. Only this time, with the pain gone, there is one less structural stress to inhibit peak performance.

If we let it, the body will take the necessary time in the Listening Phase to remove accumulated stress and strain, ultimately leaving it stress-free and ready to perform at its highest capacity. The more its latent potential unfolds, the more gracefully will the Listening Phase expand into the Performance Phase, and you will find yourself running or playing all-out, using the experience of comfort as your guide.

DISTRACTIONS

When athletes recall their peak experiences, they report that while in the Zone, they are unable to hear the crowd and are often unaware of the contest, the opponents, or the pressure. Dan Fouts, former San Diego Chargers quarterback, described it as being almost comatose—floating around and being barely aware of the body. The great Zen master D. T. Suzuki described this nonthinking state: "As soon as we reflect, deliberate, and conceptualize, the original unconscious is lost and thought interferes."

The Zone is defined by its lack of distractions. If you're thinking, you're not in the Zone. If you're trying, you're not in the Zone. If you're bored, you're not in the Zone. And if you're reading a book while exercising, you're certainly not going to find the Zone!

When a person reads while on an exercise bike, the mind has to read while the body exercises. This is directly opposed to mind-body integration that characterizes the Zone. Reading while exercising may be a more efficient use of time in the moment, but in the long run, distracting the mind from the body is not worth it. This is another of the bad habits that are a way of life for many of us, like eating and talking on the car phone while driving.

In our society, we pride ourselves on how many things we can do at one time or accomplish in one day. In ancient times, pride was taken for the quality of the accomplishment rather than for the accomplishment itself.

There is an old saying, "A painter paints with his hand, an artist paints with his hand and his mind, and a master paints with his hand, his mind, and his heart." It is the same with all things. If our entire focus isn't on what we are doing, no matter how simple the job, the result will be compromised. This is a lesson we can't learn fast enough and will probably have to learn the hard way.

Athletes often have to be injured or overtrained before they are willing to listen to that most important person—themselves. When you slow down enough and begin to listen, you will find the body to be a wealth of important feedback that, when attended to, will ensure a safe, enjoyable, and lasting fitness program.

As you apply these principles, you will soon see that it isn't possible to read a book while adhering to them. It's like flying an airplane: You are constantly navigating, monitoring instruments, keeping the plane level and straight. The last thing a pilot would do is pull out a book and start to read! Similarly, the thought of watching TV during the Three Phase Workout would never arise, because there is so much you need to do to stay on track. These principles require your mind and body to work together, if you are going to produce results such as the alpha brain waves seen in our case studies.

There are many distractions in use these days as standard exercise equipment. We've already talked about the scene in most health clubs, with their big-screen televisions mounted from the ceiling, ear phones for remote TV listening or music channels, reading stands built into the exercise equipment, and so on. Now, having read this far, you can see clearly that most of these gadgets and distractions are disintegrating to mind and body.

Music, however, is a two-way street. On the positive side, the rhythm can often be very integrating and can help coordinate mind and body, as in dance or ballet. The problem arises when the athlete becomes tired, and yet the music is still going. The body starts screaming for rest, the heart and breath rates go up, form begins to break down, and the awareness of comfort is long gone, but the mind drives the body to keep up with the music. Music can give superhuman motivation, but it can distract you from how your body is feeling, and if you're not careful, it can leave you exhausted.

IF YOU ARE ACCUSTOMED TO WORKING OUT WITH MUSIC, AND IN-TEND TO CONTINUE, SELECT YOUR MUSIC CAREFULLY, PREFERA-BLY A RHYTHM THAT WILL PROVIDE MOTIVATION FOR THE KAPHA TYPES AND MIND-BODY INTEGRATION (A CALMER RHYTHM) FOR VATA AND PITTA TYPES. PICK SOMETHING THAT SETS A RHYTHM THAT YOU ENJOY AND IS IN HARMONY WITH THE DESIRED EXERCISE PACE. AND BE CAREFUL NOT TO OVERDO IT.

LISTENING PHASE WRAP-UP

During the Listening Phase, the exercise level is gradually accelerated to the OTR, the optimum training heart rate. At this point, there should be an initial feeling of strain. The other monitors will chime in as the body tries to express its loss of comfort. The breath rate becomes labored, form breaks down, and the awareness of discomfort, although still subtle at this point, is definite.

When this happens, begin to bleed back the pace until all monitors are in their respective comfort zones. After 1 to 2 minutes of comfort, try again to go faster. If the body responds to the increased demands with more strain and discomfort, indicated by one or more monitors, then again slow down.

We continually ask the body for more, but we are not willing to violate the integrity of its inner intelligence by forcing it. In its own time, with proper training, it will accommodate any desire of the mind. As long as we keep the strain off the system, it will adjust and grant our request for better performance. When all the stress is removed, the body can begin to access its full potential and function in perfect balance.

Perfect balance means the highest intensity of exercise in conjunction with a composed body and mind. This is subjectively verified by the feeling of comfort and the regular experience of the exercise high. Objectively, this balanced state is correlated with lower heart and breath rates, lower perceived exertion, a deconditioned fight-or-flight response, and a higher percentage of alpha in the brain.

THE PERFORMANCE PHASE—THE ULTIMATE EXPERIENCE OF BODY, MIND, AND SPORT

The Listening Phase prepares the body for a competitive level of performance. After you spend the designated body-type time requirement in the Listening Phase, you will be ready for competition. The Performance Phase, although the natural extension of the Listening Phase, is a distinct experience. Please read the Level 1 description as the Performance Phase in both levels is similar.

The Performance Phase has no time limit. As you move into this phase, the only two monitors you need to be concerned with are the experience of comfort that you have trained yourself to be aware of, and the rhythm of the breath established in the Listening Phase. You may exercise as hard and as fast as you like, taking the pace to the limits. As long as the body doesn't shift into discomfort and strain and the breath rate doesn't become labored, the Performance Phase can go on indefinitely.

During this phase, if the body has been properly prepared, the athletic potential seems unlimited, while the internal experience is one of effortlessness. This is the Zone, where the hurricane is fully mature.

You have created the eye early in your training, and cultured it through higher and higher performance levels, until the coexistence of opposites became a tangible reality. In the Resting and Listening phases, this experience is delicate; it is easy to bring heart and breath rates up as you increase your performance level. With patience and careful monitoring, the body will eventually allow you to enter the Zone, where the opposites—intensity and composure—are spun together.

Experience of the exercise high is available at every fitness level and in every stage of the Three Phase Workout. As you become more fit, the intensity level in the Performance Phase will escalate each day, and the exercise high will be with you every step of the way. A time will come when the limits of comfort and breath will seem to dissolve, and you will find yourself running as fast as you can and somehow watching yourself do it, while totally relaxed, calm, and performing effortlessly. This is the Zone, where nothing is impossible and performance limits become unlimited, where records are broken, the good become great, and some find it indescribable.

Tony Gwynn said, "When you're in it, you don't hear the crowd, you don't think about the situation, you don't think about nothin'. It's something way beyond confidence. I mean, I'm usually fairly confident, but this is like—I don't even know what the word would be."

The Zone is where the difficult becomes easy, and you find yourself doing things you shouldn't be able to do. Inside, you know: "This is it, this is the way I should play every day. This it the *only* way to play!"

The teachings of the Vedas were designed to bring us to this level so that we can perform this way daily—in all that we do. This book, based on these ancient principles, provides a path to peak experience that is available to everyone who wishes to enter the Zone. This experience is our birthright, and it is within the design of our human nervous system to access it.

To push ourselves into exhaustion when we have the capacity to allow effortless, perfect performance to flow naturally, from the inside out, seems somehow primitive and a waste of time. I have never heard of a peak experience that was described as painful, grueling, or exhausting. Rather, the descriptions always fit the original definition of exercise: rejuvenating, stress-relieving, and accessing full human potential.

INTERVAL TRAINING

In the beginning of this training program, you are not going to be able to go out and do intervals and speed work while satisfying all the monitors. The body is simply not ready for it. It needs time to recondition itself to perform from balance and comfort, rather than from strain and exhaustion.

Many athletes have immediate competitive goals, however, and can't wait for this retraining to be completed before running intervals. If this is the case for you, then start every workout exactly as described above. Take yourself through each phase of the workout, and when you complete the Listening Phase, start the competition or begin intervals. Try to hold on to the nasal breath rate and comfort as long as possible, but if the interval demands more exertion, that is fine: Go for it! As long as you are properly warmed up, a degree of mind-body coordination will be carried with you and the rigors of competition won't be nearly as exhausting.

The fight-or-flight response, elicited by conventional competitive techniques, is most harmful to the body when it is frequently repeated. If the body is "maxed out" every day in training as well as during competitions, it will surely show signs of wear and eventually break down. Remember, the fight-or-flight sympathetic response is catabolic, which means that it has known degenerative effects.

To achieve your immediate competitive goals while you are mastering this program, the combination of both training styles—Invincible Athletics and conventional methods—can work well. The Zone will still be a random experience, but your chances of attaining it will be better than they would have been using conventional techniques.

Start interval training only after you successfully complete the Listening Phase. This means that if you didn't feel well during the Listening Phase, this may not be the best day for a maximal workout. Reschedule your speed work for a day when you feel better and more balanced. Remember, you can't set the workout schedule for the body without asking the body.

In this regard, coaches must realize that there are good and bad days, and they must become responsive to the daily experiences and needs of their athletes. If an athlete is just loafing, this will become obvious in time, and the coach can act accordingly.

If competitive goals are not pressing, then your sprint workouts can be as follows:

Take your sprints up to the point where the nose breathing has to shift to the mouth for more oxygen. You can do sprints up to this point, then back off. Soon the nose will be able to accommodate even the fastest sprints. I know many runners who have trained themselves to maintain nose breathing throughout a sprint workout.

If you do have immediate goals, still take your sprints to the maximum nasal-breathing pace before you shift into fight-or-flight mouth breathing.

In the beginning, it will be much harder to nose breathe when running intervals; it will clearly feel like a strain. But keep at it; this forced nasal breathing will help expedite nasal-breathing efficiency at competitive levels. With this style of interval training, 80 percent of the workout will still be within your comfort zone. When the maximum exertion comes (the interval), the body has been properly prepared for it in the warm-up and in the Resting and Listening phases.

COOL-DOWN

The cool-down for Level 2 is identical to Level 1:

5 to 10 minutes of Resting Phase
5 to 10 minutes of Sun Salute

(See the end of chapter 13 for details.)

SAMPLE RUNNING WORKOUT

This workout can be applicable to any aerobic workout.

WARM-UP
Perform 5 to 10 minutes of Sun Salutes very slowly and with deep breathing through the nose.

RESTING PHASE
Begin the run, but for the first 5 to 10 minutes run very slowly while still breathing very deeply through the nose. Remember, this is called the Resting Phase! Keep the heart rate about 30 BPM below the optimum training rate (OTR).

REMINDER: THE FORMULA FOR THE OTR (OPTIMUM TRAINING HEART RATE) IS:

220 − AGE + RESTING HEART RATE ÷ 2

LISTENING PHASE

Begin to run faster and monitor the comfortable rhythm of the breath. If the breath through the nose becomes labored, or if you find yourself having to breathe through the mouth, slow down to the pace set by the comfortable rhythm of nasal breathing.

Keep the pace at or below the OTR. When the heart begins to spike to 150 or so, slow the pace and reestablish the OTR.

Use form as your monitor. As soon as you feel the form begin to break down, slow the pace and reestablish a speed at which you can maintain proper form.

Learn to recognize the experience at the point where the heart goes over the OTR, the breath rate increases, and the form breaks down. There will be a subjective feeling of comfort becoming discomfort. The Listening Phase is partly to reeducate us to feel and respect this experience. It also prepares the body to handle a heavier workload in the Performance Phase.

The minimum times in the Listening Phase, to ensure cardiovascular benefit, are 10 minutes for Vata types, 15 minutes for Pitta types, and 20 minutes for Kapha types. This should be done at least 3 times a week for cumulative benefit.

PERFORMANCE PHASE

Here you would start the race, speed work, or any more-demanding aspect of your training. Monitor the experience of comfort you established in the Listening Phase and the comfortable rhythm of the breath.

You have a choice at this stage. You can be patient and adhere strictly to these principles by adjusting your pace to maintain a stable breath rate and the experience of comfort. However, if you have immediate competitive goals, you can do your sprints, hills, or whatever, holding on to nose breathing and comfort for as long as possible. Heart rate is not a monitor in the Performance Phase. It is the perceived level of comfort established in the Listening Phase and carried into the Performance Phase that will control the heart rate at a lower level. If mouth breathing becomes imperative at some point of peak exertion, try to regain the comfortable rhythm of the nose breath as best you can afterward. (See Performance Phase details earlier in this chapter.)

In the Performance Phase, running should be at a pace that is comfortable. There is no time limit. If you persevere, the pace will soon improve, but the exertion will stay constant.

COOL-DOWN

The cool-down consists of 5 to 10 minutes of Resting Phase and 5 to 10 minutes of Sun Salute.

MINIMUM TIME REQUIRED FOR LISTENING PHASE
FOR LEVEL 1 AND 2 WORKOUT—BY BODY TYPE AND SEASON

YOUR MIND-BODY TYPE	VATA SEASON (Winter)	PITTA SEASON (Summer)	KAPHA SEASON (Spring)
🌿	V=10 min.	V=10 min.	V=10 min.
🕯	P=15 min.	P=15 min.	P=15 min.
🍶	K=20 min.	K=20 min.	K=20 min.
🌿-🕯	V=10 min.	P=15 min.	V=10 min.
🕯-🌿	V=10 min.	P=15 min.	P=15 min.
🌿-🍶	V=10 min.	V=10 min.	K=20 min.
🍶-🌿	V=10 min.	K=20 min.	K=20 min.
🕯-🍶	P=15 min.	P=15 min.	K=20 min.
🍶-🕯	K=20 min.	P=15 min.	K=20 min.
🌿-🕯-🍶	V=10 min.	P=15 min.	K=20 min.

Find your body type on vertical axis, find the current season on horizontal axis, and cross-reference the appropriate minimum time required.

15

WEIGHT TRAINING

This chapter contains a sample workout that you can use as a model when you create your own.

LEVEL 1 WEIGHT TRAINING

For this we will use the 50 percent rule, more commonly known as the one rep max program at 50 percent. Main points:

- Find out what your 1 time maximum lift is for each exercised muscle.
- Exercise for 1 week using 50 percent of that 1 time maximum lift.
- Reevaluate maximums at the end of each week, then continue to work out using the 50 percent rule.

Before you begin your weight training, whether free weights, Nautilus machines, or any other muscle-resistance training, you will need to find out what your maximum 1 time lift is for each exercised muscle. For example, if you can lift 100 pounds during a biceps curl as a maximum 1 time lift, then for the rest of that week you will exercise at 50 percent of that weight. Your curls will be done at 50 pounds. The current thinking is that the percentage should be between 60 and 80 percent of maximum but, as we have seen, the Ayurvedic approach maintains that at 50 percent one will reap maximum fitness benefits.

If your desire is for body building, you may need to increase the weight beyond 50 percent. When doing so, be sure to follow the Three Phase Workout, as well as the Level 2 Weight Training Program outlined below.

Caution: When measuring for maximum lifts, be sure to do so only after you are properly warmed up. An approximation of maximum will suffice for most of us seeking general strength and fitness. Once you become familiar with your weights or resistance machine, you will see that you can easily approximate what a 100 percent load would be when lifting 80 percent or so. The key is to train at about half your maximum capacity. At the end of each week, your capacity can be reevaluated to accommodate your strength gains.

When weight training, be sure to follow the principles and breathing techniques explained earlier in the book. In order to keep your breath and heart rates low during weight training, you may find that you have to do very slow repetitions. You can coordinate these repetitions with your breath. As you exhale with Darth Vader breathing, slowly push the weight up (concentric.contraction). As you inhale through the nose, slowly let the weight down (eccentric contraction). This will slow down the pace, but will ensure an even breathing cadence, keep heart rate down, and allow optimal form and your mind's awareness of the muscle.

LEVEL 2 WEIGHT TRAINING (BODY BUILDING)

I decided that the best way to illustrate these principles in a more serious training program was to print a sample of Joanne Madden's body-building workout. As you may remember from chapter 3, Joanne is the former Ms. Maine and Ms. Natural New England, and she took second place in the Ms. America body-building contest. She is also the founder of the Maine Alliance of Drug Free Athletes. Following is her workout, exclusively using Invincible Athletics principles.

> On my way to the gym, as I drive or walk, I put my attention on easy breathing through the nose, gradually increasing the depth of breathing and all the time keeping it easy and without strain. I put attention on lengthening the exhalation, exhaling completely through the abdomen.
>
> Upon entering the gym, I do Sun Salutes: minimum 3 sets, maximum 6, performed slowly, putting attention on linking motion with breath. I greatly enjoy these as a physical warm-up and as an appropriate preparation for a workout, i.e., linking the movements of the body with the impulse of the mind and vice versa.

The few times I have begun a workout without performing Sun Salutes resulted in my heart rate going too high too quickly.

There was a time when I could not complete 6 sets without my heart rate going into the Listening Phase heart rate. I would do whatever I could, remaining at or near Resting Phase heart rate. Sun Salutes seem to stabilize the experience of physical balance.

RESTING PHASE (95 BPM)

Next I move on to exercises that don't require a lot of "work," i.e., exercises that I can complete with good form without breaking nose breathing or going much or at all above Resting Phase heart rate. These tend to be abdomen and calf exercises. Attention is always on the form of execution, easy breath, and completing the movement, having brought the specific isolated muscle group through its entire range of motion. I dismiss any notion of "muscling" or forcing the weight around. This training is an act of attention, respect, and, indeed, love.

The Resting Phase can also be performed on a treadmill, stair stepper, or during any such aerobic activity.

Sun Salutes and Rest Phase routines take about 20 minutes.

LISTENING PHASE—MAJOR MUSCLE GROUPS (95–125 BPM)

I vary workout routines quite a bit, as my energy, time, and changing needs require. At times I work two major muscle groups a day, 4 days in a row. Other times I will work three muscle groups 2 days in a row, then take a day off.

Workouts seem to require this flexibility in order for the body to remain attentive and responsive. Faced with the same workout, even just the same workout pattern, the body and mind grow stale and dull. I feel that if I am bored in the gym, so is my body.

I tend to work my chest/triceps, or my back/biceps, or my legs/shoulders. But I mix these up constantly, sometimes working my chest/shoulders, or my legs/back, or my arms (biceps and triceps)/legs. The choice of body part, if I've taken a rest day or two, is dictated by what I perceive as my most lagging body part. For example, if I feel that my shoulders need more mass work, then this muscle group takes priority over a more well developed biceps. Attention, overall, shifts from mass building off-season, to definition building on-season.

I do not ever work the same muscle group 2 days in a row (except abs). If I have completed a particularly challenging workout the day before and am sore, I take that into account. For example, if my chest workout resulted in some soreness through the deltoids and pectorals, I would choose to avoid working the chest the next day; I would opt to work legs and arms. I do not push beyond that soreness as I once did. I feel I need to let it heal now, and benefit greatly from the rest.

If I am working my chest, I will design a workout tailored to the need, e.g., mass building, definition, combination, as well as choosing the emphasis (upper, medial, or lower pectorals).

I generally do 4 exercises per body part but that depends on my energy level, my heart rate, and the number of repetitions I maintain. There are days when I feel exuberantly prepared to "conquer" the dumbbells, yet find that my heart spikes well out of the Listening Phase almost instantly. And there are those days quite to the contrary, when I feel honestly unambitious yet discover that my heart has seemingly infinite stability and capability, that no matter what weight I choose the heart rate remains low and constant.

It is for this reason that I faithfully wear my heart monitor. I do not trust my mind so much, whereas during aerobic activity, I can judge my heart rate more accurately by my breathing.

If I proceed with dumbbell presses on the flat bench, I do a moderate weight for the first set. This allows me to register how my heart is behaving, and it helps me decide if I will be going heavy or not. If my heart rate remains well within the Listening Phase range even after I've completed my first set of repetitions, then I take this as a green light for a heavier next set. (If I begin with 45-pound dumbbells, for example, I'll move on to 50s or 55s the next set; if my heart rate remains within Listening Phase range for that set, I might move on to 65- or 75-pound dumbbells.)

I do sets of 6 to 8 repetitions, only doing more if I feel the muscles are not experiencing the form. I do not very often do high-rep sets of 15 to 20 or more. I find these okay on occasion, but highly fatiguing and difficult on elbows, wrists, knees, etc., when used extensively.

My attention is on my heart rate during performance of the repetitions; however, I cannot allow it to go to the higher limit of the Listening Phase range because the heart raises its "output" after the reps are completed. For example, performing dumbbell presses will probably bring my heart up to 117 to 119 BPM by the sixth or seventh rep; when I put the weights down there is a second or two lag time and then it may max out at 120 BPM or more.

It comes down quickly now. If it doesn't, I close my eyes, bring my attention within, and the heart rate quiets. That "postrep rise" in heart rate was the trickiest aspect of adopting this program. Here are several accommodations I utilize in response to this phenomenon:

1. I do not go all the way to the top range of Listening Phase heart rate. During reps, I "allow" for this postexertion rise.

2. I will often remain lying flat or seated in/on the equipment after I've completed my reps. Jumping up will spike the heart rate, as will quickly adjusting the weights. This behavior, by the way, has resulted in people referring to me as acting in an unmotivated way!

3. If needed, I close my eyes for a few moments and settle down.

4. I always allow heart rate to be as near to Resting Phase as possible when I initiate a set. I let the heart rate fall way back before resuming another set.

5. I decide the number of reps I complete by how my heart responds.

Frequently I will rack a weight prior to exhaustion or prior to my prede-termined number of reps, simply because my heart rate is approaching the maximum range. (This behavior also leads to confusion and dismay from gym members who wonder why I don't "give it my all.")

Having begun with flat dumbbell presses, 3 to 4 sets, I will move on to 3 more chest exercises, perhaps:
• incline bench or dumbbell press
• decline bench or dumbbell press
• isolation movement for pectorals, i.e., chest fly of some sort; ma-chine, cable, or dumbbell

This chest workout takes about 25 to 35 minutes to complete.

Now, typically, I would move on to triceps. I am at a point in the routine where I could move into Performance Phase, but I only use this phase if it is necessary to accommodate the exercise, i.e., working biceps and triceps or legs often requires greater output from the heart, so I will work these during this phase, allowing heart rate to go up if necessary, but dictating the endurance of the movement or set by ease of breath and bodily comfort.

At times I also choose to do heavier sets for the initial muscle group at this point—any movement that seems to require a higher heart rate.

Biceps exercises are particularly challenging to accomplish at lower heart rates. When I first began I would complete reps that felt particularly light and so easy, yet would send my heart rate soaring. This has changed a great deal over time, and now I can complete heavy bicep curls within (or close to) Listening Phase range. I have found that whatever I sacri-ficed in poundage I gained in good form and intensity—the clear sensa-tion of working an isolated muscle through its entire range of motion.

Triceps—3 or 4 exercises, 6 to 10 reps, performed slowly—often opting to do them seated or prone to help reduce heart rate. I usually do 1 or 2 exercises (3 to 4 sets each) in Listening Phase/Performance Phase, and then shift back to Listening/Rest Phase, depending on how my heart behaves. Some work can be done at the lower rate, some not.

If I've completed all sets in Listening Phase, I go back to Rest Phase with some ab or calf work again for 5 to 10 minutes.

I complete the workout with more Sun Salutes performed slowly, min-imum of 3, maximum of 6.

When I have less time available, I do basically the same cycle of routine; however, I modify it by doing 2 to 3 exercises per muscle group, 6 to 8 reps, or working one major muscle group, not two.

I find my own energy to be optimum between 8:00 A.M. and 11:00 A.M.; after that it diminishes. After 4:00 P.M. I possess only "virtual" energy!

Throughout the year, I have varied how many days per week I trained. In the off-season, I trained 5 days a week, taking weekends off except for light aerobic activity such as walking, cycling, or rowing. At times I trained 2 days on, 1 day off. It depended on my working heart rate at rest, the emphasis of my training (mass vs. definition), and my commitments outside the gym.

Prior to the Invincible Athletics seminar I would prepare for a contest by doing 1 hour daily, 7 times a week, of aerobic activity (running, stairclimbing, biking, rowing, etc.), with 45 minutes minimum all out. This year, since the course, I did aerobics 4 to 5 times weekly, 20 to 45 minutes in Listening Phase.

I also made every attempt to get out of the gym to do this, to be amid pleasant surroundings, so I could enjoy the fragrances of flowers and the scents carried in the air, and I never went so fast that I couldn't hear the birds or the wind through the grass. Often I would simply walk—something I would not have conceived of doing a couple of years ago. I would not have been able to slow down. It would have seemed too "wimpy."

16

JET FUEL

In 1983 I found myself training for an Ironman-length triathlon. For those unfamiliar with the event, this is a grueling combination of a 2.4-mile ocean swim, immediately followed by a 112-mile bike ride, and then a refreshing 26-mile marathon run—all in one day. The best do it in 9 hours.

I had been in the sport since 1981 and was used to the long hours of training needed to compete as a triathlete. Between swimming, biking, and running, I would log an average of 3 to 5 hours of training per day.

I remember finding myself getting dizzy in classes, probably from sheer exhaustion. The dizzy spells got so strong at times that I would have to leave class and lie down. I was consoled by some of the more experienced ultramarathoners, who assured me that dizziness was part of the process of developing endurance and was a good sign, a sign restricted for those who were willing to pay the price. My fear and concern were immediately placated. Thinking that this was a positive training effect, I felt a new sense of motivation to go out and push myself even harder. I figured that the "no pain, no gain" formula was really paying off!

Despite all this training, I found myself plateaued at a competitive level I somehow couldn't break through. No matter how hard I trained, I simply couldn't shave off any more minutes, whether during the bike, swim, or run.

At first, the sport was so new that it didn't really matter how well you did; just finishing was considered accomplishment enough. By 1983, however, the sport was in full swing. The United States Triathlon Series was well under way, and former swimmers, runners, and cyclists were becoming triathletes. The competition had gotten a lot tougher in the two years I had been in the sport, but I wasn't improving with the pack.

At the time I was carrying quite a full load as a student and really had no right to expect competitive results in a sport that demands full attention. I was enrolled at the Los Angeles College of Chiropractic and had to study 2 to 4 hours a day. That, on top of 7 hours of classroom time a day plus 3 to 5 hours of training, didn't leave much time for socializing. To say the least, I was pushing myself to the limit, yet blindly went right on pushing.

Fortunately, I was in the natural-health-care field, and was exposed to many different systems of natural medicine. Although I was studying health, it was really athletic fitness that I was developing. For some reason, I never thought to contrast my excellent fitness with my slipping health. I was clearly fit, but was I healthy? Are dizzy spells a sign of good health? Probably not, although I had convinced myself that they were the positive results of good work. Looking back, I wonder if I could have passed the same standard health-related physical fitness test we discussed in chapter 3, the one that New Hampshire high school state champions were unable to pass. What was it going to be for me—health or fitness?

Around this time, a friend gave me a 100-page essay on the science of Ayurveda. He told me it was India's natural system of medicine and probably predated all other known systems. Very interested, I began reading about this "science of life." I was fascinated by the body-type system at the heart of Ayurveda. Its focus on prevention made total sense to me. So did its emphasis on treating *people*—their constitution, lifestyle, diet, etc.—not just their diseases.

The more I studied, the more I liked about this science. And I began to see that anything that was working in the world of natural medicine had roots somewhere in the Vedic understanding of health care. Acupuncture, for example, had its roots in certain South Indian vital points called *marma* points. Also, Ayurveda prides itself on having the largest herbal pharmacopia in the world. I even spent time with Ayurvedic doctors who specialize in the practice of spinal manipulation, a blend of chiropractic and osteopathy. The only bone I had to pick with this science was regarding exercise.

Most sources agreed that exercise should be moderate, not to exceed 50 percent of one's capacity, and that there should be no strain. Some even said a person shouldn't sweat or breathe heavily! Well, I did more sweating and heavy breathing every day in training than I'd like to remember, and I just couldn't accept this teaching. How did they expect people to unfold their unlimited potential—something Ayurveda preached—and yet limit exercise to only 50 percent? In those days, the recommended maximum heart rate percentages were 85 to 90 percent. The only time you might be guided toward 50 percent was if you were 70 years old, noncompetitive— and recovering from bypass surgery!

At that time, I never would have believed that the 50 percent formula would provide the performance key for everyone, whether 6, 16, or 66, whether Olympic athletes or recovering couch potatoes. Nor would I have imagined that only ten years later, the so-called experts would begin recommending heart rates as low as 60 percent. I believe it won't be long now before 'the 50 percent formula set more than five thousand years ago will be the accepted key to developing our enormous physical potential.

At the time, I continued my studies in Ayurveda with enthusiasm, but I also kept up my strenuous workouts and competitions. If I was going to cut down, I'd have to hear it in person from an expert, and he would have to prove the logic to me!

Around that time, a small group of Ayurvedic physicians came to the United States. While visiting Washington, D.C., they got their first look at American physical fitness practices. One sultry summer day they were caught in traffic, driving very slowly up one of the hills near the White House. They all had their windows rolled down because they rejected the use of "environmental refrigeration," as they called it. As they slowly climbed the hill, drinking in the humidity-soaked exhaust fumes, they came up next to a runner who was paced with them for the next 200 to 300 yards.

The slightly overweight runner, not in the best shape, was perspiring profusely. His face was beet red, he grimaced in pain, and he was breathing and panting like an exhausted horse. "What is this poor man doing?" the doctors asked. When told that he was doing a common sort of physical exercise that people do to stay healthy, they responded, "Yes, exercise is a good thing, but this man is in pain, he might hurt himself."

They were reassured that this was a common sight, as many doctors recommended running to their patients. At this the doctors howled in laughter. They simply couldn't compute the notion of such torture in the name of health. Their idea of exercise was miles away from the grimacing red face of that Capital City runner.

Their exercise philosophy was closely allied to the science of Yoga. Yoga, with its slow stretches and long-held postures, is clearly not aerobic in the conventional sense, but it can certainly produce an extraordinary state of health and fitness. My goal at that time was neither health nor fitness; I guess I was too young for that. Although my training regimen made me remarkably fit, what I wanted was *performance*, and I was more than willing to pay any price.

In 1983 I had a chance to consult with a well-respected Ayurvedic expert. Having heard the story of the Washington runner, I could well imagine the expert's probable reaction when I started to describe the triathlon! With little hope for satisfaction, I found myself near the back of a line of people waiting to talk to him after the lecture. I waited about a half-hour while he patiently answered questions. When I reached the front of the line, he turned to me, and I started to describe my situation:

"I do triathlons, and I train 3 to 5 hours every day for this sport." I could see by his expression that he had no idea what a triathlon was, and was concerned about someone exercising for 3 to 5 hours.

"It's a competition," I continued, "in which you swim, bike, and run in consecutive order." His stare grew blank. "First you swim 2.4 miles, then ride a bicycle for 112 miles, and then run 26 miles. All in one day, one right after the other."

With that he perked up. "Are you being punished? Or is someone chasing you? Why would you do such a thing?"

"Oh no, this is a competition, where you train for a particular event. We do it because . . ." I suddenly realized I had no idea why I did it. "There is no one chasing us. It's a sporting event.

"My question is this," I continued. "I've been doing a lot of reading about Ayurveda, and wondering about its concept of exercise." Starting to feel quite foolish now, I gingerly asked, "Is all this exercise I do good for me according to Ayurveda?"

He paused in silence for a minute or two. I began to think my ridiculous question was unworthy even of being answered. But finally he responded: "Do you meditate?"

"Yes," I said. "I learned Transcendental Meditation (TM) a few years ago to help deal with the stress of school."

"Do you sleep when you meditate?"

I proudly responded, "Oh yes, I'll come home from a long training run, shower, and start to meditate. Next thing I know I've fallen into a really deep black-out sleep. I wake up sometimes 2 or 3 hours later, wondering if it's morning or night, totally out of it! I feel it's some of the very best rest I get."

His reply surprised me. "Yes, of course you're getting rest—but you're exhausted. But the purpose of meditation is not to fall asleep, it's to maintain a state of restful alertness, where your body is deeply relaxed and your mind is totally alert—not sleeping. Research on TM has shown many health benefits, including enhanced mind-body coordination and physical performance in sports, when this state of restful alertness is maintained [see appendix].

"When you continually fall asleep as you've been doing," he continued, "it means you're too exhausted to maintain the state of restful alertness, and you would reap more of the benefits of TM if you were not so tired."

I got the feeling that he knew that if he came right out and said, "Don't exercise so much," I would probably do it anyway, so he was trying to be diplomatic.

I asked, "Do you mean that if I can maintain this state of restful alertness while I meditate, then I can do as much exercise as I want?"

He smiled and said, "Yes, that's exactly right," and turned to greet the next person in line.

So began the first taste of my less-is-more training. I really had nothing to lose, as my competition results weren't improving, and I was getting to the point where I had to decide whether I was going to *be* a pro athlete or treat them. Both were full-time commitments, so giving this a shot in the name of experience was well worth it.

I figured that all I had to do was stay awake when I meditated, and I could exercise as much as I wanted. It sounded simple, but it turned out to be easier said than done! Even to get a glimpse of the state of restful alertness, I had to cut my training by half. The funny thing was that cutting back was a relief. I now had an excuse to miss those midnight 10-mile runs.

When I began my quest for restful alertness, I had little idea that I was searching for the very same experience that a decade later I would be describing as the formula for the Zone: the coexistence of opposites, mental and physical composure in the midst of vigorous exercise.

I kept cutting back my training, hoping to taste the experience of restful alertness. I adjusted my training level according to my ability to experience this state. If I fell asleep during TM, I took that to mean I was overtraining, and I would cut back. If I felt myself relaxed and rested but remained alert, I would pick up the pace a little. After a few months, I was still training at about half my previous level, and I was able to lock in to the restful alertness state on a fairly regular basis.

Monitoring my experiences in this way, I began to respect my body's need for rest. It was much greater than my ambitious mind had been willing to admit!

As a result of this experiment, the most interesting and totally unexpected thing began to happen: My performance started to improve. I hadn't bought a new bike or adopted any fancy new training techniques. All I was doing was training less! Yet, I was getting so much stronger that some of my friends began to suspect me of steroid use. It was definitely uncommon to improve as much as I did in a few short months.

I went from being a top 10 percent triathlete to regularly placing in the top ten. I took a few fourth and fifth places in fields of 800 to 1,000. In my last really competitive year, 1984, I began competing as a pro. No one could believe me when I told them how little I was training, considering how well I was competing.

Before starting with the new method of training, I had sometimes trained in a health club with a group of basketball and volleyball players who worked out with one goal in mind—a higher vertical jump. As part of the workout, we would hop up and down the bleacher steps on one leg, going up and down until the leg gave out. Then we would hop up and down on the other leg until it, too, was completely exhausted. Each step was about a foot and a half high. After both legs were rendered useless we would go beat up the rest of our bodies with dumbbells and Nautilus machines.

I was a skier and runner most of my competitive life, but was never much of a jumper. I was not especially good at this hopping routine, which is probably why I rarely trained with those guys. I would struggle on each step while they would kind of float up as if they were playing hopscotch.

After several months, I walked into that gym with zero stair-hopping time logged since I had begun my "train less" program, and joined in on another bleacher-hopping contest. This time, to my total surprise, I found myself floating up the steps. For some reason, it had become the easiest thing in the world. I was going up and down, up and down, completely effortlessly.

I was hopping faster than anyone else, and, what was more amazing, I couldn't fatigue my right leg. My friends couldn't believe it; they thought I was on drugs. When they had totally worn out both their legs, they sat patiently watching as I continued hopping up and down, trying to fatigue my right leg. Eventually I just stopped.

For the first time in my life, I felt invincible, with unlimited, literally inexhaustible physical potential. One friend said afterward, "What got into you in there? I've never seen you jump like that before." All I could say was that I was training less and meditating more, and as a result I was performing better. I was as surprised as he was.

Another of my friends was so impressed by this display that he went out and learned TM that week.

Looking back, it seems that what probably happened is that the rest I got from cutting back on my training allowed me to integrate into my exercise the silent composure I felt in meditation, and thus to enter the Zone. Without realizing it, I had stumbled onto the coexistence of opposites—rest and alertness, composure and vigorous exercise—the formula for the Zone.

That day I performed at a level I had never dreamed possible, and it was effortless. I couldn't be fatigued. There was no strain or pain, which was usually associated with my hard workouts. It was all so easy and natural that I became convinced that we are all designed to enjoy that place on a regular basis. That was the experience I had, and I wanted it back!

But what could I do to get it back? I wasn't sure; all I knew was that this unorthodox new program was working beyond my wildest expectations. Sure, I still wanted to be competitive, but somehow the TM helped me let go of the goal and just begin enjoying the process. I wasn't exhausted anymore, my workouts became fun again, and I was performing better than ever before. Without knowing it, I had tapped the mental techniques of our formula for the exercise high—dynamic activity and silence in the form of restful alertness.

To consistently re-create the experience of the Zone for myself, over the next ten years, with extensive study in India, I researched and developed the physical techniques I have described in this book. These techniques will help you to do less and accomplish more. With less training, and by monitoring the experience of comfort through form, awareness, and lower heart and breath rates, you too can regularly reproduce the elusive experience of the Zone.

When you combine these physical and mental techniques you are training the mind and body, both during rest (TM) and activity (exercise) to be silent in the midst of dynamic activity. This is the formula for success.

As I discussed, our case studies have shown an enhanced production of alpha waves in the brains of athletes using these techniques, as compared to conventional exercise. The alpha bursts, as well as the lower breath and heart rates, provide an objective measure of the subjective experience of the Zone. We now know that vigorous exercise can be associated with mental and physical composure.

With these opposites in place, the body is constantly nourished during vigorous exercise by the quiet equanimity of a mind at rest. The strain of conventional exercise is replaced by the body's innate, God-given ability for natural excellence. The trick is: "Just listen."

The bleacher-hopping experience hooked me on the "less is more" concept. I continued my training and study of this principle, and even began writing about it, but at that time, nobody wanted anything to do with it. Less was definitely not more back in 1983! In 1986 and 1987 I submitted the first draft of this book to a couple of publishers and was politely turned down.

Sometimes I would wonder if this stuff really worked or was just something I had cooked up in my own head. There were many instances when I was just about to drop the whole program due to lack of interest when without fail I'd receive a letter or a phone call from someone telling me how wonderful the program was, and how it had changed their life. This refueled my tanks, and I was compelled to keep the program alive.

In 1987 I was invited to spend two weeks visiting the World Centre for

Maharishi Ayur-Ved outside New Delhi, India. At the time, Maharishi Mahesh Yogi had invited hundreds of the very best Ayurvedic doctors in India to a new hospital, to rejuvenate and authenticate this science of life according to the original Vedic texts and the discoveries of modern science.

This new framework is called Maharishi Ayur-Ved, giving credit to the great (*maha*) seers (*rishis*) who originally cognized it and to Maharishi for reviving it as such.

My invitation was unexpectedly extended, and before I knew it I was closing my Boulder practice from a scratchy phone in New Delhi. A year or so later, I was back in the United States with a deep commitment to this program.

I began working with local athletes in the Boston area, workshopping these principles until I could see them working for everyone. Soon we had hundreds of case studies in hand and a program that seemed to have a life of its own.

After working with these athletes for a couple of years, and further integrating these principles into the twentieth century, I developed a seminar called *The Invincible Athletics Course*, which I've since taught to thousands of people, including professional athletes, around the world, including at the former USSR State Committee for Physical Culture and Sports in Moscow.

During my first months back in the United States I was asked to be on a local Boston talk show called the *Nancy Merrill Show* to talk about my Invincible Athletics program. Without warning, Nancy asked me a question I hadn't heard since 1983, when the Ayurvedic expert first told me about restful alertness:

"What makes people want to compete in these grueling sporting events like the triathlon? Why do you do it?"

Once again, and this time on the air, I drew a blank, and awkwardly skirted the issue.

After blowing two chances to answer that question, I would now like to take the opportunity to answer it properly. Actually, the long-form answer is this book. Here is the short form:

The reason why people challenge themselves in such a physical way is that it is human nature to seek perfection. Some will be more inclined to seek physical perfection, and some mental perfection, based on the dictates of their body type, but it is human nature not to stop short of perfection. The problem is that perfection is hard to come by! It is especially so for athletes, for whom the road to perfection has become painful. Even those who accomplish grueling feats of endurance rarely find lasting satisfaction and quickly turn to another challenge.

If we seek perfection only through outer accomplishments, whether in a sport or a career, we will invariably come up short. Yes, we will often reach our goals, but in time we lose interest and redirect our energy. One challenge after another is the road we travel, searching for fulfillment, happiness, and perfection, but rarely do we succeed.

The real challenge is not on the top of a mountain or the finish line of a race, it is within. To harness the potential of the mind and body to win any race or accomplish any goal while remaining inwardly calm, silent, and composed, to be restfully alert while running a marathon, climbing a mountain, putting for par, or even while in the deepest sleep, is the goal not only of the athlete but of humanity itself.

A WAY OF LIFE

To reap the maximum benefits of exercise, we must look beyond fitness and even beyond health, to a place where these are the results rather than the goal. Health and fitness are certainly important, but experience shows that these goals alone don't provide sufficient motivation to make exercise a way of life. The vast majority of people simply don't do it.

To make exercise a way of life, we have to go one step further. To the ancient Greeks, exercise was a tool used to harness an even greater potential than the physical skills derived directly from it. Exercise was designed to take the integrated mind, body, and spirit established at rest into dynamic physical activity, and then into daily life.

The exercise high or peak performance state, sometimes thought to be exclusively athletic in nature, can become a regular experience, whether you are washing the car, vacuuming the rug, raising your kids, or closing a business deal. It is easier to keep the mind and body connected during the motion of exercise, or at rest in meditation, but more difficult in the routine activity of daily life, where the motion isn't fast enough to create a rhythm, or slow enough to shut it all down. However, if you combine the mind-body techniques of exercise with the restful alertness of meditation, the formula for the Zone can be with you in every aspect of your daily life.

THE FLOW

What does it mean to experience the Zone throughout the day? Is it that your every thought, action, decision, and spoken word is a Michael Jordanism? Well, not exactly. It's more a question of living your life either with the grain or against it.

Have you ever felt that everything you do is an upstream battle? Living in the Zone means just the opposite. It means that you are living in the flow. It's like swimming downstream, without resistance.

In chapter 4 we described the unique characteristics of each body type. The Sanskrit translation for the word "body type" is "nature." Your body type is your nature, and knowing it is the first step to the daily experience of the Zone. You've got to know who you are. Your individual nature will determine exactly how to maintain balance within yourself, as well as with the environment.

The second step is to recognize that we are intimately connected to the powerful environmental cycles of nature. The birds fly south and the whales migrate, without choice. They are compelled by their instinctual connection to the cycles of nature to breed, migrate, and raise their young.

Our own nature, our constitutional type, can be either disconnected from these cycles or connected to them. We too have instincts, but they have frequently been suppressed by the mind's free will, which gives us the unique ability to live against the grain of nature. No other species can do this.

Nature functions according to daily, monthly, and seasonal cycles. We are as connected to them as are the swallows of San Juan Capistrano, and we must give them a chance to be heard in our lives. If we do, we soon find ourselves naturally living in tune with nature's cycles, without strain or discipline.

While the body is by nature connected to these rhythms, the mind is not. The purpose of this program is to tie the two together, to qualify the desires of the mind with the needs of the body and the intelligence of nature. Only when the mind and body are functioning as one integrated whole, from the inside out, can the Zone be a reality both on and off the field.

On the field, there are viable techniques to bring us into the Zone. Off the field, the key is to recognize the connection of human nature to Mother Nature, and to respond to it. There are times to eat, sleep, and study, and times to exercise. The whole thing has been mapped out ahead of time. All we need to do is understand our individual natures and plug in properly, in harmony with these cycles.

Living in accordance with nature is like living in the eye of the hurricane, surrounded by the storm. It is a place that remains protected and calm. Surrounded by stress, pressure, and problems, there is an internal silent composure that puts it all into perspective.

An intelligence beyond comprehension lies behind this balance of nature. We are a part of that balance. With our intellect, which allows us to choose to swim either up- or downstream, we can go with or against the grain of nature. This inherent ability to choose gives us the capability, unlike animals, to access and harness the invincible power of nature, from which we come.

There is nothing man-made that can be considered truly invincible. The Romans or maybe the Yankees may have seemed invincible, but history has proved that they were not. The only lasting source of nature's invincibility is within each and every one of us. It is the same force that hurls the earth around the sun and makes the seasons come and go. It's been doing it for millions of years, without fatigue. There is no motor, no effort, just an infinite array of dynamic activity, silently coordinated from every atom to every cell to every universe.

Don't sell yourself short. Human life has the software and hardware to go the distance. All we need to do is know our nature, and mimic Nature's Way. "Do less and accomplish more; do nothing and accomplish everything" is nature's secret to the miracle of life.

For more information about John Douillard's Body, Mind, and Sport programs, call 1-800-ALL-VEDA or write to him at P.O. Box 344, Lancaster, MA 01523.

REFERENCES

Anderson, R. 1980. *Stretching.* New York: Random House.

Atha Vale, V. B. 1980. *Basic Principles of Ayur Veda.* Bombay, India: Town Prinery.

Banquet, J. P. 1973. Spectral analysis of the EEG in meditators. *Electroenceph. clin. Neurophysiol.* 35:143–151.

Bhishagratna, K. L. 1981. *Sushruta Samhita.* Vol 1, 2. Varanasi, India: Chowkhamba Sanscrit Series Office.

Borg, G. and H. Linderhom. 1967. Perceived exertion and pulse rate during graded exercise in various age groups. *Acta Med. Scand.* 472:194–206.

Boutcher, S. H., and D. M. Landers. 1988. Effects of vigorous exercise on anxiety, heart rate, and alpha activity of runners and non-runners. *Psychophysiology* 25(6):696–702.

Burwash, P. 1983. *Vegetarian Primer.* New York: Atheneum.

Cohen, J. 1977. *Statistical Power Analysis for the Behavioral Sciences.* New York: Academic Press.

Chopra, D. 1991. *Perfect Health.* New York: Harmony Books.

Cooper, K. H. 1985. *Running Without Fear.* New York: Evans.

Gardiner, E.N. 1925. *Athletics of the Ancient World.* Oxford: Clarendon Press.

Gilbey, M. P., D. Jordan, D. W. Richter, and K. M. Spyer. 1984. Synaptic mechanisms involved in the inspiratory modulation of vagal cardio-inhibitory neurons in the cat. *J. of Physiol.* 356:65–78.

Grossman, P., J. Karemeker, and W. Wielsing. 1991. Prediction of tonic parasympathetic cardiac tone using respiratory sinus arrhythmia. *Psychophysiology* 28:201–216.

Kyle, D. G. 1987. *Athletes in Ancient Athens.* Amsterdam, Netherlands: Leiden E. J. Brill.

Hirsch, J. A., and B. Bishop. 1981. Respiratory sinus arrhythmia in humans: How breathing patterns modulate heart rate. *J. of Applied Physiology* S1:H620–H629.

Jennings, J. R. 1987. Editorial policy on analysis of variance with repeated measures. *Psychophysiology* 24:474–478.

King, B. J. 1992. *Billie Jean.* New York: Viking Press.

Lorig, T. S., G. E. Schwartz, K. B. Herman, and R. M. Lane. 1988. EEG activity during nose and mouth breathing. *Psychobiology* 16:285–287.

Miller, S. G. 1979. *Areie.* Chicago: Ares Publisher.

Murphy, W, 1978. *The Psychic Side of Sports.* Reading, Mass.: Addison-Wesley.

Niedermeyer E. 1987. The normal EEG of the waking adult. In *Electroencephalography: Basic Principles, Clinical Applications and Related Fields,* ed. E. Niedermeyer and R. Lopes da Silva, 97–118. Baltimore: Urban & Schwarzenberg.

O'Brien, J. 1985. *Running and Breathing*. Lakemont, Ga.: CSA Press.

Porges, S. W. 1984. Heart rate oscillations: An index of neural meditation. In *Psychophysiological Perspectives*, ed. M. Coles, J. R. Jennings, and J. A. Stern, New York: Van Nostrand Reinhold.

Porges, S. W. and N. A. Fox. 1986. Developmental psychophysiology. In *Psychophysiology: Systems, Processes, and Applications*, ed. M. G. H. Coles, E. Donchin, and S. W. Porges, 611–625. New York: Guilford.

Porges, S. W., P. M. McCabe, and B. G. Yongue. 1988. Respiratory-heart rate interactions: Psychophysiological implications for pathophysiology and behavior. In *Perspectives in Cardiovascular Psychophysiology*, ed. J. T. Caccioppo and R. E. Petty. New York: Guilford.

Rama, Swami, Rudolph Ballentine, and Alan Hymes. 1981. *Science on Breath*. Monesdale, Pa.: Himalayan Institute.

Saraswati, S. M. 1985. *Hatha Yoga Pradipika*. Bihar, India: Bihar School of Yoga.

Sharma, P. V. 1981. *Caraka Samhita*, Vol 1, 2. Varanasi, India: Chaukhambha Orientalia.

Stamford, B. 1992. Exerting yourself. *The Physician and Sports Medicine* 20:187–188.

Wallace, R. K., H. Benson, and A. F. Wilson. 1971. A wakeful hypometabolic physiological state. *American Journal of Physiology* 221:795–799.

Yamamoto, Y., R. L. Hughson, and J. C. Peterson. 1991. Autonomic control of heart rate during exercise studies by heart rate variability spectral analysis. *J. Appl. Physiol.* 71(3):H1136–H1142.

Appendix

Research on TM

Change in Metabolic Rate

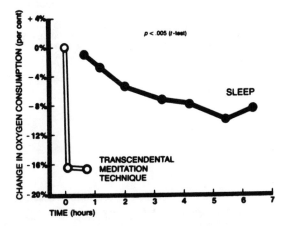

Reference: Robert Keith Wallace and Herbert Benson, "The Physiology of Meditation," *Scientific American* 226 (1972): 84–90.

More Efficient Physiological Functioning

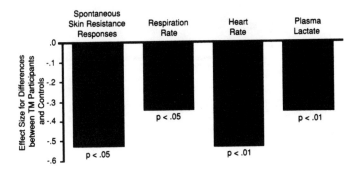

Reference: 1. M. C. Dillbeck and D. W. Orme-Johnson, "Physiological Differences Between Transcendental Meditation and Rest," *American Psychologist* 42 (1987): 879-881.

Change in Running Speed

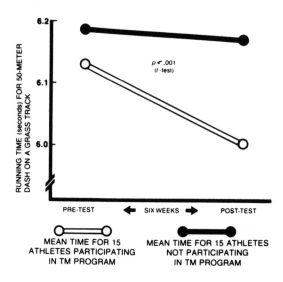

Reference: *Scientific Research on the Transcendental Meditation Program: Collected Papers*, Volume 1. West Germany, MERU Press, 1976.

Change in Reaction Time

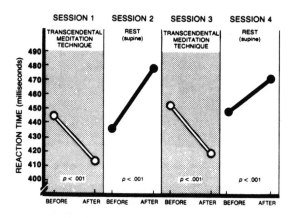

Reference: *Scientific Research on the Transcendental Meditation Program: Collected Papers*, Volume 1. West Germany, MERU Press, 1976.

INDEX

Simeon," he said slowly, with a glance at his father. "Why did you stay in Jerusalem? Why didn't you escape when we did?"

"I was a Zealot, a freedom fighter," said Simeon. "I was young and wanted to fight Romans. We called those who left cowards, but I wish now. . . . You were right, Mordecai. In the terrible days that followed I often cursed myself for not listening to you."

Mordecai nodded sadly.

Jonathan gave Tigris a piece of gravy-soaked bread. "Simeon," he said. "Was my mother with you in Jerusalem?"

"Yes, of course," said Simeon. "Susannah was my younger sister."

"What happened to her? After Titus sacked Jerusalem."

"I don't know. I was telling your father earlier that they separated the men and women. There was terrible confusion. It was the last time I saw her alive."

"Do you know why she stayed? Did she ever tell you why she didn't?"

"Jonathan." Mordecai's expression was grim. "Please don't pursue this subject. I told you already why she didn't come with us."

Nubia saw the injured expression on Jonathan's face. He hung his head and stroked Tigris. Suddenly the puppy stiffened and gave a single bark. A moment later they heard pounding on the front door.

"You must hide at once, Simeon," hissed Mordecai, as Miriam ran to answer the door. "It may be the magistrate again."

SCROLL V

'It's not the magistrate, Father. It's Gaius." Mi
of a tall, fair-haired man.

Everyone breathed a sigh of relief and N
Lupus. "You can give Simeon the signal to com

"Did you find a house, Uncle Gaius?" asked

Her uncle shook his head. Despite his bro
across one cheekbone, Flavia still thought hin

Gaius smiled down at Jonathan.

"I'm sorry I'm late for your dinner pai
birthday!" He extended a flat wooden object
blue stripes. "It's just a wax tablet but I thou
stripes."

"I do," said Jonathan reaching to take it
. . . useful."

"Jonathan!" cried Flavia. "You've hurt yo

A strip of white linen was wrapped rour
left hand.

"It's nothing," Jonathan flushed and put

Mordecai gave his son a sharp look, bu
and Simeon came back into the dining ro

"Gaius," said Miriam, "this is my Uncl

After the introductions had been

The ram's horn trumpet sounded again, a long blast followed by nine staccato bursts and a final long note.

"It's coming from the synagogue, isn't it?" said Flavia.

Mordecai nodded. "We celebrate our New Year today," he said. "We call it the Day of Trumpets."

"But I thought you were Christians," said Flavia with a frown.

"We are," said Mordecai. "We haven't abandoned our customs and festivals. We have merely added to them our belief in a Jewish prophet we call the Messiah."

Miriam came back into the dining room with a platter.

"It's apple and honey. For the festival," she said. "Happy New Year, everyone!"

"Happy New Year!" they replied.

A warm breeze drifted in from the dusky garden, bringing with it the shofar's haunting call.

"Why do they blow it?" asked Flavia, crunching a piece of apple.

"To get our attention," smiled Mordecai. "To remind us that today we can make a fresh start. Have our sins wiped away."

"What is arsons?" asked Nubia.

"Our sins," said Mordecai. "Things we've done wrong. We remember them over the next ten days, which are called the Days of Awe. Then on our most holy day, Yom Kippur, we fast and pray and say sorry to God and to our fellow man."

Simeon looked around at them. "I'm sorry I frightened you. Especially you, Jonathan. Will you forgive me?"

Jonathan shrugged, not even bothering to look at his uncle. Flavia realized he had hardly touched the stew.

Mordecai frowned at Jonathan's rudeness, and said to Simeon. "Of course we forgive you."

Simeon smiled, took a piece of apple, dipped it in the honey and ate it.

"Does anyone else want to say sorry?" said Mordecai. "Perhaps you, Jonathan?"

"Why are you asking me?" Jonathan scowled and glanced around. "What about Lupus? He has plenty to be sorry about."

Lupus's head jerked up. He stared at Jonathan, then rose slowly to his feet and took out his wax tablet. His ears deepened from pink to bright red as he wrote on it. Finally, he threw it down onto the table with such force that it sent a wine cup flying. Then he ran out of the triclinium. A moment later they heard the sound of the back door slamming shut.

Miriam burst into tears. A pink wine stain was spreading across the front of her white tunic.

Abruptly Jonathan got up and ran out of the room. Flavia was surprised to hear his footsteps going upstairs instead of to the back door, so she got up, too, and hurried through the twilit garden.

"Lupus!" she called through the open door. "Come back!" But the sky above the graveyard was such a deep blue that she could barely make out the tops of the umbrella pines. Flavia closed the door and ran back to the triclinium.

"It's too dark," she said breathlessly. "I couldn't see which way he went. Shall we light torches and go after him?"

Mordecai shook his head. "You know Lupus often loses his temper and runs off like that. He'll come back when he's ready."

Gaius was comforting Miriam while Nubia dabbed at the wine stain with her napkin. Simeon held the wax tablet that Lupus had thrown down.

"What does it say?" asked Flavia.

Jonathan's uncle silently handed her the tablet.

"Oh, no," murmured Flavia, and read aloud what Lupus had written:

GOD SHOULD SAY SORRY
FOR WHAT HE'S DONE TO ME!!

■ ■ ■

Lupus ran through the purple twilight. Angry tears blurred his vision as he plunged into the pine woods.

He was only wearing his linen dining slippers and the stones and sharp twigs hurt the soles of his feet. He was not as tough as he had been a few months earlier. Living in Jonathan's house had made him soft.

He could barely see now, for dusk was becoming night and the moon was the merest sliver. Black shapes of pine trunks loomed up suddenly like an advancing army of dark opponents. He veered left and right, silently daring them to catch him.

At last something did catch him. But it was not a tree.

Flavia scratched softly on the wall beside Jonathan's doorway. There was no reply, so she pushed the curtain aside and entered.

By the light of the oil lamp in her hand, she could see Jonathan lying on his bed. He had his back to her.

"Jonathan?" she whispered.

There was no reply.

"Jonathan, what's the matter?" said Flavia. "You really upset Lupus, not to mention your father and Miriam. This isn't like you."

"Yes, it is. I ruin everything." His voice was muffled.

Flavia carefully set the oil lamp on a low table and perched on the edge of his bed. Tigris looked at her over Jonathan's shoulder and thumped his tail.

"It's my fault Lupus ran off," Jonathan continued. "It's my fault that Miriam's new tunic is ruined. I insulted our guest and I upset Father."

Flavia hugged her knees. "Well, it's only partly your fault that Miriam's tunic has a wine stain on it and Lupus didn't have to storm off into the graveyard. Your father is upset, but you know he loves you."

"No, he doesn't," said Jonathan. "Father hates me."

"Of course he doesn't hate you. What are you talking about?"

Jonathan turned and looked up at her. In the dim light his brown eyes looked almost black. "He hates me because it's my fault that Mother died."

Lupus swung gently in the darkness, his feet higher than his head, his right arm twisted awkwardly behind his back, the net tight around him.

He knew it was a trap for wild boar. When an animal stepped onto a certain rope the whole net rose up into the trees. This one was particularly well made. It was designed to withstand the thrashings of a creature twice his weight and strength.

Lupus waited until his heart stopped pounding. Then he took several deep breaths and tried to ease his right arm into a less painful position.

In the cave of the Cyclops, Odysseus's faithful wife, Penelope, sat at her loom. A waterfall splashed somewhere nearby. As Jonathan entered the cave, she turned and looked at him.

Though it was dim, he could see that she was very beautiful. She had pale skin and dark blue eyes and her straight black hair was as smooth as silk. When she smiled, she looked like his sister Miriam.

"I weave all day, and undo what I've woven at night," she whispered to Jonathan. "I wait for him every day."

Jonathan took a step into the cave, terrified that the Cyclops might return. Penelope held out a handful of yellow wool. "Do you want to smell it? It's my favorite."

The scent of lemon blossom filled the cave.

"Mother?" said Jonathan, "Is it you? Are you still alive?"

She smiled at him and nodded.

Then Jonathan woke up.